Religion and Schooling in Contemporary America

Source Books on Education
(Vol. 50)
Garland Reference Library of Social Science
(Vol. 1127)

Religion and Schooling in Contemporary America

Confronting Our Cultural Pluralism

Edited by
Thomas C. Hunt
James C. Carper

GARLAND PUBLISHING, INC.
New York & London
1997

Library of Congress Cataloging-in-Publication Data

Religion and schooling in contemporary America : confronting our cultural pluralism / edited by Thomas C. Hunt, James C. Carper.
p. cm. — (Garland reference library of social science ; v. 1127. Source books on education ; vol. 50)
Includes bibliographical references and index.
ISBN 0-8153-2472-3 (alk. paper)
1. Church and education—United States. 2. Religion in the public schools—United States. 3. Church schools—United States. 4. Education and state—United States. I. Hunt, Thomas C., 1930– . II. Carper, James C. III. Series: Garland reference library of social science ; v. 1127. IV. Series : Garland reference library of social science. Source books on education ; vol. 50.
LC111.R43 1997
379.2'8'0973—dc21 97–2439
CIP

Printed on acid-free, 250-year-life paper
Manufactured in the United States of America

Thomas C. Hunt dedicates this book to two long-time close friends, Sister Kathleen O'Connell, OP, and Father Ray Runde. Their support and encouragement, during good and difficult times, was constant, consistent, and sometimes vital. He herein publicly and gratefully acknowledges their highly valued friendship.

James C. Carper dedicates the book to those committed to the proposition that parents have the primary right and responsibility to direct their children's education.

Contents

Acknowledgments ix

Introduction xi

Chapter One
Religious Pluralism in the Public School Curriculum 3
Charles R. Kniker

Chapter Two
Religious Practices in Public Schools 31
Charles R. Kniker

Chapter Three
Culture, Religion, and Education 59
E. Vance Randall

Chapter Four
Religious Schools in America 83
Worldviews and Education
E. Vance Randall

Chapter Five
Cross-National Analysis of Religious Schools 107
Institutional Adaptation from Four Perspectives
Bruce S. Cooper and Rita E. Guare

Chapter Six
Law and Church-Related Schools 139
Mary Angela Shaughnessy, S.C.N.

Chapter Seven
Public Policy, Religion, and Education in the United States 159
William F. Davis, O.S.F.S.

Chapter Eight
Mission and Money 181
Religious Schools and Their Finances
Michael J. Guerra

Contributors 199

Index of Persons 203

Index of Subjects 205

Acknowledgments

We acknowledge with gratitude the assistance of a number of people whose help was indispensable in creating this book. In particular, we wish to thank David Starkey of the Word Processing Center of Virginia Tech's College of Education, Ms. Bonnie Guthrie, Dr. Hunt's secretary at Virginia Tech and Mr. Nick Compagnone, for his work on the indexing. Finally, we acknowledge Dean Patricia First of the School of Education of the University of Dayton for her generous assistance that enabled this project to be completed.

Thomas C. Hunt
James C. Carper

Introduction

The title of this book, *Religion and Schooling in Contemporary America: Confronting Our Cultural Pluralism,* reflects the editors' view of the book's purpose and what we hope will be its accomplishment. In company with authors like Stephen Carter[1] and Warren Nord,[2] we believe that the United States has become publicly a secular nation, largely devoid of theistic religious influence in its institutions, including its schools. This, despite the fact that most Americans embrace, in diverse ways, a theistic belief system.

We do not advocate government espousal of any confessional interpretation, nor of any combination of them. At the same time, we must voice our protest against the ever-growing tendency to relegate theistic religion to the status of the peripheral and the realm of the private, whether due to ignorance, bias, a fear of controversy, or a combination thereof.

This book is the seventh, the sixth under the auspices of Garland Publishing, on which the editors have collaborated in the last twelve years. This volume contains eight chapters. The first two, both written by Charles Kniker, address questions related to the place of religion in the curriculum and activities of the nation's public schools. The remaining six chapters deal with religious-affiliated schools from a variety of perspectives: their place and role in American culture; a comparative view; their political setting; international perspective; their legal status; and their means of fiscal support. All are authored by scholars widely respected in their fields.

It is well to note at this point that religious-affiliated schooling has a long and rich history in the educational annals in the United States. Prior to the rather well-known "Ould Deluder Satan" Law of Puritan Massachusetts in 1647, there were schools that operated under Catholic auspices in what is now Florida, Louisiana, and the Southwest.[3] The reader is referred to the 1993 Hunt-Carper book on religious schools for brief historical overviews of the educational endeavors of eleven denominations, plus home-schooling (which counts the majority of its participants as religiously motivated).

Some denominations, as our 1986 book revealed, no longer participate in hosting schools, for a variety of reasons. Those who do counted (in 1993–1994) a total of 20,531 institutions, of which 8,331 were Catholic, with an enrollment of 4,202,194, of which 2,516,130 were in Catholic schools.[4] Thus, using numbers alone as a measuring rod, these schools constitute an important part of the American educational landscape, and deserve our attention.

The editors concluded their 1993 book with an epilogue. While the movement for choice in American schooling has broadened and deepened in the last three years, we still believe little else has changed in that time to cause us to alter our thoughts on the critical challenges facing religious schools in the United States. These three challenges are: (1) keeping them affordable, yet paying a living wage to their personnel; (2) maintaining their religious identities despite the growing numbers of students who are not members of the sponsoring denomination; and (3) keeping their religious uniqueness if public support, e.g., a voucher-like formula, becomes available.[5]

It is our hope that this book will enhance the knowledge of its readers as to pivotal issues involving religion in our schools—both those in the public sector and those sponsored by religious groups. Hopefully, *Religion and Schooling in Contemporary America: Confronting Our Cultural Pluralism* will contribute to a growing dialogue on religion and schooling in our democratic society.

Notes

1. Stephen L. Carter. *The Culture of Disbelief: How American Law and Politics Trivialize Religious Devotion* (New York: Basic Books, 1993).
2. Warren A. Nord, *Religion & American Education: Rethinking A National Dilemma* (Chapel Hill: The University of North Carolina Press, 1995).
3. Harold A. Buetow, *Of Singular Benefit: The Story of U.S. Catholic Education* (New York: Macmillan, 1970), Ch. 1.
4. National Center for Educational Statistics, *Digest of Educational Statistics 1995* (Washington, D.C.: U.S. Department of Education, Office of Educational Research and Improvement, 1995), p. 58.
5. Thomas C. Hunt and James C. Carper, eds. *Religious Schools in the United States K–12: A Source Book* (New York: Garland Publishing, 1993), pp. 445–446.

Religion and Schooling in Contemporary America

Chapter One
Religious Pluralism in the Public School Curriculum

Charles R. Kniker

Religious pluralism is a reality in the nation's schools today. It affects the formal and informal curriculum in many ways. A Muslim student in California, given a ceremonial knife to indicate his manhood, wears his sheathed blade to school. African American students in St. Louis celebrate Kwanza. A Chicago school sets aside a prayer room for Islamic children. Teachers in a Florida school district are asked by conservative Christians not to observe Halloween. Native American parents at a Southwestern school voice their displeasure over the lack of positive references about tribal leaders in history textbooks. Buddhist families in Iowa provide materials for a "culture kit" developed by a university extension program for schools.[1] These incidents are illustrative of the surprising religious pluralism found in the tapestry of our nation's schools, rural as well as urban.

This diversity has contributed to a growing consensus on the part of religious, civic, and professional education groups of the need to agree on what and how teaching about religion should occur in public education. Such support for guidelines was evident when President William Clinton issued recommendations on religion in the curriculum and religious practices in public schools in July 1995.[2] Not all, however, want to acknowledge or accept the diversity of students in schools; some are opposed to accommodations to turn the "melting pot" into a "round table," where all perspectives are respected and given opportunities for dialogue.[3]

Overview

The first purpose of this chapter is to provide an overview of the complex issue of religion in the curriculum, beginning with definitions of religion and pluralism. The second purpose of the chapter is to provide an historical, legal, and philosophical background to the academic study of religion in public schools, most frequently described as "religion studies" hereafter. More specifically, the background material will include a brief history of religion in the public school curriculum, a review of significant court cases (primarily *Abington v. Schempp*), a recounting of pedagogical issues related to the "objective teaching of religion," an identification of groups supporting and groups questioning the academic study of religion, and an update of state laws and guidelines. The third and final purpose of the chapter is to survey current teaching practices and resources related to religion in the curriculum. The four curriculum areas to be highlighted are Bible as/in literature, social studies/history, world religions, and others (art, music, health, economics, and science).

Definitions of Religion and Pluralism

The emphasis of this chapter is clearly upon what the U.S. Supreme Court identified in *Abington v. Schempp* as "the objective teaching of religion."[4] Since 1963, several other expressions have gained more frequent usage—the academic study of religion, teaching about religion, or religion studies. What is meant by "religion"? Generally speaking, religion is defined from a sociological or phenomenological basis; that is, it is a human activity related to a deity, with a founder (who may or may not claim to be God), disciples, a set of beliefs, sacred literature (here understood to be in either oral or written form), and behaviors consistent with the beliefs. Some scholars suggest that broader definitions be used. They argue that some religions do not meet the criteria listed above; some, for example, do not believe in a god but have a reverence for life. Some agree with the theological stance of Paul Tillich, that everyone is religious (because we all value something ultimately).[5] Most curriculum materials are based on the narrow definition rather than the broader one.

Pluralism, for this author, is a descriptive term, referring to the demographics of the country's different populations, racially, ethnically, linguistically, religiously. It does not have a positive or negative connotation, although it acknowledges that there will be more than one world view, one truth perspective. Others, wanting to differentiate between diversity and pluralism, argue that pluralism is a positive term, implying it is a constructive goal for society to more fully achieve. While I agree with Warren Nord's observation that religious pluralism made religious liberty necessary and possible, I resist efforts to make it more than descriptive.[6] Multiculturalism, to me, is a curriculum strategy to increase and enrich students' awareness of and appreciation for the contributions made by diverse groups in the nation's history. In practice, the focus in many teacher education multicultural courses is upon information about racial and ethnic groups and improving communication and interaction between members of the dominant culture group (white) and members of the groups studied. While I endorse the goal of multiculturalism, I am aware that some view it negatively, because they have concluded it promotes "one world-ism," which they believe downplays the unique history and role of the United States.[7]

Topics Not Covered

This chapter cannot discuss all topics which relate to religion in the curriculum. Specifically excluded are informal religious studies although some policies, like school-sponsored prayer and observation of religious holidays, will be covered in the next chapter. Censorship of textbooks on religious grounds is also omitted. Religion in the school curriculum of other countries or in the curriculum of parochial and private or independent schools is not covered. Teacher preparation in religion studies is given minimal consideration.

Background: Historical, Legal, and Philosophical Perspectives on Religion Studies

Formal instruction in America from the 1600s to the early 1800s most often was conducted in private schools founded by religious groups; the curriculum in such schools was based on the Bible and denominational doctrines.[8] After the Revolutionary War, a number of the infant nation's political leaders suggested that a new form of education was needed, schools whose primary goals would be promotion of civic values and business-related knowledge and skills. The "common" school movement emerged by the 1830s and 1840s. The leaders of the movement, including Horace Mann of Massachusetts and Henry Barnard of Connecticut, believed that certain types of moral instruction and Bible readings were acceptable in the curriculum, but resisted what they called sectarian textbooks.[9]

The modern assumption that a monolithic Judeo-Christian hegemony existed then can be easily refuted. As early as the 1840s, a court case over the use of public monies for Catholic schools occurred in New York State. At mid-century, Philadelphia was the scene of a bloody riot where Catholics had objected to reading the King James Version of the Bible in the common schools. By the early 1900s, a number of court cases in the Midwest over Bible reading were further indications of the growing diversity of the country. Judges in these cases ended Bible reading in public schools because it too often reflected a pan-Protestant perspective. Even before the onset of the twentieth century, the U.S. Commissioner of Education's reports were filled with articles and letters from administrators and teachers advocating that the Bible could be used for moral guidance, or better yet, as a treasure trove of various types of literary masterpieces.[10]

The most famous textbook series from the mid-1800s to early 1900s was the McGuffey Readers. Originally published in 1836, the editions of the late 1800s had omitted almost all references to God. Moral lessons were abundant, although the Calvinist theological underpinnings were reduced in later editions. Just as textbooks were becoming "less religious," due in part to the growing recognition of the increase of different religious traditions in the schools, so some religious practices were minimized in the nineteenth century. By 1900, only one state had a law requiring prayer and Bible reading in the public schools. That would change. By 1923, twelve states had such laws.[11]

Significant Court Cases

Concerned that too many immigrants were being allowed into the country and that the nation's values would be eroded by involvement in World War I, many states passed legislation which tried to omit private schools. The Court ultimately upheld the right of private and religious schools to exist (*Pierce v. Society of Sisters*, 1925). Until the end of World War II, with the *McCollum* decision (1948), local control prevailed; that is, schools reflected the dominant religious ethos of their communities with little state intervention. In the *McCollum* decision (1948), the U.S. Supreme Court banned religious instruction within the Champaign, Illinois, public schools even when taught electively by local clergy. Of note is Justice Robert Jackson's concurring opinion mentioning the importance of religion studies in the curriculum,[12] thereby emphasizing the distinction made between religious instruction and religion studies.

Four years later, the Court (*Zorach v. Clauson* 1952) approved "released time" classes, allowing students to receive religious instruction at their houses of worship during school hours. Shortly before that decision, which seemed to have a minimal impact, the National Education Association issued a report, *Moral and Spiritual Values in the Public Schools*, which endorsed what some might label religion studies. In their view, it was a mistake to link religion studies with moral instruction.[13]

In 1963 (*Abington v. Schempp/Murray v. Curlett*), the Court ruled on two cases, one from suburban Pennsylvania (reading of Bible verses at the start of the school day) and the other from Baltimore, Maryland (prayer), concluding that such practices were unconstitutional if done for a nonacademic purpose. Reporting by the media and reaction by religious groups focused on the negative—the Bible had been "kicked out" of the public schools, prayer was "outlawed." Justice Jackson's sentiments in *McCollum* were echoed in several opinions. Justice Tom Clark, writing the majority opinion, stated:

It might well be said that one's education is not complete without a study of comparative religion or of the history of religion and its relation to the advancement of civilization. It certainly may be said that the Bible is worthy of study for its literary and historic qualities. Nothing we have said here indicates that such study of the Bible or of religion, when presented objectively as part of a secular program of education, may not be effected consistently with the First Amendment.[14]

A concurring opinion by Justice William Brennan included the following:

The holding of the Court today plainly does not foreclose teaching about *the Holy Scriptures or about the differences between religious sects in classes in literature or history. Indeed, whether or not the Bible is involved, it would be impossible to teach meaningfully many subjects in the social sciences or the humanities without some mention of religion.*

To what extent, and at what points in the curriculum, religious materials should be cited are matters which the courts ought to entrust very largely to the experienced officials who superintend our Nation's public schools. They are the experts in such matters, and we are not.[15]

Similar remarks were offered by Justice Arthur Goldberg. ". . . it seems clear to me . . . that the Court would recognize the propriety of . . . teaching *about* religion, as distinguished from the teaching *of* religion in the public schools."[16]

Support and Opposition to Religion Studies

In the wake of the *Schempp/Murray* decision, some individuals, organizations, and higher education institutions realized that a golden opportunity had been offered. In 1971 the National Council on Religion and Public Education (NCRPE) was formed.[17] A coalition of religious and educational groups which met in Chicago agreed that its sole agenda of advocacy was for teaching about religion in public schools. Professional education groups such as the National Council for the Social Studies (NCSS) passed guidelines regarding the study of religion and sponsored sessions at their national meetings on topics related to instructional techniques, philosophical issues, and preparation of teachers. One of the most active organizations was a special interest group of the American Academy of Religion (AAR), which produced several books and monographs. Several institutions, such as Florida State University, Harvard University, Wright State University, Indiana University, and Western Michigan University designed programs in religion studies to prepare teachers for certification, assisted educators in preparing teaching materials, or offered in-service programs and workshops for teachers.[18]

The publication of legal, pedagogical, and policy materials was fostered in the 1980s by the work of several institutions and organizations. The J.M. Dawson Institute for Church-State Studies at Baylor University, directed by James Wood Jr., published the *Journal of Church and State* and sponsored occasional conferences. Charles Kniker of Iowa State University, with the assistance of long-time NCRPE Newsletter Editor, Thayer S. Warshaw of Andover, Massachusetts, founded *Religion & Public Education.* Later, the NCRPE Distribution Center was also begun at Iowa State University, disseminating curricular materials and teacher resources produced by NCRPE and others.[19]

One of the high water marks for the movement for religion studies in public education occurred in July 1988. At a press conference in Washington, D.C., a flyer was released which reflected the consensus of a number of groups regarding what could be taught in public schools about religion. Sixteen groups supported the document; they reflected a wide range of religious perspectives and included many mainline education groups.[20]

The remarkable consensus which emerged led to many statements by other organizations, educational as well as religious; in 1995, the president of the United States and his Secretary of Education summarized their views on religion in the public schools. In the late 1980s and early 1990s the Association for Supervision and Curriculum Development (ASCD), which has a broad-based educational membership, became active in the religion studies area.[21]

There have continued to be some challenges to religion being taught in public schools. The charge most frequently leveled is that textbooks are promoting the "religion" of secular humanism.[22] Most notable were cases from Hawkins County, Tennessee, and Mobile, Alabama. However, it is noteworthy that the plaintiffs did not challenge the concept of the objective teaching of religion. In the 1990s, there has been little organized opposition to religion studies.[23]

Pedagogical Issues Involving Religion Studies

Even the most ardent supporters of religion studies can raise issues and problems which relate to the academic study of religion. They include:

1. Separating Teaching about Religion and Moral Education. A common assumption is that to teach about religions is to inculcate students with some specific values and theological doctrines. To do so is to violate what the justices called for—objectivity. Asked another way, can the teacher be descriptive rather than prescriptive? Or, stated in a concrete way, while teachers may realize intellectually they are to present the facts of religious phenomena, can they in practice avoid endorsing the moral imperatives they themselves support or criticizing the explicit or implicit values they reject?

2. Promoting Neutrality and Avoiding Hostility. When religion is central in the lives of some persons, they expect discussions in the public schools to reflect their faith; expectations are that teachers will be supporters of the dominant group, including a dash or two of criticism of "minority" traditions. Persons from other traditions may recognize that it is not fair, considering the impressionable natures of the "captive audience," to present one perspective in the most favorable light and others in less positive terms. Some may be tempted to believe, however, that religion in general could be favored over no religion. The Court has been very clear regarding that matter. School leaders and teachers cannot favor one religion over others, nor can they favor religion over "irreligion."[24] Warren Nord supports what the Court has done. He advocates what he calls "fairness."[25] Charles Haynes and others have developed guidelines for teachers. In an article for teachers on how they might accommodate the religious diversity of their students, Charles Kniker developed what he called the "CARTS Checklist."[26] The guidelines are that they need to be Comprehensive in coverage, Accurate with information, Respectful in attitude, to stress Typical rituals and behaviors, and to be Sensitive to the diversity of students.
3. Teacher Preparation. How much do teachers need to know of the religions about which they teach? Are they conscious of their own biases and aware of the religious backgrounds their pupils bring to class? There have been few studies which provide answers to these questions. Various religion professors and several teacher educators have written about the need for better preparation of teachers. In this area, there are some skills as well as knowledge which should be mastered prior to teaching about religion. Some states have developed certification areas and, as indicated earlier, several university programs have been created in religious studies.[27]
4. Content and Materials for Teaching about Religion. There are some pedagogical questions to be answered. When studied academically, should religion be offered as a separate course or "naturally included" as units within classes in geography, literature, history, or science? What about methodology? Should there be a direct comparison of various beliefs and practices from world

religions in a world history class? Should the course make generalizations about religion as a universal human phenomenon? Should religious topics be offered only through elective courses, with the clear understanding that students will share their own faith perspectives? How important in this type of class would it be to take field trips, or to have religious leaders from various denominations as resource persons?

5. The Faith Perspective. Some have argued that only a person from a religious tradition can truly teach about that faith. They say that it is not possible for religion, so freighted with meaning(s), to be clinically (objectively) studied. I beg to differ. The educational enterprise collapses if that argument is carried to the extreme. The teacher of economics cannot be an advocate for all positions, but must narrate past and current theories as fairly and as objectively as possible. Likewise, the literature instructor who wishes to engage the class in sampling poets of Japan, Africa, and South America can not be a native of all nations or continents.[28]

Related to this area is the issue of how much can or should the schools encourage students to experiment with different religious traditions. As Guntram Bischoff has argued, the power of religion will attract some students to do more than just study it; they may want to "try it out."[29] While common sense would dictate that mention might be made of churches which practice snake-handling, no responsible administrator or teacher would demonstrate that practice in the classroom or encourage students to handle reptiles. Yet, where is the line drawn? Jonathan Kozol has said:

Words on an ethical issue which do not compel to action are: inert, nonearnest and dishonest. Schools . . . fend off the intensities of grief, the tangible realities of unjust power, and the necessity for taking sides. . . . They teach us how to trim the sails of our most deep and serious convictions, to limit the fury, to water down the passion and to understate the pain.[30]

The Public Education Religion Studies program at Wright State gave us the best solution to the questions raised in this section, the "pair word" concept. The teacher is to teach about religion, not teach religion; the teacher is to provide information, not indoctrination.[31] Other instructional issues remain to be faced. The limited amount of time in the school day places restrictions on course content. In a course in world religions, how can the teacher offer a comprehensive curriculum that is not superficial? When studying religion in Western history, should the emphasis be upon ancient, medieval, or modern events? When religion is included in American history instruction, how much of the curriculum should be based on primary source materials rather than secondary? Subsequent to the creation of guidelines for religion studies, the need remains for careful and puposeful curriculum development.

Survey of State Materials, Regulations, and Guidelines

In the years since *Abington v. Schempp* was decided, several states have developed materials or passed guidelines on religion studies. Pennsylvania developed a course on religious literature of the West. In the 1970s and 1980s, California and Florida prepared material on the Bible as literature, although other states like Wisconsin developed guidelines for religion in social studies. More guidelines were created in the 1990s.[32] Because of interest or controversy, local districts also developed guidelines. One of the most elaborate statements was done by Dallas, Texas, which received extensive feedback from a large citizens' committee.[33] In 1989, a study of the fifty states and the District of Columbia (with only Hawaii not participating) found that ten states specifically endorsed or required teaching the Bible as literature, twelve states mentioned world religions, and thirteen states specified that religion in history could be taught. Currently, the most active efforts regarding religion studies are found in California, Georgia, Florida, North Carolina, Utah, Texas, and Pennsylvania.[34]

Current Curriculum, Teaching Practices, and Resources in Religion Studies

Thayer S. Warshaw has defined religion studies as "the academic study of religions and of religion as a phenomenon."[35] Barbara Swyhart has provided a similar but somewhat amplified description about the scope of religion studies.[36] Considering the amount of material which could be covered, teaching about religion in the curriculum is an awesome task. It begins with the acknowledgment that religious forces have shaped every culture, literally as well as figuratively. Buildings, languages, organizational structures, family roles, and food customs show the impact of religion on daily life.

Although the comments just made suggest that religion is decidedly present, some persons will assume that due to secularization, religion is more of a phenomenon of the past. This section of the chapter argues that religion studies has four goals, regardless of whether it is done in separate classes or naturally included as units within other courses. The first goal is to promote literacy about religion—religion is a fact of life (the *what* question). Second, religion studies can and should promote passionate inquiry, by that is meant that such studies seek to promote tolerance first, but also the willingness to listen actively to other perspectives. Here the role of the teacher is paramount, not merely to share sterile facts, but with "passion" explain to students *why* people act as they do.[37] Third, religion studies should promote open and accurate communication. Realizing that many religions are mission-oriented, and seek through a variety of means to spread their "good news," teachers and students can become aware of *how* people communicate what is of deepest importance to them. Fourth, religion studies should demonstrate to students that persons of faith are committed to *action*. Consequences, good and bad, occur as a result of religious decisions and actions. As Michael Novak stated, "Action is the starting place of inquiry. . . . Action is our most reliable mode of philosophizing. In action we declare our cosmology, our politics, our convictions, our identity. Who am I? I am what I do."[38]

These four goals for the study of religion can be met from within many disciplines. The *Schempp/Murray* decision underscored three such disciplines, and most curriculum developed has been in one of these areas—the Bible as literature, social studies, and world religions. These three areas will be examined below. A fourth section will summarize curriculum resources in other areas, especially science, but also health, economics, art, and music.

Religion Studies in Literature

No other book has influenced American culture, its values and institutions, more than the Bible. The Court, in a 1948 decision noted:

Certainly a course in English literature that omitted the Bible and other powerful uses of our mother tongue for religious ends would be pretty barren. . . . The fact is that, for good or for ill, nearly everything in our culture worth transmitting, everything which gives meaning to life, is saturated with religious influences.[39]

As the paragraph above suggests, the Court and others have assumed that students in the public schools should study culturally significant literature and the Bible is therefore worthy of study.[40] How is the Bible to be studied? As Warshaw and others have developed their approach, they teach about the Bible *for* literature, *as* literature, *in* literature, and the Bible *and* literature. The Bible *for* literature presents Bible stories and some often-quoted passages just to familiarize children with what the book actually says, so that they may recognize allusions in our culture. This approach may be used at the elementary school level, as well as the secondary school level. It lends itself to pupil projects and contributions from the fine arts, music, and popular culture. Using the Bible *as* literature technique, a teacher might examine verses in Proverbs or Psalms as an example of literary parallelism. The Bible *and* literature approach makes use of biblical texts in studying literary genres or themes. For example, a teacher offering a unit on poetry might include an excerpt from Job or the Song of Solomon. Another instructor might organize a unit on life-crises that speak to young people and include the Gospel of Luke's story of the Prodigal Son.

The Bible *in* literature is based on the fact that secular literature is filled with biblical references. Milton's *Paradise Lost* or T.S. Eliot's "Journey of the Magi" are examples. Other secular literature recreates Bible stories; for example, Hemingway's *Old Man and the Sea* or Archibald MacLeish's *J.B.* Shakespeare's plays are filled with biblical references.

Certainly there are problem areas in this academic arena, as in any discipline. Students will be prone to ask the teacher if the biblical story is true, especially "miracle" stories. The teacher may respond that historically people have offered at least four kinds of explanations for stories such as the Great Flood, the Exodus, and the Virgin Birth. First, the story is literally true; second, it is an embellished story, making a point about the power of a divine being; third, the story is primarily a myth (in the strict literary sense), embodying a people's experiences and values; or fourth, such stories are devices writers use to challenge humans to seek meanings in their own lives.

Another question or problem increasingly raised in our pluralistic world is whether sacred texts other than the Bible should be taught in literature courses in the public schools. Some authorities in English literature will argue that the answer is no, because there is a dearth of good teaching materials and more importantly, no other sacred texts have had the same impact upon our culture. The counter argument is that as more materials become available they should be introduced.[41]

Teaching resources for the Bible in literature classes are numerous. While most will focus on content materials, several will discuss methods and suggested activities. The basic book is James S. Ackerman and Thayer S. Warshaw, *The Bible as/in Literature*, 2nd edition. Another text is John B. Gable and Charles B. Wheeler, *The Bible as Literature: An Introduction.* The Society of Biblical Literature has produced an excellent series providing insights into the role of the Bible in popular culture, American arts and letters, law, politics, rhetoric, education, and social reform; the six-volume set, geared for scholars, is entitled *The Bible in American Culture.* Indiana University, with support from the Lilly Endowment, offered summer institutes for a number of years on teaching the Bible as/in literature. From lesson plans developed at those workshops, Linda Meixner has selected and revised a number of plans which are appropriate for schools today. Her work, developed with the assistance of Thayer Warshaw, is *The Bible in Literature Courses: Successful Lesson Plans.* Charles and Bernard Suhor have written *Teaching Values in the Literature Classroom: A Debate in Print.* The journal *Religion & Public Education* has published over twenty articles on this topic between 1987 and 1990.[42]

That Bible as literature can be taught in public schools, legally speaking, is no longer an issue. Whether it should be will continue to be debated. Even with the problems discussed above, it appears that it will continue to grow in popularity.

Teaching about Religion in History and Social Studies

Any tribe, community, or nation which has endured has a history. Its name, food, currency system, allies and enemies, immigration and emigration patterns, governmental structures and formal and informal covenants among its members, reveal its values and its fears, accomplishments and failures. The meaning to this mosaic of events is often shown through its religions. History is more than a chronicle, it is the "story of human suffering and human flourishing and what causes each of them. How historians and teachers tell that story is [can be] deeply controversial."[43] To deprive persons of a valid history is to give them cultural amnesia.

Much has been written in the past fifteen years about the limited treatment of religion in American history textbooks.[44] Many liberal and conservative authors and organizations agree that religion has been absent, inexcusably, from texts. To quote just one of the reports, "These texts simply do not treat religion as a significant element in American life—it is not portrayed as an integral part of the American value system or as something that is important to individual Americans. . . ."[45] Pilgrims and Puritans, the religious background of Abolitionist leaders, the response to Darwinism by church leaders (pro and con), the involvement of clergy and laity in the Social Gospel movement or the Civil Rights movement were minimally discussed. More recently, probably reflecting the California "framework" decision, which required textbook publishers to include more material on religion in their books if they expected their books to be adopted, some improvement has been noted.[46] Another factor which has increased the academic study of religion has been the attention given to the First Amendment. The three R's of religious liberty promoted in one popular program are rights, responsibilities, and respect.[47]

The National Council for the Social Studies (NCSS) produced a statement in 1984 which called for a greater commitment by the public schools to including religion in the social studies/history curriculum.[48] Note its reference to diversity:

Knowledge about religions is not only a characteristic of an educated person, but it is also absolutely necessary for understanding and living in a world of diversity. Knowledge of religious differences and the role of religion in the contemporary world can help promote understanding and alleviate prejudice. . . . Omitting study about religions gives students the impression that religions have not been and are not now part of the human experience. Study about religions may be dealt with in special courses and units or wherever and whenever knowledge of the religious dimension of human history and culture is needed for a balanced and comprehensive understanding.

That statement was followed in 1990 by the Williamsburg Charter, developed by a group of individuals and organizational representatives who espoused concepts also linked closely to religious liberty. The Association of Supervision and Curriculum Development became a leader in this field in the mid-1980s. One of its publications, *Religion in the Curriculum*, noted that textbooks had few references to Jewish people, and virtually no mention of the Holocaust. The NCRPE Distribution Center and *Religion & Public Education* published numerous articles for teachers on the topic of teaching about religion in the social studies.[49]

What is the current state of religion studies in social studies/history classes in America? California leads the country in the training of teachers. At several grade levels study about religion is mandated, and as noted earlier, religion must be mentioned in the textbooks which are adopted by the state. North Carolina has mandated preparation of history teachers in this area. The University of Florida began offering summer workshops for teachers in world history after the state strengthened its requirements for students in the history area.[50] Utah and Georgia have instituted programs of teacher preparation. Texas and Pennsylvania are in the initial stages of developing new programs. The Illinois legislature recently passed a bill permitting (encouraging) teachers to use religious documents in their history classes.[51] State departments of education over the years, with either state or federal funds, have developed curriculum units which incorporate religious information relevant to their state's history.[52]

In 1994 standards for teaching American and world history in grades 5–12 were published by the National Council for History Standards. There has been much debate about these standards. In his analysis of the standards, Nord concluded that religion is "increasingly marginal after 1750" in world history and its role in American life is minimized after 1850.[53] For example, of 191 components for the study of world history after 1750, only six deal chiefly with religion; only seven of the 256 components of standards for the study of American history after 1850 deal primarily with religion. Nord concludes that religion will not get sufficient attention through the natural inclusion approach and therefore advocates that students in high schools ought to have a minimum of one course in religion.

Assuming that teachers are interested in teaching about religion, but cautious about how to do it, what advice have they been given? One article, by Sister Mary Jessica Karlinger, stressed the use of primary source materials. John Simmons has used media projects to help students comprehend the pervasiveness of religion in common life, both past and present. A survey of Iowa social studies teachers revealed a number of creative ways teachers incorporated insights about the role of religion in culture. One teacher, for example, focused on reasons for immigration. Steven Stein, who directed the Indiana University summer seminars for social studies teachers, reported a variety of methods used by teachers who attended the summer sessions. Authors of *Religion & Public Education* articles have emphasized that autobiographical and biographical stories are often effective. Haynes and Kniker have both cautioned that role-playing, potentially quite effective, can have drawbacks in the area of religion, such as when students are given roles critical to their own religious tradition.[54]

Standard works in this field include: *Living with Our Deepest Differences: Religious Liberty in a Pluralistic Society* (Williamsburg Charter Foundation); *Pathways to Pluralism: Religious Issues in American Culture*; *Religion in American History: What to Teach and How*; and *The Role of Religion in U.S. History.* For teacher guidelines, see Thayer S. Warshaw, "Preparing Social Studies Teachers to Teach about Religion." That article and others are noted in a bibliography available from Webster University.[55]

World Religions in the Public School Curriculum

Consider these signs of the diversity of America. A study of the nation's forty-four largest school districts revealed that over 100 different "home" languages were spoken by the students in those districts. Over one million Muslims reside in California alone; one estimate is that 2,500 mosques have been built in the United States in the past decade. In its "Calendar of Religious Holidays and Ethnic Festivals," the National Conference lists approximately 100 events per year (usually the calendar covers two academic years) which schools could observe. The religious groups mentioned include Buddhist, Baha' i, Sikh, Hindu, Islamic, Jewish, Jain, Mormon, and Christian groups such as Eastern Orthodox, Protestant, and Roman Catholic. We live in a global village and the American public favors the study of world religions in the public schools.[56]

The *Schempp/Murray* case identified "comparative" religions as one of the three areas in which to teach. That is understandable, considering the number of students who take world history and world civilization courses at the secondary school level and elementary and middle school pupils who are exposed to geography units or area studies. As supportive as many educators are of including some treatment of world religions as units in such courses or of having an elective course in world religions in high schools, there are two general concerns to be raised. First, comparisons between religions are both difficult and inappropriate pedagogically. As James Carse has noted, it is hard to distinguish one religion from another on the basis of belief.[57] Second, such comparisons tempt teachers and students alike to rate religions. In an attempt to be fair, the teacher is prone to say that all religions are about the same or that all are equal (when there are different perspectives). Some critics of the public schools, from the religious right, are especially concerned about diminishing the Christian faith. The stance the teacher should favor is to let adherents speak for their faith if they volunteer to do so.[58]

The cautions just mentioned may strike readers as clear warnings to avoid including world religions in the curriculums. There is both anecdotal and empirical evidence to the contrary, that world religions can be dealt with quite effectively. Robert Dilzer, of Newtown High School, Connecticut, has offered a most successful elective course on world religions for many years. Similarly, a teacher of the year from Oregon, Dorothy Sawyer, has also taught such a course.[59]

Two teachers from St. Louis Park High School in Minnesota, Lee Smith and Wes Bodin, developed a high school program on world religions which was titled *Religion in Human Culture.* Professors at the University of California at Santa Barbara, working with area school districts, developed a series of curriculum materials about the influence of world religions in that state's history. Called *Reli-*

gious Contours of California, it became the template for expanded resources developed by John Simmons of Western Illinois University, which is now distributed by Public Broadcasting System as *Beliefs and Believers*.[60]

Because of the interest expressed in this area, the NCRPE and *Religion & Public Education* developed many helpful resources, both on content and teaching methods, for secondary school and middle school teachers. Unfortunately, there are only a few references for elementary school teachers.[61] A commercial textbook, *World Religions in America: An Introduction*, has been published for lower college/upper high school student populations.[62]

Religion Studies in Other Fields

Interestingly, the guideline statements which support teaching about religion in public schools say little about disciplines and fields beyond the three mentioned above. One discipline which has generated wide debate, from newspaper columns to academic journals and in legislative hallways, is science. Scientific creationism will be discussed in some detail later.

Art

The visual arts in the past two centuries, as Diane Apostolos-Cappadona reminds us, have extended beyond painting and sculpture.[63] Photography, movies, television, picture magazines provide new ways to "see." Theological worldviews are found in such traditional works of religious art as Jan van Eyck's *Annunciation* and architecture such as the cathedral at Chartres. In their way, Andy Warhol's *16 Jackies* and Maya Lin's sculpture of the Vietnam Veteran's Memorial incorporate religious motifs, albeit more secular, from more recent times. An outstanding resource for teachers which identifies over 3,000 slides of biblical images is found in the Warshaw Slide Collection at Indiana University.[64]

Music

The area of the performing arts, especially vocal music, is another powerful way societies over the centuries have communicated their religious faiths. In 1987 a committee of the Music Educators National Conference issued a statement endorsing the study of religion as an essential part of the music curriculum. Lenola Allen-Sommerville, a teacher educator, provided suggestions to those public school educators who wished to incorporate African-American music into the classroom.[65] The issue of religious music at special concerts and commencement services will be discussed in the next chapter.

Economics

Warren Nord persuasively argues that many economic theories reflect religious world views. To ignore how various cultures have been based on such perspectives (how often have we heard the term "Protestant work ethic"?) is to offer students an incomplete education.[66]

Health

Charges of secular humanism are often focused in the health area, where teachers or school counselors provide students with ways to improve self-esteem, gain skills in conflict resolution, or understand more clearly issues related to human growth and development. As noted elsewhere, in two court cases secular humanist charges were based upon family values, gender roles, and human sexuality education. The plaintiffs were concerned that public schools promoted critical thinking skills which encouraged students to challenge the values received from their parents.[67] Educators in these areas are discovering that it will be harder to dismiss or ignore religious perspectives; parents from the secular left and the religious right as well as the middle will insist that recognition be given to alternative perspectives.

Science

The debate about changing the way that science is taught in American schools is both of long duration and reflects a number of issues. Those who believe that science is an academic discipline argue that it follows a specific methodology which is at odds with the way that truth (revelation) is obtained religiously. Those who wish "creation science" or "scientific creationism" introduced into the school curriculum posit that evolution, presented as a theory, is less than that. Further, they use the argument of "fairness," suggesting that different points of view about creation and the scientific enterprise at least deserve a dialogue rather than a monologue in the public school classroom. A number of sources are available for those who wish to explore the "creationism" issue.[68] There are numerous sources published now by both pro and con advocates.[69] The lower courts and Supreme Court have ruled that, when state legislatures have clearly been attempting to introduce the specific religious view of creation as presented in the book of Genesis into the schools, that reflects a religious tradition and is not consistent with what is offered in science. Accounts of a special/spontaneous creation, common to many religious communities, can be properly discussed in literature classes.

There are many other dimensions of the interaction of religion and science which should be discussed in public schools. The stereotype that science and religion have always been at war needs to be deconstructed. Clergy of the past, frequently the most highly educated in their communities, were careful observers of nature. In today's scientific world, there are issues of truth and ethics—in the realm of genetic research, for example—which should be examined. The use of empirical research alone is insufficient to provide answers to what is researched and what is to be done with the results of such research. Likewise, it can be argued that there needs to be greater discussion between religionists and scientists about what Douglas Sloan has called the "two truth" approach to knowledge.[70]

Conclusion

This chapter supports the position that it is legal and pedagogically desirable to have religion studies in the public schools. Legally, the Court has decided that it must be done objectively and in the thirty plus years since the *Abington v. Schempp/Murray v. Curlett* decision there have been no significant challenges to that ruling. Indeed, there has come about a significant consensus of support, reflecting liberal and conservative voices in the public square, in addition to professional educators and religious organizations.

As the result of the efforts of individuals and groups described above, curriculum materials consistent with Court guidelines and sensitive to diverse religious traditions have been and are being developed. Teacher pre-service and in-service programs, following action by state legislatures aware of the growing pluralism in our communities, are gradually helping teachers become better able to be effective in the religion studies area. Religious literacy is increasing, passionate inquiry is being nurtured, open and accurate communication about religious differences is being enhanced, and constructive student actions revealing their religious decisions are being demonstrated.

Notes

1. Derek H. Davis, "Religious Pluralism and the Quest for Unity in American Life," *Journal of Church and State* 36, 2 (Spring 1994): 245–259, offers an excellent analysis of issues related to pluralism. The 1993 enrollment figures for American elementary and secondary schools by race and ethnicity are, by percentage: white 66.1, Black 16.6, Hispanic 12.7, Asian and Pacific Islands 3.6, and American Indian/Alaskan Native 1.1. All percentages except white have increased since 1986. Source: National Center for Educational Statistics, *Digest of Education Statistics*, 1995 (Washington, D.C.: U.S. Department of Education, Office of Educational Research and Improvement, 1995), 60. Many of the accounts about students, and similar ones, have appeared in the News section of *Religion & Public Education*, a journal published from 1983 to 1994 by the National Council on Religion and Public Education (hereafter identified as NCRPE). In 1995 the journal changed its name to *Religion & Education*; it is now published by Eden Theological Seminary and Webster University of St. Louis, Mo. All citations to articles from the journal will be noted as *R&E*. [Note: For copies of past issues, contact *Religion & Education*, Department of Religion, Webster University, 470 E. Lockwood Ave., St. Louis, MO 63119.]
2. *Religion in the Public Schools: A Joint Statement of Current Law, April 1995.* Available from 15 East 84 St., Suite 501, New York, NY, 10028; e-mail "listproc@ajcongress.org." For a report of what nineteen groups, including the Christian Coalition, Citizens for Excellence in Education, the National Association of Evangelicals and more "mainline" groups agreed to, see "Coalition Issues Guidance on Religion in Public Schools," *Education Week* (April 19, 1995) 9; for a printed copy of their brochure, "Religious Liberty, Public Education, and the Future of American Democracy: A Statement of Principles," write The Freedom Forum, First Amendment Center, 1207 18th Avenue South, Nashville, TN 37212. The Forum also has reprints of President William Clinton's remarks made on July 12, 1995, as does the U.S. Department of Education.
3. Norman J. Bauer, "The Round Table and Our Civic Religion," *Viewpoints* (March 1995): 1–6, ERIC No. ED 380909; Joe L. Kincheloe, *Understanding the New Right and Its Impact on Education* (Bloomington, Ind.: Phi Delta Kappa Educational Foundation, 1983); Lori Forman, *The Political Activity of the Religious Right in the 1990s: A Critical Analysis* (New York: The American Jewish Committee, March 1994). For liberal voices against religion studies, see Edd Doerr, "Does Religion Belong in Our Public Schools?" *USA Today*, September 1987, 48–50; available as a reprint from Americans for Religious Liberty, P.O. Box 6656, Silver Spring, MD 20906; see also Jon G. Murray, representing American Atheists, *USA Today*, November 30, 1989, who stated "only an atheist could conduct an objective, non participatory classroom evaluation of religion."
4. *Abington School District v. Schempp (PA)/Murray v. Curlett (MD)*, 374 U.S. 203 (1963). Two helpful resources analyzing this and other court cases are: Eugene T. Connors, *Religion and the Schools: Significant Court Decisions in the 1980s* (Bloomington, Ind.: Phi Delta Kappa Educational Foundation, 1988) and Terry Eastland, ed., *Religious Liberty in the Supreme Court: The Cases That Define the Debate over Church and State* (Washington, D.C.: Ethics and Public Policy Center, 1993), 147–168. Eastland begins with a summary of each case, provides

excerpts of opinions, and concludes with media responses of the day. See also Martha McCarthy, "Church and State: Separation or Accommodation?" *Harvard Educational Review* 51, 3 (August 1981): 373–394.

5. John Lyden, ed., *Enduring Issues in Religion*, from the Opposing Viewpoints Series (Green Press: San Diego, Calif., 1995). Lyden offers seven definitions of religion. See also "How Should Religion Be Defined for Public School Study?" (unnumbered pages) in *Public Education Religion Studies: Questions and Answers*, a 1990 reprint by the NCRPE Distribution Center of the Wright State University Public Education Religion Studies guidebook (1974). This booklet and other NCRPE materials are available now from the Butte County Office of Education, 5 Country Center Drive, Oroville, CA 95965, telephone (916) 538–7231.
6. Warren A. Nord, *Religion & American Education: Rethinking a National Dilemma* (Chapel Hill: University of North Carolina Press, 1995), pp. 101–102. See also Charles H. Whittier, *Religion in the Public Schools: Pluralism and Teaching about Religions*, (Washington, D.C.: Congressional Research Service, the Library of Congress, February 15, 1989); Robert Spivey, Edwin Gaustad, and Rodney Allen, *Pathways to Pluralism* (Menlo Park, Calif: Addison-Wesley Publishing, 1990). For a "mainline" church perspective, see Daniel F. Romero, *Our Futures Inextricably Linked: A Vision of Pluralism* (Cleveland: United Church Board for Homeland Ministries, 1994). A conservative perspective is found in Michael Cromartie, ed., *Disciples & Democracy: Religious Conservatives and the Future of American Politics* (Washington, D.C.: Ethics and Public Policy Center/ William B. Eerdmans Publishing Co., 1995).
7. James A. Banks, *Teaching Strategies for Ethnic Studies*, 3rd ed. (Boston: Allyn and Bacon, 1984); Theresa E. McCormick, "Teaching about Religious Diversity as a Multicultural Issue," *R&E* 18, 1–3 (1991): 117–128; Nord, *Religion*, pp. 225–229. For liberal reactions to the religious right, see Americans United for Separation of Church and State, *Reflections on Religious Liberty*, 2nd ed. (Washington, D.C.: Americans United, 1995). A sociological perspective is found in Thomas Robbins and Dick Anthony, eds., *In Gods We Trust: New Patterns of Religious Pluralism in America* (New Brunswick: Transaction Publishers, 1990).
8. Robert Cummings Neville, "Religious Diversity and Cultural Inclusion in America," *R&E* 22, 2 (Fall 1995): 28–39; Charles R. Kniker, *Teaching about Religion in the Public Schools* (Bloomington, Ind.: Phi Delta Kappa Educational Foundation, 1985), 8–11; Richard L. Christensen, "Reflections on a Historical Relationship: Religion and the Public Schools," *New Conversations* 17, 2 (Summer 1995): 29–31. [Note: *New Conversations* is a publication of the United Church Board for Homeland Ministries, United Church of Christ, Cleveland, Ohio.]
9. Harvey G. Neufeldt, "Religion, Morality and Schooling: Forging the Nineteenth Century Protestant Consensus," and Seymour W. Itzkoff, "Religious Pluralism and Public Education," in *Religion and Morality in American Schooling*, eds. Thomas C. Hunt and Marilyn M. Maxson (Washington, D.C.: University Press of America, 1981).
10. James Dunn, "Defending the Common School," *R&E* 22, 2 (Fall 1995): 49–57; Charles R. Kniker, "Reflections on the Continuing Crusade for Common Schools: Glorious Failures, Shameful Harvests, or . . . ?" in *Religious Schooling in America*, eds. James C. Carper and Thomas C. Hunt (Birmingham, Ala.: Religious Education Press, 1984), 169–206; Nord, *Religion*, 71–74.
11. John Westerhoff, *McGuffey and His Readers* (Nashville: Abingdon Press, 1978); Christensen, "Reflections," 30; Carl F. Kaestle, "Moral Education and Common Schools in America: A Historian's View," *Journal of Moral Education* 13 (May 1984): 101–111.
12. *Pierce v. Society of Sisters*, 268 U.S. 510 (1925). Robert Michaelsen, *Piety in the Public School* (New York: Macmillan, 1970) and Richard C. McMillan, *Religion in the Public Schools: An Introduction* (Macon, Ga.: Mercer University Press, 1984)

provide helpful historical context and case interpretations from this period. See Eastland, *Religious Liberty*, 83–104, on *McCollum*, 333 U.S. 203 (1948).

13. Nord, *Religion*, 243–244; Nicholas Piediscalzi and Barbara Ann Swyhart, *Distinguishing Moral Education, Values Clarification, and Religion-Studies* (Missoula, Mont.: American Academy of Religion, 1976). See also Educational Policies Commission, *Moral and Spiritual Values in the Public Schools* (Washington, D.C.: National Education Association, 1951) and *Zorach v. Clauson*, 343 U.S. 306 (1952).
14. Eastland, *Religious Liberty*, 152, American Association of School Administrators, *Religion in the Public Schools* (Arlington, Va.: American Association of School Administrators, 1986), 18–21. For the fundamentalist reactions to *Schempp*, see James R. Durham, *Secular Darkness: Religious Right Involvement in Texas Public Education, 1963–1989* (New York: Peter Lang, 1995); also Thomas C. Hunt and Barbara K. Bellefeville, "The Bible in the Schools: The *Edgerton and Schempp* Decisions Revisited," *R&E* 15, 3 (Summer 1988): 321–330.
15. Justice Brennan's concurrence was forty-four pages in length. See Eastland, *Religious Liberty*, 153–164, for excerpts of his remarks and other commentaries. Not many years before the decision, national discussions about religion studies were taking place in education circles. One massive effort involved over twenty higher education institutions; see A.L. Sebaly, ed., *Teacher Education and Religion* (Oneonta, N.Y.: American Association of Colleges for Teacher Education, 1959).
16. Justice Goldberg's opinion is found at 306 in *Schempp*. For a more recent rationale which makes many of the same points the justices made, see Cheryl B. Aspy and David N. Aspy, "Why Religion Should Be an Integral Part of Public School Education," *Counseling and Values* 37, 3 (April 1993): 149–155.
17. *The Religious Educator* II, 1 (January 1972): 1, 4. The Religious Education Association (REA) was one of the major sponsors of NCRPE; today the REA and the Association of Professors and Researchers in Religious Education (APRRE) through the journal *Religious Education* publish occasional articles on religion studies. See also Nicholas Piediscalzi, "Public Education Religion Studies 1950–2000," *R&E* 15, 4 (Fall 1988): 403–416.
18. Nicholas Piediscalzi, "Back to the Future?: Public Education Religion Studies and the AAR in the 1970s and 1990s—Unique Opportunities for Development," *R&E* 18, 2 (1991): 237–251. *R&E* 17, 2 (Spring-Summer 1990) contained several articles on preparing teachers, including a description of a program at Western Michigan University. Adrianne Nagy, "Where Education Meets Vocation: The Program in Religion and Secondary Education at HDS," *Harvard Divinity School Bulletin* 23, 2 (1994): 3. Florida State University was a pioneer in producing religion studies curriculum materials; for a history of its successes and failures, see Robert A. Spivey, "After the Fall," *R&E* 15, 4 (Fall 1988): 417–422.
19. The NCRPE Distribution Center moved from Iowa State University to Indiana University of Pennsylvania in 1993, and in 1994/1995 to Butte County Office of Education, Calif. Others publishing articles and producing or distributing student and teacher materials include but are not limited to: A committee of the American Educational Research Association, the Special Interest Group on Religion and Education, which publishes the *Religion & Education Forum* (a newsletter); the Association of Supervision and Curriculum Development (ASCD) of Alexandria, Va., which publishes the *Religion and Public Education Network Newsletter;* the Freedom Forum, First Amendment Center at Vanderbilt University; National Conference (New York, N.Y.); and National Organization of Legal Problems in Education (NOLPE).
20. *Religion in the Public School Curriculum: Questions and Answers.* Published in Washington, D.C., by the following groups: American Academy of Religion, American Association of School Administrators, American Federation of Teachers, American Jewish Committee, Americans United Research Foundation, ASCD, Baptist Joint Committee on Public Affairs, Christian Legal Society, National Association of Evangelicals, National Conference of Christians and Jews,

National Council of Churches, NCRPE, NCSS, National Education Association, National School Boards Association, and Church of Christ of Latter Day Saints. In subsequent printings, additional groups were added.

21. Diane Berreth of the ASCD assumed a leadership role in NCRPE in the 1980s. A number of materials on religion studies were published. In 1995, ASCD released "A House Divided . . . Religion and the Public Schools," two audio cassettes featuring interviews with liberals and conservatives on a variety of topics including pluralism, character education, and school choice (Stock #295066V84). Charles Haynes, who was a principal writer of ASCD materials, has more recently edited *Finding Common Ground: A First Amendment Guide to Religion and Public Education* (Nashville: The Freedom Forum, 1994). Haynes and others became very active in California training teachers after the Social Studies framework was adopted in that state.
22. Connors, *Significant Court Decisions*, 31–36; James E. Wood, Jr., "Church-State Issues in Education in the 1980s," R&E 12, 3 (Summer 1985): 75–81; Durham in *Secular Darkness* has as one of his major themes the fear of secular humanism.
23. Stephen Bates, *Battleground: One Mother's Crusade, the Religious Right, and the Struggle for Control of Our Classrooms* (New York: Poseidon Press, 1993); Robert Boston, *Why the Religious Right Is Wrong about Separation of Church and State* (Buffalo, N.Y.: Prometheus Books, 1993), 93–122; Eugene F. Provenzo, Jr., *Religious Fundamentalism and American Education: The Battle for the Public Schools* (Albany: State University of New York Press, 1990), 31–50.
24. *Everson v. Board of Education* 330 U.S. 1 (1947), at 15–16.
25. Nord, *Religion*, 236–261, provides a series of arguments—epistemologically, politically, morally, and constitutionally—regarding neutrality. He concludes that it is necessary to have "curricular neutrality" to meet legal guidelines, adding, however, that there are many difficulties for teachers in carrying out the letter of the law.
26. Charles C. Haynes and Charles R. Kniker, "Religion in the Classroom: Meeting the Challenges and Avoiding the Pitfalls," *Social Education* 54, 5 (September 1990): 305–309. Charles C. Haynes, ed., *Finding Common Ground: A First Amendment Guide to Religion and Public Education* (Nashville: Freedom Forum, 1994): 7.1–7.17. See also Charles R. Kniker, "Accommodating the Religious Diversity of Public School Students: Putting the 'CARTS' Before the Horse," *R&E* 15, 3 (Summer 1988): 304–320, and Haynes, *Finding*, 7.1–7.10.
27. Paul J. Will, ed., *Public Education Religion Studies: An Overview* (Chico, Calif.: Scholars Press, 1981), includes articles on practices in Michigan, Minnesota, and a national survey of certification policies by Frank Steeves and Joseph Forcinelli. (See also n. 18.)
28. Philip Phenix, "Perceptions of an Ethicist about the Affective," 86, in Louise M. Berman and Jessi A. Rodenick, eds., *Feeling, Valuing, and the Art of Growing: Insights into the Affective* (Washington, D.C.: Association of Supervision and Curriculum Development, 1977). The hermeneutical questions which can be raised are nicely treated in David L. Barr, *New Testament Story: An Introduction,* 2nd ed. (Belmont: Wadsworth Publishing Co., 1995), when he discusses how a text needs to be interpreted through at least four lenses.
29. Guntram G. Bischoff, "The Pedagogy of Religiology," in Anne Carr and Nicholas Piediscalzi, eds., The *Academic Study of Religion, 1975* (Chico, Calif.: American Academy of Religion, 1975) 134–135.
30. Jonathan Kozol, *The Night Is Dark and I Am Far from Home* (New York: Houghton Mifflin, 1975), 166, 126.
31. This statement was developed by staff of the Public Education Religion Studies Center (PERSC) at Wright State University in Dayton, Ohio, in 1974. It has been reprinted frequently, including appearing in the AASA, *Religion* and recently in Haynes, *Finding Common Ground.*

32. John R. Whitney and Susan Wiltowe, *Religious Literature of the West* (Minneapolis: Augsburg Publishing House, 1971); *Religious Studies Guidelines* (Madison: Wisconsin Department of Public Instruction, 1982), Bulletin No. 2385; Michigan State Department of Education, *Humanities in Michigan Schools: A Position Statement* (Lansing: Michigan State Board of Education, 1987); Mirko Strazicich, ed., *Moral and Civic Education and Teaching about Religion Handbook on the Legal Rights and Responsibilities of School Personnel and Students* (Sacramento: California State Department of Education, 1990).
33. Dallas Independent School District, *Helpful Information on Religion-Related Issues*, a booklet issued by the District in 1992. For a partial reprint, see Haynes, *Finding Common Ground*, 13.2–13.3. For other samples of local district statements, see Haynes, Appendix B.
34. Charles R. Kniker, "A Survey of State Laws and Regulations Regarding Religion and Moral Education," *R&E* 16, 3 (Fall 1989): 433–457. Recent information is based on a phone conversation with Charles C. Haynes, January 9, 1996.
35. Thayer S. Warshaw, "Religion Studies, Moral Education, and Values Clarification in American Public Schools: Definitions," a paper provided for AAR members in 1976. Warshaw also contributed to one of the first major background texts in this field, Nicholas Piediscalzi and William E. Collie, eds., *Teaching about Religion in Public Schools* (Niles, Ill.: Argus Communications, 1977).
36. Barbara Ann Swyhart, "Paradigms-of-Reality-in-Process: A Methodology for Interdisciplinary Religion-Studies," *Religious Education* LXXII, 4 (July-August 1977): 425. She posits religion studies is a commitment to a neutral academic methodology accompanied by a detached academic enthusiasm and appreciation of religion and religious experience, and includes diverse methodologies conditioned by the context.
37. Quoted in a brochure developed by the Task Force on Religious Pluralism and Public Education, a unit of the New Mexico Inter-Church Agency, 1982.
38. Michael Novak, *Ascent of the Mountain, Flight of the Dove* (New York: Harper and Row, 1971), 1–3, 46–47.
39. *Illinois ex rel. McCollum v. Board of Education* 333 U.S. 203 (1948).
40. Charles R. Kniker, "Should the Bible be Taught in Public Schools? Yes!" *Bible Review* XI, 3 (June 1995): 36–39; John M. Swomley, "Should the Bible be Taught in Public Schools? Yes . . . But," *Bible Review* XI, 3 (June 1995): 36, 39. For a more extensive treatment, see Thayer S. Warshaw, *Handbook for Teaching the Bible in Literature Classes* (Nashville: Abingdon, 1978). Some instances of teachers and groups using *Schempp* to get confessional materials in the schools do exist. For a brief review of several cases, see Perry A. Zirkel, "Teaching the Good Book," *Phi Delta Kappan* 71, 10 (June 1990): 814–815.
41. Thayer S. Warshaw, "Teaching about Religions in Public Schools," *Religious Education* 81, 1 (Winter 1986): 79–86 raises many of the issues for teachers that Swomley (see n. 40) poses. They include being sensitive to the many backgrounds of students (the number of faith traditions they come from as well as their levels of knowledge about their traditions). Swomley asks which version or versions of the Bible should be used.
42. James S. Ackerman and Thayer S. Warshaw, *The Bible as/in Literature*, 2nd ed. (Chicago: Scott Foresman, 1976); John B. Gabel and Charles B. Wheeler, *The Bible as Literature: An Introduction* (New York: Oxford University Press, 1986); Society of Biblical Literature, *The Bible in American Culture* (Chico, Calif.: Scholars Press, 1982); Linda L. Meixner with Thayer S. Warshaw, *The Bible in Literature Courses: Successful Lesson Plans* (Ames, Iowa: NCRPE, 1992). [Note: Meixner's book is available through the Butte County Office of Education; see n. 5.] Charles Suhor and Bernard Suhor, *Teaching Values in the Literature Classroom: A Debate in Print* (Washington, D.C.: ERIC-REC, 1992).
43. Warren A. Nord, "Taking Religion Seriously," *Social Education* 54, 5 (September 1990): 289.

44. ASCD Panel on Religion in the Curriculum, *Religion in the Curriculum* (Alexandria, Va.: Association of Supervision and Curriculum Development, 1987), was among the most widely quoted of textbook studies. John W. McDermott Jr., "The Treatment of Religion in School Textbooks: A Political Analysis and a Modest Proposal," *R&E* 13, 4 (Fall 1986): 62–77, did a comprehensive review of the studies by Paul Vitz, People for the American Way, and others. James W. Loewen, *Lies My Teacher Told Me: Everything Your American History Textbook Got Wrong* (New York: The New Press, 1995) has only a few references to religion.
45. Tony Podesta, "The Uphill Battle for Quality Textbooks," *R&E* 13, 3 (Summer 1986): 60.
46. Gilbert T. Sewall, *Religion in the Classroom: What the Textbooks Tell Us* (New York: American Textbook Council, 1995).
47. The California 3Rs Project is a Teacher and Community Civic Education Project of The Freedom Forum, First Amendment Center at Vanderbilt University, Peabody College at Vanderbilt University, and the California County Superintendents Educational Services Association. See also Charles C. Haynes, *Religious Freedom in America* (Washington, D.C.: Americans United Research Foundation, 1986).
48. See *Social Education* 15, 4 (September 1990), 310 and 280.
49. Haynes, *Finding Common Ground* (2.1–2.8 and appendix A.1-A.14). Over fifty articles have been published in *R&E* related to subject matter and methods in the social studies area.
50. Austin Creel, "Teaching the Teachers: A University-Public School Partnership," *Social Education* 54, 5 (September 1990): 291–293. See Nord, *Religion*, p. 316.
51. "[Illinois] Bill Would Authorize Teachers to Use Religious References," *St. Louis Post Dispatch*, March 26, 1995.
52. Curriculum units developed by teachers and state departments of education in Nebraska, North Dakota, Oklahoma, Iowa, and others are in the author's collection.
53. Nord, *Religion*, 384.
54. Sr. Mary Jessica Karlinger, S.N.D., "Teaching the Role of Religion in American History: A Case Study," *Social Education* 54, 5 (September 1990): 298–299; John K. Simmons, "A Religious Contours Course: A Media Update," *R&E* 20, 1–3 (1993): 134–139; Charles R. Kniker, "Teaching About Religion in Today's Social Studies Classrooms: An Iowa Survey," *R&E* 14, 1 (Winter 1987): 85–100, and 101–102, which contained a list of student activities. Another survey was conducted by Steven J. Stein, "The Indiana Religion Studies Project: A Participant Survey," *R&E* 12, 3 (Summer 1985): 87–98. For teacher guidelines, see Thayer S. Warshaw, "The Bible as Textbook in Public Schools," *R&E* 17, 1 (Winter 1990): 130–132. See n. 26, Haynes and Kniker citation.
55. Contact either the First Amendment Center at Webster University or the Butte County Office of Education for resources. (See n. 2 and n. 5 for addresses.) The Department of Religion at Webster University has both back issues of the journal, *Religion & Public Education*, and indexes on religion studies topics for sale. (See n. 1 for address of *Religion & Education* office.) See also *Social Education* 54, 5, (1990): 299, for additional references and Thayer S. Warshaw, "Preparing Social Studies Teachers to Teach about Religion," *R&E* 13, 1 (Winter 1986): 15.
56. To obtain a calendar, write National Conference, 71 Fifth Avenue, New York, NY 10003, or contact one of its regional offices. See the 26th Annual Gallup poll on education, in *Phi Delta Kappan* 76, 1 (September 1994): 41–56, which indicates a support for world religions in the public schools.
57. James Carse, "Diversity in the World's Religions," *National Forum* LXXIV, 1 (Winter 1994): 26–27.
58. Kniker, "Teaching about Religions," *R&E* (1987), 30–32; Kniker, "Accommodating . . . ," *R&E* (1988): 317.
59. Robert J. Dilzer, "Connecticut High School's Most Popular Elective Course—Comparative Religions," *R&E* 13, 2 (Spring 1986): 41–44; Dorothy Sawyer, "Reli-

gion Classes: A Public School Success," *R&E* 15, 4 (Fall 1988): 441–444; Paul E. and Beth Stroble, "'Religion is a Personal Thing': Students' Portfolio Reflections in a World Religions Course," *R&E* 20, 1–3 (1993): 6–12.

60. Contact World Religions Curriculum Center, 6425 West 33rd St., St. Louis Park, MN 55426 for more information on *Religion in Human Culture*. For a video series prepared for college audiences, see John K. Simmons, *Beliefs and Believers* (Washington, D.C.: Public Broadcasting System, 1990). Another media resource is *The Long Search: A Study of Religions*, a BBC production distributed in the U.S.A. by the Miami-Dade County College, Auxiliary Services, 11011 S.W. 104 Street, Miami, FL 33176.

61. Wes Bodin and Lee Smith, eds., *NCRPE Resource Packet on Teaching about World Religions* (n.d., c. 1990 or 1991), available from Butte County Office of Education. Selected articles on this topic in *R&E* were printed in 1985, 1987, 1989, and 1990. Dorothy Dixon, *World Religions for the Classrooms* (Mystic, Conn.: Twenty-third Publications, 1975), a text written for the elementary level.

62. Jacob Neusner, ed., *World Religions in America: An Introduction* (Louisville: Westminster/John Knox Press, 1994). *R&E* has published numerous articles regarding religion studies in the classrooms of many counties.

63. Diane Apostolos-Cappadona, "Art of Seeing Cultural Values: Religion and Art in Public Education," *R&E* 15, 4 (Fall 1988): 423–433.

64. Indiana University Biblical Studies Slide Collection, Department of Religious Studies, Sycamore Hall Room #230, Bloomington, IN 47405.

65. Music Educators National Conference, "Religious Music in the Schools," *R&E* 15, 4 (Fall 1988): 435–440; Lenola Allen-Sommerville, "African American 'Church Music' in the Classroom: A Cultural Portrait," *R&E* 20, 1–3 (1993): 76–83.

66. Nord, *Religion*, 31–32, 144–147, 297–298.

67. AASA, *Religion* (1986), 38–40; Susan D. Rose, "Gender, Education, and the New Christian Right," in Robbins and Anthony, *In Gods We Trust*, 99–117; James E. Wood, "Religious Fundamentalism and the Public Schools," *R&E* 51, 1 (Winter 1988): 51–63; Mark Pitts, "In Search of Middle Ground: An Evangelical Approach to Issues in Public Education," *R&E* 14, 2 (1987): 157–165; Charles J. Russo, et al., "Sexuality and AIDS Education in the Schools—An Ongoing Controversy," *R&E* 18, 1–3 (1991): 257–313; Richard P. Manatt, *When Right Is Wrong: Fundamentalists and the Public Schools* (Lancaster, Pa.: Technomic Publishing Co., 1995).

68. Eugene Bjorklun, "Evolution and Creationism in the Public School Curriculum," *R&E* 19, 1 (Winter 1992): 57–66; Verlyn L. Barker, *Creationism, the Church, and the Public School* (Cleveland: United Church Board for Homeland Ministries, 1995); Jerry Bergman, *Teaching about the Creation/Evolution Controversy* (Bloomington, Ind.: Phi Delta Kappa Educational Foundation, 1979); Provenzo, *Fundamentalism*, 51–64.

69. For support of evolution, see National Academy of Sciences, *Science and Creationism* (Washington, D.C.: Academy Press, 1984); Molleen Matsumura, ed., *Voices for Evolution*, rev. ed. (Berkeley: National Center for Science Education, Inc., 1995), includes statements from a number of organizations; Stan Weinberg, ed., *Reviews of Thirty-One Creationists Books* (Syosset, N.Y.: National Center for Science Education, Inc., 1984). For advocates for creationism, see Richard A. Baer Jr., "They *Are* Teaching Religion in the Public Schools," *Christianity Today* (February 17, 1984): 12–15, with responses on 16–19; also American Scientific Affiliation, *Teaching Science in a Climate of Controversy* (Ipswich, Mass.: American Scientific Affiliation, 1986).

70. Ronald S. Cole-Turner, *An Unavoidable Challenge: Our Church in an Age of Science and Technology* (Cleveland: UCBHM Distribution Center, 1992); Douglas Sloan, *Faith & Knowledge: Mainline Protestantism and American Higher Education* (Louisville: Westminster/John Knox Press, 1994), 143–144.

Chapter Two
Religious Practices in Public Schools

Charles R. Kniker

The American public, the courts, and professional educators have recognized the important role of religion in past and contemporary societies. As chapter one indicated, a growing consensus of support for religion studies in public schools has emerged. Curriculum materials which meet Supreme Court guidelines, that are pedagogically appropriate, and that increasingly reflect the religious pluralism of the nation are being developed. State departments of education, regional educational service units, and local districts are offering teacher in-service workshops and programs for school board members and administrators to help them become familiar with religion studies curriculum and sensitive to the diverse religious backgrounds of today's students.

What then of the "informal" or what some call the "hidden" curriculum? How willing are our schools and courts to be open to religious practices that are outside the mainstream, the traditional? What is to be done about a school which has a prayer as its official song? What of the student discouraged from praying prior to lunch in the cafeteria? Was it proper for a school board to dismiss a teacher for reading his Bible during the students' free reading time? Should a student who wished to do a research paper on Jesus have been denied that request? What action should have been taken regarding the principal who encouraged public prayers prior to sports events? Should the Bible study club be recognized as having the same standing as the scouting troop when school facilities are opened to the community after school hours? What prohibitions, if any, should be placed on distribution of religious literature?

The guidelines for religious expression that President William Clinton announced in July 1995 attempted to answer some of these policy questions. The guidelines received widespread support, but they did not and will not answer all questions regarding religious freedom. Indeed, church-state debates have been one of the top news stories of the year.[1] Those who thought Clinton did not go far enough were encouraged when Representative Henry J. Hyde of Illinois introduced a "Religious Equality Amendment." Its text reads, "Neither the United States nor any state shall deny benefits to or otherwise discriminate against any private person or group on account of religious expression, belief or identity; nor shall the prohibition on laws respecting an establishment of religion be construed to require such discrimination."[2] Proponents argue it restores protection of religious liberties weakened in recent decades and could be interpreted, if passed, as providing support for vouchers. Opponents argue it is not needed and goes too far.

The purpose of this chapter is to examine religious practices to which public school teachers, administrators, staff, school board members, and concerned citizens ought to be sensitive. The chapter explores typical situations, examines current state and local school district policies and rules, describes media resources and groups providing resources, and offers projections of future areas of concern. While lower and Supreme Court decisions are cited when necessary, it should be understood that more extensive treatment of legal issues is left to other sources as well as later chapters in this book.

For this chapter, topics include: (a) school-sponsored prayers, moments of silence, and graduation prayers; (b) equal access and use of school facilities; and (c) observance of religious holidays. Both whether or not schools should recognize or in some way commemorate major religious holidays and the excusals of teachers and students missing school for religious reasons are discussed here. In addition, because of the increasing diversity of students and faculty in public schools and the increase in religious fundamentalism in the country, these topics are included: (d) distribution of religious material; (e) religious diet and dress; and (f) display of religious art and symbols.

Although of some relevance, there are other aspects of religious expression and religious practices which will not be covered, at either the public school or higher education levels. Topics omitted include financial support of nonpublic schools, censorship, and released time. Released time programs are those which permit students to be dismissed for part of the school day to receive religious instruction at their houses of worship. A practice popular in the 1940s and 1950s, it may be receiving additional attention in the future.

Background and Religious Guideline Resources

The United States of America has a unique "church and state" relationship, although more precisely this is an interface of government, religion, and education. The concept of religious freedom was immensely important for those who came from Europe in the 1600s. Some colonies developed established churches, a policy not completely abandoned until the 1830s. Others opted for religious tolerance. That religion was still a critical matter for the new nation is evident in the prominent place it is given in the First Amendment to the Constitution. In part this amendment states: "Congress shall make no law respecting an establishment of religion, or prohibiting the free exercise thereof." As Jan Robbins notes, while the language is clear, no clear guidelines result for education policymakers. The Establishment Clause prohibits government from assisting religion; the Free Exercise Clause prohibits it from hindering religion. While the number of cases on government, religion, and education have increased markedly in the past fifty years, one overarching principle has been affirmed: "If there is any fixed star in our constitutional constellation, it is that no official, high or petty, can prescribe what shall be orthodox in politics, nationalism, religion, or other matters of opinion or force citizens to confess by word or act their faith therein."[3] The Court's position regarding both religion in the curriculum and religious practices was stated most forcefully in *Abington v. Schempp* in 1963. Speaking for the majority, Justice Tom Clark wrote: "In the relationship between man and religion, the State is firmly committed to a position of neutrality."[4] Concurring, Justice William J. Brennan, after providing an extensive historical review of church-state relations, commented: "The State must be steadfastly neutral in all matters of faith, and neither favor nor inhibit religion. . . . Government cannot sponsor religious exercises in the public schools without jeopardizing that neutrality."[5]

Space limitations do not permit review of the history of legal decisions related to this area or a debate about whether the schools today need to be more "accommodating" to students' religious beliefs and practices. One trend to be noted is that local districts, states, and the courts are clearly granting greater recognition to students' expressions of religious faith. This chapter will include mention of policies, laws, and resource materials from local schools, state government, federal government, education organizations, and religious and civic groups.

Local School Districts

With over 15,000 school districts in the country, it should be acknowledged that most decisions regarding religious practices, historically as well as today, are made at the local level. There are some outstanding examples of local school districts which have taken on the task of preparing guidelines for a number of areas which will be addressed in this chapter. They include Dallas, Texas; St. Louis Park, Minnesota; Dubuque, Iowa; Des Moines, Iowa; Indianapolis, Indiana; and Wicomico County Board of Education, Salisbury, Maryland.[6]

State Government

In the United States, education is a responsibility of state government. Why? Because the Tenth Amendment to the Constitution states that anything not previously mentioned is a state matter, and the words "education" or "school" do not appear earlier. As a result, today educational practices can vary widely from state to state. Policies mandated in one state or a publicized case from one area can not be assumed to set precedent elsewhere.[7] In most states, the department of education will have its own legal staff, although in a few states, education matters are handled from the office of the State Attorney General.

There are different levels of legislative and bureaucratic actions in states. These definitions should be kept in mind: common law—a law upheld through court decisions but never passed by a legislative body (also known as case law); statutory law—a law established through legislative action; regulation—condition(s) that specify how the law is to be interpreted, usually developed by a nonlegislative body; and guideline—specifications that are recommended but not required.[8] Of these four categories, statutory laws are the most commonly used method to address religion practices.

Most surveys of state laws address one issue, for example, home schooling or funding for nonpublic schools. The last comprehensive study of state regulations related to religion in the curriculum and religious practices was published in 1989. At that time twenty-three states had legislation and guidelines related to excused absences for religious holidays, twenty-two permitted observance of a moment of silence, nineteen made specific mention of freedom of speech for students, nineteen had a requirement that students were to recite the Pledge of Allegiance, fifteen granted equal access for student meetings, fourteen allowed distribution of religious materials, fifteen indicated schools should be sensitive to students' religious diets and prayers, and fourteen prohibited invocations at school events.[9]

It is wise to consult one's State Department of Education to learn about local or regional guidelines. As discussed in the previous chapter, states have made efforts to bring about curricular changes in specific areas, such as character education. In the past 20 years, Wisconsin and California are among the states which have developed guidelines in the religious practices area. Other states are now engaged in this field.[10]

Federal Government Sources

The president and executive branch of the government make pronouncements about religion and the schools from time to time. As indicated in Chapter 1, in July 1995 President William Clinton announced guidelines for religion studies and instructed the Secretary of Education to send copies to all the school districts in the country. The U.S. Department of Education is one source for this guideline.[11]

The U.S. Supreme Court and the federal courts make decisions which sometimes have a major impact and at other times a minimal impact upon behaviors of local schools. Ironically, some of the most frequently mentioned decisions may be largely ignored. Another truism is that the Court's decisions are often inaccurately or incompletely reported. To receive the most current information on court decisions, several sources are recommended.[12]

The Congress of the United States, reflecting citizens' concerns about religion, has certainly attempted to legislate in this area from time to time. One of the most persistent issues has been school-sponsored prayer. In 1994, a prayer amendment was again declared a high priority for congressional leaders. Since the early 1960s, over 200 attempts have been made by Congress to amend the First Amendment to include prayer. As will be discussed later, Congress did pass the Equal Access Act in 1984 and in 1993 legislated the Religious Freedom Restoration Act (RFRA). The latter was done because of the feeling that government had too often in recent years prohibited individual expression of religion. Until 1990 the standard used was that a governmental unit (such as a state department of education or a local school district) could prohibit a religious practice if there was "compelling state interest." The RFRA places more of a burden on the governmental agency to make its case to prohibit or limit a religious activity.[13] The significance of this act is that it makes it necessary for the State to have the burden of proof to stop a religious practice because to deny accommodation is to deny personal religious liberty.

Education Organizations

Periodically, national organizations of professional educators will issue helpful resources for their members. The American Association of School Administrators (AASA) and the National School Board Association have been among the most active groups in this field.[14] The National Education Association and the American Federation of Teachers, the largest teacher organizations, have participated in developing some of the pamphlets and brochures previously described.[15] Two professional societies, the Association of Supervision and Curriculum Development (ASCD) and Phi Delta Kappa (PDK) have a history of creating resource materials on religious practices; the ASCD now produces the *Religion and Public Education Network Newsletter*. Occasionally, policy statements are developed by "guild" groups, such as the National Council for the Social Studies (NCSS) and the National Council for Teachers of English (NCTE).

Civic and Religious Organizations

"Civic" here means both groups which historically have been concerned about legal issues relative to church-state matters as well as groups which have been formed because they have a particular concern about constitutional rights and educational practice. Groups in these categories include: American Civil Liberties Union (ACLU), Americans United for Separation of Church and State (Americans United), American Center for Law and Justice (ACLJ), and People for the American Way (PAW). Higher education-related groups include, for example, Baylor University's J.M. Dawson Center for Church-State Studies and the First Freedoms Center at Vanderbilt.[16] The National Council on Religion and Public Education (NCRPE), before its dissolution, was related to several universities; the journal it founded, *Religion & Public Education*, is now located at Webster University, St. Louis, Missouri.

Certain groups with religious ties or interests also prepare materials on First Amendment issues. They include the Anti-Defamation League (ADL), the American Jewish Committee (AJC), and the National Council of Churches (NCC). Some Protestant denominations, including the Methodists, Presbyterians, Lutherans, and the United Church of Christ, have issued pronouncements and position papers on public education. In the past decade, groups associated with what is frequently called the Religious Right, have spoken out on religious practice issues in public schools. They include the Christian Coalition, Focus on the Family, and the Council for Excellence in Education. One organization, the Rutherford Institute, was founded to help students who had difficulties in the public schools when they expressed their religious faith.[17]

School-Sponsored Prayers and Moments of Silence

Today there is no "hotter" political issue involving religion and the schools than prayer, more precisely, school-sponsored prayer. There is still much confusion about what the courts have allowed or not allowed, and which practices are permissible. Among those who write about this or seek to legislate school prayer today, there is little disagreement that voluntary (student-initiated) prayers have never been "outlawed." For example, a student can pray before a test or meal. The crux of the matter has been the extent to which the school, a government agency, can organize, mandate, or provide support for prayer groups. Hence the issue is about organized or school-sponsored prayer. This section begins with a retrospective, including an examination of popular beliefs about reasons to have prayer in the schools. Three dimensions of the prayer issue will then be explored: what can or cannot occur in the classroom (teacher-led prayers) and moments of silence, student-led prayers in other school settings, and prayers at commencement and baccalaureate services.

School prayer is an important issue for some because it symbolizes the past greatness of America, beginning with the belief that the country was built upon a Judeo-Christian foundation. To lose that foundation is to abandon the moral compass and source of ethical authority the nation needs. For those who hold this view, the absence of prayer in schools is the sign, if not the root cause, of the moral decline of America. To return prayer to schools, they argue, would reduce crime, improve family life, and bolster the economy, because it would teach discipline and lift ethical standards. One counter argument is that school-sponsored prayer is not "magical." Another is that the battle over prayer is not a religious matter, but actually a conflict to determine who belongs and who doesn't, in terms of ethnicity, class, and status. Others argue that on religious grounds, it makes no theological sense to support "generic" prayers, for religion is not religion if it is not specific. It makes little sense, further, pedagogically and politically, to force students to pray.[18]

The polls consistently show that a large percentage of Americans (70 percent to 80 percent) favor prayer in the schools. However, a survey of educators indicated that less than half favored school-sponsored prayer.[19] Responding to popular opinion, the House of Representatives and Senate have made numerous attempts to amend the First Amendment since 1963. President Ronald Reagan spent considerable effort in his early years in office to promote a prayer amendment. The Republican-dominated Congress of 1994 indicated its first priority was a school prayer amendment. Why such efforts have failed have been analyzed by many; a chief reason offered is that the pluralism of the country ultimately has brought its defeat.[20]

Why has this issue been so persistent? Why the outrage about its perceived omission from schools? First, an historical perspective. At the local school level, prayers were not the controversial issue, Bible reading and hymn singing were more likely to cause disputes. School-sponsored prayer is not as long standing a custom, nor as widespread as commonly assumed. Prior to the *Engel v. Vitale* decision in 1962, studies reveal that twelve states required prayers and another twelve did not permit school prayer.[21] In *Engel v. Vitale* the Supreme Court found that a nondenominational prayer prepared for use in the public schools of New York by a Regents committee was unconstitutional; it established a religious practice. A year later in *Abington v. Schempp* and *Murray v. Curlett*, two separate cases reviewed by the Court as one, the justices decided that school prayer and Bible reading, when required of students, violated both the First and Fourteenth Amendments to the Constitution. The reactions to the 1962 decision began the series of attempts by congressional leaders to add the prayer amendment. President Reagan's proposal was advanced in May 1982 but defeated in 1984.[22]

Those wishing to gain more detailed information about the legal cases already discussed and those to be treated below will find a number of excellent references available, including some produced by the educational, civic, and religious organizations already mentioned. Cited here are additional items related to the three topics about to be explored.[23]

Certainly some dimensions of school prayer are confusing. However, the majority of cases which relate to prayers led by the teacher in an individual classroom or by an administrative staff member over the public address system at the start of the school day have consistently been found to be unconstitutional. Any doubts about that were put to rest when the *Wallace v. Jaffee* decision from Mobile, Alabama, was made by the U.S. Supreme Court in 1985.[24]

A number of cases on school prayer occurred during the 1980s and 1990s. In Michigan, Bible stories were read in an elementary classroom followed by the Lord's prayer. A "New Age" meditative exercise at a California elementary school was challenged because to some it seemed a prayer. In South Carolina and New Jersey parents questioned whether the "new" moments of silence were actually "old" prayers in a different format. An assistant principal in Alabama filed a lawsuit in early 1996 challenging a number of religious practices still allowed in the DeKalb County school system, including school prayer. A school principal in Mississippi who advocated teacher-led prayers was fired although he had much community support.[25]

The trend has been for states to pass legislation permitting moments of silence. In Georgia a state law on moment of silence was upheld recently. One study in the early 1980s indicated that twenty states at that time had such legislation on the books. Most legal authorities believe that, if the intent of the legislation is clearly shown to provide a moment of reflection and is not a back-door attempt to reintroduce prayer, it is acceptable.[26]

Those who have opposed school-sponsored prayer have included a number of Jewish and Protestant groups as well as representatives from some fundamentalist traditions. Statements against organized prayer have been written by conservative columnists George Will and James Kilpatrick, as well as representatives of Buddhist and Islamic groups. The National Association of Evangelicals, for example, opposed the 1962 *Engel* decision. Some argue that prayer will not be a unifying force for American society, but will in fact increase ethnic and religious strife. Stephen Carter begins his discussion of school prayer by summarizing what the Court did and did not say. "What the First Amendment does not allow, according to the Justices, is organized classroom prayer, whether led by a teacher or by a student, as a part of the regular school day. . . ." He adds,

> *It does not mean that God is not allowed in the classroom, a metaphorical banishment that would be a metaphysical impossibility. It does mean that the state, in the person of the teacher, the classroom's authority figure, cannot tell the students whether to believe in God, whether to worship, or how. Organized classroom prayer is forbidden because there is no way to organize it without having the state do just those things.*[27]

Another trend is for states to pass school prayer bills that allow student-initiated prayers. Mississippi passed such a law in 1994; its law has been challenged and has now been overturned.[28] In 1995 and early 1996, Oklahoma, North Carolina, Florida, Texas, Virginia, and Kentucky passed or were about to pass such legislation. The emphasis is unmistakable—the students are demonstrating their right to Free(ly) Exercise their religion. That means, they are "free to pray, read their Bibles, and even invite others to join their particular religious groups as long as they are not disruptive of the school or disrespectful of the rights of other students."[29] Other types of religious expression for students which are permissible would be prayer before meals, reading a Bible passage during study hall, creating art projects with religious themes, and having the opportunity to invite other students to attend their house of worship.

One of the most popular student-initiated activities observed in the past few years has been the "prayer at the flagpole" event. Students organize the event, gathering at the flagpole to have a prayer prior to the start of the school day.[30] Prayers at sporting events, such as football games, have been under legal challenge for some time. The courts have consistently decided against school districts when such prayers were offered at public events or when school officials and coaches led prayers prior to games. Some schools blatantly choose to ignore court decisions, others find ways to circumvent the law. For example, the band at one school played "Amazing Grace" after the national anthem.[31]

Suffice it to say that students' religious rights are being acknowledged now more than they have been in the past. Consider the issue of prayers at graduation ceremonies and invocations at other school programs. School boards are encouraging voluntary (in terms of attendance) baccalaureate services which are held off the school grounds and which are organized by the students. The cases which most impact this area in recent years are *Lee v. Weisman* and *Jones v. Clear Creek*.[32]

The facts of the *Lee v. Weisman* case can be stated briefly. Deborah Weisman was scheduled to graduate from Nathan Bishop Middle School in Providence, Rhode Island, in June 1989. Her father sought a temporary restraining order in federal district court to prevent a rabbi from delivering an invocation or benediction. Due to time constraints, the judicial order was not given. Following the graduation service, the trial court granted his request for a permanent injunction prohibiting prayer at public middle and secondary schools in Providence. When the case reached the Supreme Court, and was decided 5–4, it was Justice Kennedy who wrote the majority opinion. His two basic points were that school officials had acted improperly, including directing the rabbi on how the rabbi was to prepare the prayers and second, that students, while not required to attend graduation, were in fact coerced to be present and to participate. The strongest dissenting opinion came from Judge Scalia, who argued that the school had taken precautions so that persons would not be coerced into participation. Discussions of this decision have drawn both praise and criticism.[33]

The *Jones v. Clear Creek Independent School District* case, a year later, seemed to bring more confusion than clarity. The Supreme Court refused to grant an appeal from the lower court. The case had been decided in the Fifth Federal Circuit Court (i.e., Texas, Louisiana, and Mississippi). In this case, some students had voted to have a prayer at graduation, the prayer was student-led, and it was "non-sectarian" and "non-proselytizing." Because this practice was upheld by the lower court, it has been promoted by those who advocate prayer in the schools as the "new law of the land." Indeed, some recent state efforts appear modeled after the *Jones* guidelines. The Ninth Circuit Court, responding to a case from Idaho which had similar circumstances to the Texas case, barred student-led prayers. This ruling, which the High Court chose not to hear when it was appealed, adds to the confusion. The concern about coercion has not been settled. A practical problem is who determines if a prayer is "nonsectarian;" school officials do not want to be placed in the position of judging the merits of a religious statement.[34]

Where does that leave us? It seems that the answer in many schools is to have a privately sponsored, voluntarily attended baccalaureate service off the school grounds during non-school hours. Although the *Jones* decision may slow that trend down, it appears to be one that will continue to grow as it has since the mid-1980s.[35]

Equal Access/Use of School Facilities

Although advocates of school prayer legislation may be disappointed, they can take some comfort in the rights students have been given to hold religious meetings in public schools. Some legal authorities came to the conclusion that the Establishment Clause was being used to block religious expression. They reasoned that the Free Exercise Clause and the Free Speech provision of the Bill of Rights could be used to increase access. In the context of the debate about participation in the Vietnam War and the *Tinker v. Des Moines School District* decision on student free speech, those wanting the public schools to offer a better forum for religious ideas believed that there should be a greater opportunity to express religious ideas.[36]

Today, some persons and groups, including religious conservatives who hailed the passage of the Equal Access Act and cheered when the *Mergens* case was decided in 1990, are wondering if the victory gained came at too high a price—too many groups are being given access. In one western state, for example, a gay and lesbian group of students requested to meet prior to school, and their request was accepted. For those families whose values do not accept those sexual orientations, a real sense of discomfort has emerged.

Prior to the passage of the Equal Access Act, public school administrators had frequently turned down requests for religious groups, both student-led and community-based, to use school facilities, because they and school attorneys concluded it would establish a religious practice. Two Court decisions, *Widmar v. Vincent* (1981) and *Bender v. Williamsport Area School District* (1983), challenged that rationale.[37] The Court in *Widmar* found it inappropriate that a student religious club at the University of Missouri at Kansas City was not granted space at the student union building. In *Williamsport* some students, including Deborah Bender, had been denied permission to have meetings for their religious group, "Petros." That ruling was also overturned. A key point at issue in both cases related to the ability of students to discern. At what age do students, who in their younger years are an impressionable "captive audience," develop the intellectual abilities to analyze accurately that just because a school board or school administrators allow groups to meet on school grounds, they are not endorsing the religious tenets and behaviors advocated by such groups?

Members of Congress evidently believed that the confusion about access needed to be ended. In 1984 Congress passed the Equal Access Act, which was then signed by President Reagan. The Act, in section a, provides that any public secondary school receiving federal financial aid and that has a "limited open forum" cannot lawfully "deny equal access or a fair opportunity to, or discriminate against, any students who wish to conduct a meeting within that limited open forum on the basis of the religious, political, philosophical, or other content of the speech at such meetings."[38] The major features of the Act, as stated in section c, are that the meetings: (1) must be voluntary and student initiated; (2) must not be sponsored by the school; (3) may have school officials present only in a nonparticipatory role; (4) must not materially and substantially interfere with the orderly operation of the school's educational activities; and (5) must not be directed, conducted, controlled, or regularly attended by nonschool persons. One of the chief concerns of school officials in the years which followed was the "limited open forum" aspect of the Act. One option, of course, was for the school not to permit any groups to use the school facility before or after school hours. Most schools choose to have their facilities available to students and other community groups. In doing so, they must allow any group meeting the above conditions to have access.[39]

The major legal challenge to the Equal Access Act occurred at the Westside School District in Omaha, Nebraska. A Bible study group was not permitted to meet. Noting that other student clubs were allowed to meet, the Court ruled in *Board of Education v. Mergens* that this "non-curricular" club should be granted access. In later cases, which focused on outside religious groups using public school facilities, the Court has affirmed that such groups cannot be denied access if a limited forum is established.[40]

Despite the widely distributed guidelines, and the decisions rendered in cases mentioned above, local contexts and circumstances will continue to offer challenges for school officials and the legal community. In 1992, cases from Idaho, Ohio, New York, and Pennsylvania, and other states made the news.[41]

Like most cases, the one from Buffalo, New York, has been resolved. The teacher who was the "moderator" of a Bible Club there offered some reflections recently.[42] There appears to be a growing consensus on student-led groups. Perhaps there is less clarity on opening school facilities to non-school related groups, although as various commentators make the case, the schools do have a right to exercise control over what can take place on the school grounds.[43]

Religious Holidays

Three dimensions of religious expression related to holidays will be discussed. First, how religious holidays are observed in the public schools, in both classrooms and school-sponsored programs. Second, the issue of when the school should close relative to religious holidays celebrated in the community will be explored. Third, school policies related to excusals for teachers as well as students will be examined. This relates to participation in school curriculum and events and excusal to participate in religious services off-campus.

School Programs

Can or should public schools in this pluralistic world do anything about the religious holidays which are celebrated by and, we assume here, have deep meanings for the students and staff of the school? Michael Woodruff has stated that "civilization is somehow measured not by the observance of ritual events or traditions . . . but by the adherence to the spirit and values of those traditions."[44] He adds that it is the public school's role to introduce only the themes of these holidays, so that those students who are not of that tradition will begin to understand others. Further, he warns that teaching about various holidays will inevitably make some people feel different; what is to be avoided is to make them feel second-class. Others would agree, adding that to give in to those who believe that any acknowledgment of religion should be ignored seems illogical on historical grounds alone, and to bow to those who wish only to recapture a past time when Christian holidays were celebrated is grossly insensitive to the many other traditions now represented in our schools. There are many! As noted in the prior chapter, the National Conference calendar of religious and ethnic holidays includes almost 100 such dates per year. A broad coalition of organizations published a brochure in 1989/90 which offered, in question-and-answer format, legal, theological, and pedagogical guidelines for religious holidays. Since then, the brochure has been widely reprinted.[45]

The consensus today is that public schools may teach about religious holidays. They may not observe the holidays as religious events, that is, celebrating them as adherents of the faith world. Study of the holidays enhances pupils' understanding of the history and cultures of various peoples and the traditions of particular religions. Sacred music may be sung or played, but it, like art, drama, or literature with religious themes, needs to have a sound educational goal when included in the curriculum.

Most of the attention regarding religious holidays has focused on Christmas. The proverbial "December dilemma" has resulted in some districts trying to offer "equal time" by including teaching material or songs related to the Jewish holiday of Hanukkah. Educators and legal authorities have had problems with that approach. First, it recognizes holidays with quite different meanings in their traditions; it is hardly a matter of balance. Second, while school concerts and programs may attempt to be objective, they usually drift toward the extreme of providing a mini-worship experience. One humanist has called for schools to be "Yule free." Considering the attention given to these two religious holidays, some critics wonder if similar school time should be given to other holidays?[46]

The case most frequently cited in this regard is *Florey v. Sioux Falls School District*. In 1977 Christmas programs by two kindergarten classes brought a parent's complaint. The superintendent set up a citizen's committee which developed a policy that specified that in future school programs "no religious belief or nonbelief should be promoted by the school district or its employees, and none should be disparaged." That change did not please the complainant, who with the assistance of the American Civil Liberties Union (ACLU), filed a lawsuit in federal district court. That court upheld the school board policy which was later affirmed by the federal appeals court.[47]

Many examples could be given of cases involving other religious and social holidays which have generated opposition. Historically, honoring the flag in school ceremonies has changed. In our own time, in a Midwestern community, a winter play was called off because some parents objected to words in the play which spoke about Greek gods. In Florida, one school cancelled Halloween-related activities because of complaints that such activities promoted witchcraft. At the time of the celebration of "Columbus' discovery" of America, some schools were asked to downplay Thanksgiving because of the poor treatment of Native Americans.[48]

How can current policy best be described? If observances of religious holidays have a clear instructional purpose, and if there is no attempt to endorse or diminish a religion, and if students and staff are not made to feel inferior if they are not part of the tradition being noted, then such observances are permissible.

Closing Schools for Religious Holidays

A brief word about what schools do regarding their days of closing.[49] Many districts have changed the names of the traditional break times at Christmas and Easter; they are now "administrative holidays." A recent court decision banned a long-standing practice in Illinois which allowed all public schools to close on Good Friday. School staffs received pay for that holiday.[50] It should be noted that the federal government recognizes Christmas as a holiday and that it is unlikely that Christmas, because of its commercial and secular ties, will be challenged for being a school holiday. Anecdotes abound about neighborhood schools with large Jewish populations in major cities which close at the time of Jewish holidays, although other schools in the city remain open. If true, will that practice be criticized? Considering the rapid growth of the Islamic faith in some parts of America, and increases in Buddhist or Hindu populations in certain communities, school officials will need to ask this question more frequently, Should the school be closed for "new" holidays?

Excusals for Students and Teachers—For Religious Reasons

Common sense should prevail in this area. As the *Questions and Answers* brochure on religious holidays recommends, schools should be sensitive to the religious needs of students (and we might add, teachers and staff). Students should be allowed a reasonable number of excused absences without penalties. There is growing recognition of the needs of school employees in policy articles regarding excusals.[51]

States have recognized that employees and students do have Free Exercise religious rights which the schools should respect. In one survey, twenty-three states had a specific law or regulation on students being excused to attend or otherwise observe religious holidays. In that same survey, nine states had a similar rule for teachers.[52]

Religious holidays are part of the culture. They reflect what gives individuals some of the deepest meanings of their lives. The public schools cannot ignore them; neither can they unduly promote the observance of religious holidays.

Distribution of Religious Materials

Can religious materials be distributed in public schools? In many parts of the country several generations ago, it appeared the answer to the question was a definite "no." Readers may recall members of the Gideon Society handing out Bibles just beyond the boundaries of the school yard. During the 1960s and 1970s the issue of distribution of non-school prepared materials centered on student underground newspapers and neon-colored flyers. In the 1980s, the distribution of religious materials became an issue. What do the courts say is permissible today? Is it an unrestricted "yes?"[53]

The answer depends upon several variables—who, what, where, and when. Students have the right to disseminate religious materials to their peers. Such literature is, however, subject to what the courts have seen as reasonable standards of time, place, and manner of distribution. For example, a school may decide that all distribution of student-prepared material should be done just before or just after school, and near the school library or cafeteria. Some courts have decided that schools can ban the distribution of any publication that is not sponsored by the school. Most courts take a different view. Because of decisions relating to free speech, students in many schools can distribute material prepared by others. It should be clear, however, that the courts do grant school officials the right to prohibit literature which creates substantial disruption, attacks or harms the rights of others, is obscene, or in some way negatively influences the educational mission of the school. Clearly, there can be limitations on distributing materials in the classroom. Limitations have been placed on student newsletter distribution and what students may distribute or display during "show and tell." One key is whether students are attempting to proselytize their peers.[54]

Based on several decisions, it is clear that outsiders are not automatically given access to classrooms to distribute religious or antireligious literature. In *Berger v. Rensselaer Cent. School Corp.*, a federal district court upheld a school policy that permitted members of the Gideon Society to distribute Bibles in school classrooms because other groups like the Boy Scouts and Little League distributed their literature. However, the Seventh Circuit Court reversed the lower court's verdict, based on the Establishment Clause. Generally speaking, school officials are not required to admit non-students to the schools during instructional time.[55]

As Oliver Thomas has suggested, one goal of the public school should be to model First Amendment principles. Students should have the right to free speech as well as religious expression. They should be taught, too, that these rights have responsibilities and that they are not absolute. While students may invite their peers to church, synagogue, and mosque programs, for example, they may not harass other students to join their faith groups. Time-wise and space-wise, they do not have unlimited access to their classmates nor can they be disruptive of the educational mission of the school.

Religious Dress and Diet

One of the greatest challenges facing schools of tomorrow in the area of religious practices is dress and diet. What people wear and what they eat are basics of life and in many cultures have deep spiritual connections.[56] As America faces a future with increased religious and ethnic diversity, its schools must face that reality.

Dress codes for students, and teachers, have existed forever, or so it seems. Interestingly, recent court cases and reported confrontations over religious garb have been about teachers. In Pittsburgh, two teachers, one a Muslim and the other a Sikh, had their employment terminated because they refused to refrain from dressing in religious garb. Commenting on these firings, Jacqueline A. Stefkovich noted first that a number of states including Pennsylvania have statutes forbidding religious dress (Iowa, Nebraska, New York, and New Mexico were cited). She argued laws like these need to be changed. In today's school world, where multiculturalism is to be taught and diversity celebrated, it is inconsistent to deny teachers their right to religious dress. She discounts the argument that children are so impressionable that such garb would be a vehicle for proselytizing. A counter argument is given by Lawrence Rossow and Sheila Barnes, who claim that such dress can be disruptive to the educational process. They conclude: "dress for success, don't dress for God."[57]

Several sources offer guidelines to schools on dress and diet restrictions. The Dallas, Texas, Independent School District has prepared a helpful chart indicating what dietary and dress practices adherents of their faith must meet. In April 1995, a coalition group offered this statement on student garb: "Religious messages on T-shirts and the like may not be singled out for suppression. Students may wear religious attire, such as yarmulkes and head scarves, and they may not be forced to wear gym clothes that they regard, on religious grounds, as immodest." The key in this area, as in others, should be a genuine effort to accommodate religious diversity. Arranging special diets or making sure that students are properly dressed (religiously speaking) remains the responsibility of parents. School officials may not be able to meet the requests to have the school cafeteria prepare special foods, but they can carefully label the foods which are provided and perhaps suggest alternate dishes for students.[58]

Religious Displays (Art Work/Symbols)

A child does a finger painting in Sunday School class and wants to bring it to school for "show and tell" on Monday. Permissible? Yes. A Michigan public high school wants to have a permanent display of religious art, including a picture of Jesus Christ, in one of its hallways. No, said a U.S. district judge. Can the Ten Commandments be posted in a public school? No, said the Court. Religious artwork and use of symbols, such as a cross, menorah, or crescent, legal voices are saying, may be used in the schools if they have an instructional purpose and if they are on display temporarily.[59]

Guidelines developed by several school districts are instructive at this point. Des Moines, Iowa, prohibits the non-instructional use of religious symbols. St. Louis Park, Minnesota's policy first defines what religious symbols are and how they may be used, in the classroom and in other settings (such as posters). Wicomico County, Maryland, from Salisbury, succinctly states: "The use of religious symbols, provided they are used only as an example of cultural and religious heritage, is permitted as a teaching aid or resource. These symbols may be displayed only for the length of time that the instructional activity requires."[60]

Conclusion

Religious practices in the public schools are a reality and need to be given serious attention by teachers, administrators, school officials, and the community. A major goal of education is to be a marketplace for ideas and, if teachers and school leaders are serious about that, there will need to be greater recognition and provision for accommodating the range of faith beliefs and practices of students and staff, including recognition of those who are non-believers. Some states mandate instruction be multicultural and nonsexist. It cannot be said too strongly, one of today's educational imperatives is a recognition of religious pluralism.

In the abstract, it is easy to call for educators to be more aware of and more active in promoting respect for religious practices. How can that be translated into specific policies and instructional strategies? Throughout this chapter, numerous legal cases, anecdotes, and resources have been shared which provide some answers. Do recall that this chapter is not intended to be a reference work for judicial findings regarding religious practices. It has sought to point out trends and court issues. In the past decade, there has been an increase in school-related cases involving the Free Exercise Clause and a decline in the number based on Establishment Clause violations. Several other trends noted include students clearly being seen as having more ability to discern religious content and schools being expected to be more accommodating of religious groups in the communities.

To make summary remarks about the main topics of this chapter is dangerous, because generalizations don't hold in specific cases. With that caveat in mind, the attempt will be made. School-sponsored prayers are illegal. Spontaneous individual prayers by students have never been illegal and are still permissible. Student-initiated prayers for groups ("meet at the flagpole") and for graduation ceremonies are more likely to be allowed now, but can be problematic. Many states now have moment of silence laws and they appear unchallenged for the most part. The Equal Access Act followed by *Mergens* seemed to clarify some points, but the "devil is in the details." Clearly, student-led religious groups can meet under the limited forum rules developed. Outsider participation is still restricted. Religious holidays have strong emotional ties for many and still create hard feelings for those who are denied their requests (to either include or exclude them). A growing consensus appears in this area, which still must be handled very sensitively. Distribution of religious materials and religious dress and diet regulations are areas which will receive much more attention in the years to come.

Religion is a fact of life. Religion, for many, is the linchpin in their interpretation of the meaning of life. Beyond individual faith, religion has communal ramifications. It influences how civilly or cruelly we treat others. Religious perspectives determine what we are willing to discuss and how we will carry on our conversations. Potentially, our different religious perspectives can help us see the richness within the nation and reveal something of the worthiness of our civilization.

Notes

1. *Christian Century*, December 20–27, 1995, p. 1235. See also Louise Adler, "'Clinton' Memorandum on Religious Expression in Public Schools," *Religion & Education* 22, 2 (Fall 1995):10–11. Hereafter, *Religion & Education* citations will be identified as *R&E*. [Note: Past issues of *R&E* may be purchased through the

Department of Religion, Webster University, 470 E. Lockwood Avenue, St. Louis, MO 63119.]

2. Joseph L. Conn and Rob Boston, "Scaling the Wall: Religious Right Activists Urge Congress to Lower the Barrier between Church and State," *Church & State,* 48, 7 (July–August 1995): 4–5.
3. Jan C. Robbins, *Voluntary Religious Activities in Public Schools: Policy Guidelines* (Bloomington, Ind.: Phi Delta Kappa Educational Foundation, 1987), 10–11. Robbins quotes from *West Virginia State Board of Education v. Barnette,* 319 U.S. 624 (1943). He goes on to discuss the "accommodation" position, found in *Zorach v. Clauson,* 343 U.S. 306 (1952). *Abington v. Schempp* 374 U.S. 226; Brennan's quote is at 299.
4. *Abington v. Schempp,* 374 U.S. at 203 (1963; *West Virginia State Board of Education* v. *Barnette,* 319 U.S. 624 (1943).
5. *Abington v. Schempp,* 374 U.S. at 203 (1963); 374 U.S. at 322 (1963); Brennan's quote is at ibid. of 299 (1963).
6. Charles R. Haynes, ed., *Finding Common Ground: A First Amendment Guide to Religion and Public Education* (Nashville: Freedom Forum, First Amendment Center at Vanderbilt, 1994), Appendix B. Dubuque, Iowa, and Indianapolis, Indiana, statements should be available from the school districts. Ralph D. Mawdsley, "*Clever v. Cherry Hill Township Board of Education*: Religion of Religious Diversity in Public Schools," *West's Education Law Reporter* 3, 3 (July 1994): 505–517, reports that a federal district court recognized a local district's efforts to teach about religious diversity and approved its policy.
7. Donald E. Boles, *The Bible, Religion and the Public Schools* (Ames, IA: Iowa State University Press, 1985), provides a comprehensive historical overview of local, state, and federal relationships, For an accurate "snapshot" of state laws, regulations, and guidelines in the 1950s, see Don Conway, "Religion and Public Education in the States," *International Journal of Religious Education* 32, 7 (March 1956): 34–40.
8. Charles R. Kniker, "A Survey of State Laws and Regulations Regarding Religion and Moral Education," *R&E* 16, 3 (Fall 1989):433–434. When doing a study of all states, I found it was necessary to use all these categories to understand what states were requiring or permitting.
9. Kniker, ibid.; 433–437.
10. *Religion Studies Guidelines* (Madison: Wisconsin Department of Public Instruction, 1982), Bulletin No. 2385, also can be found under ERIC Document No. ED 218188. For a more contemporary state document, see Mirko Strazicich, ed., *Moral and Civic Education and Teaching about Religion: Handbook on the Legal Rights and Responsibilities of School Personnel and Students* (Sacramento California State Department of Education, 1990). Contact Bureau of Publications Sales, P.O. Box 271, Sacramento, CA 95802–0271.
11. The United States Department of Education: The Secretary (August 10, 1995). The speech by Clinton was given July 12, 1995.
12. For "slips" of U.S. Supreme Court decisions, call or write the U.S. Supreme Court Public Information Office, One First St., N.E., Washington, D.C. Phone (202) 479–3000. For legal opinions, consult *West's Education Law Reporter* and publications of the National Organization of Legal Problems in Education (NOLPE). See also Barry Lynn, Marc D. Stern, and Oliver S. Thomas, eds. *The Right to Religious Liberty,* 2nd ed. (Silver Spring, Md.: American Civil Liberties Union, 1995). The Bar Association of Metropolitan St. Louis and the American Jewish Congress, *Religious Issues in the Schools and Work Place* (St. Louis: The Bar Association of Metropolitan St. Louis, May 19, 1994) provides a readable summary of many cases.
13. Jacqueline A. Stefkovich and Patricia A.L. Ehrensal, "The Religious Freedom Restoration Act and the Free Exercise Rights of Students in Public Schools," *R&E* 21 (1994): 28–35.

14. American Association of School Administrators, *Religion in the Public Schools* (Arlington, Va.: American Association of School Administrators, 1986); Naomi E. Gittins, ed., *Religion, Education, and the U.S. Constitution* (Alexandria, Va.: National School Boards Association, 1990); Cathryn Ehrhardt, "Religion in Public Schools: Free Exercise, Information and Neutrality," *Updating School Board Policies* 21, 1 (January 1990): 1–3; J.B. Morris, "Guidelines and Compatible Components on Religion in the Public Schools," *R&E* 16, 1 (Winter 1989): 131ff.
15. *Questions and Answers* brochures are described in chapter 1. The first was on religion in the curriculum, the second on holiday observance, and the third on equal access.
16. For more specific information about these organizations consult *The Encyclopedia of Associations* available at most libraries.
17. Lori Forman, *The Political Activity of the Religious Right in the 1990s: A Critical Analysis* (New York: American Jewish Committee, March 1994). A more extended analysis of many of the same groups is found in David Cantor, *The Religious Right: The Assault on Tolerance and Pluralism in America* (New York: Anti-Defamation League, 1994). See also Eugene F. Provenzo Jr., *Religious Fundamentalism and American Education* (Albany: State University of New York Press, 1990).
18. Martin Marty, "Galactic Consistency," *Christian Century* (June 16, 1993): 655; Jacob Neusner, "School Sponsored Prayer: A Judaic Reading," *R&E* 22, 2 (Fall 1995): 67–71. Also see Provenzo *Religious Fundamentalism and American Education*, 116, for a quotation regarding the centrality of school prayer as an issue and "Big-City Blacks Join in Push for Prayer in Schools," *Education Week*, April 27, 1994, 1, 8.
19. Phi Delta Kappa, in conjunction with the Gallup organization, has conducted annual polls on education. The prayer question frequently is included; see Stanley M. Elam and Lowell C. Rose, "The 27th Annual Poll of the Public's Attitudes Toward the Public Schools, *Phi Delta Kappan*, 77, 1 (September 1995): 50–52. See *R&E* 15, 1 (Winter 188):12 for article on a survey of educators; also Thayer S. Warshaw, in *R&E* 15, 2 (Spring 88): 120–122 for methodological criticisms of Gallup poll questions. See also Keith E. Durso, "The Voluntary School Prayer Debate: A Separationist Perspective," *Journal of Church and State* 36, 1 (Winter 1994): 79–96, citing 1991 Time/CNN poll indicating 78 percent were in favor of prayer, 89 percent in favor of moment of silence and Eugene H. Methvin, "Let us Pray," *Reader's Digest*, November 1992, 75–80, citing a survey indicating 80 percent of Americans disagree with the Court's prohibitions on religious practices.
20. Bruce Dierenfield, "The Amen Amendment: Doomed to Failure?" *R&E* 22, 2 (Fall 1995): 40–48; John Leo, "Praying for Sanity in Schools," *U.S. News & World Report*, November 28, 1994, 38; "A Matter of Conscience," *Church & State* 48, 3 (March 1995): 10–11, includes pro and con statements from a number of groups.
21. Elliott Wright, "Protestant-Catholic-Jews and Public School Prayer: Past and Present," a paper presented to the Church/State Study Group, American Academy of Religion, Washington, D.C., November 18, 1995; for a somewhat similar interpretation, read Boardman W. Kathan, "Prayer and the Public Schools: The Issue in Historical Perspective and Implications for Religious Education Today," *Religious Education* 84, 2 (Spring 1989): 232–249. See also Conway survey mentioned in n. 7. Another national survey referred to in these sources was conducted by Richard Dierenfield in 1962.
22. Provenzo, *Religious Fundamentalism*, 75–86; Mary E. Anthrop, "The Controversy over School Prayer," *OAH Magazine of History* 5, 1 (Summer 1990): 40–47; Dean M. Kelley, "School Prayer Decisions: Religious Toleration or Religious Liberty," *R&E* 10, 4 (Fall 1983): 28–37, provides an extended analysis—four major reasons—for the reaction to the court decisions.

23. Albert J. Menendez, *School Prayer and Other Religious Issues in American Public Education* (New York: Garland Publishing, Inc., 1985), offers extensive bibliographic listings; John W. Whitehead, *The Rights of Persons in Public Education*, rev. ed. (Wheaton, Ill.: Crossway Books, 1994); Robert Sikorski, ed., *Prayer in Public Schools and the Constitution, 1961–1992,* 3 vols. (New York: Garland Publishing, Inc., 1993): a three-volume set; Lyndon G. Furst, "Bible Reading and Prayer in the Public Schools: Clearing Up the Misconceptions," a paper delivered at the American Educational Research Association Convention, San Francisco, March 27–31, 1989, available as ERIC document ED 306665. Americans United for Separation of Church and State has produced a pamphlet, "What's Wrong with a School Prayer Amendment?—25 Questions and Answers" (not dated). AU also produced, in 1995, another pamphlet, *"A Matter of Conscience: Why Faith Groups Oppose Government-Sponsored Prayers in Public Schools,* containing statements from twenty-eight groups.
24. *Wallace v. Jaffee*. 105 S. Ct. 2479, 2483 (1985). See AASA, *Religion in the Public Schools*, 16–18. See also Robert Sikorski, ed., *Moments of Silence in Public Schools*, vol. 2 in his series cited in the preceding note.
25. David Schimmel, comments in *R&E* 13, 3 (Summer 1986): 49–51; *R&E*, 16, 1 (Winter 1989): 13; *R&E* 15, 3 (Summer 1988): 220; *R&E* 13, 3 (Summer 87): 213. Francis J. Beckwith, *Public Education, the First Amendment, and the Influence of New Religious Movements: A Policy Analysis* (Reno: Nevada Policy Research Institute, 1993), 8. "Suite Challenges Religious Practices in Ala. District," *Education Week*, February 7, 1996, 3.
26. *R&E* 10, 4 (Fall 1983): 7; Patricia M. Lines, "Prayer, the Bible, and the Public Schools," *R&E* 10, 3 (Summer 1983): 16–17. See *Bown v. Gwinnett County* (1995). In this decision, a federal court ruled that the moment of silence practice authorized by the state legislature of Georgia met the three prongs of the *Lemon* test; for more details see *West's Education Law Reporter* 103, 1 (November 2, 1995): 207–229. For pro and con statements about moment of silence, see *R&E* 11, 1–2 (Winter/Spring 1984): 17–20. For a con statement, see John M. Swomley, "Profaning This Holy Practice," *Christian Social Action* (February 1995):25–28.
27. Stephen L. Carter, *The Culture of Disbelief* (New York: Basic Books, HarperCollins Publishers, 1993), 186; Peter J. Riga, "Prayer in Public Schools Would Split Our Nation," *The National Law Journal* (December 12, 1994): 17, 15, A 21, Column 3; Islamic Society of North America, "The Needs of Muslim Children in Public Schools," *R&E* 22, 2 (Fall 1995): 90–94; "School Prayer/A Moment of Silence," reprinted from *tricycle, the Buddhist Review*, 1995, in *R&E*, 22, 1 (Spring 1995): 48–49.
28. The Mississippi statute was challenged in *Ingebretsen v. Jackson Public School District* and decided in September, 1994. A federal district judge ruled that the practice was in violation of the Establishment Clause. A three-judge panel of the Fifth Circuit Court on January 10, 1996, affirmed the district court's decision. See *West's Education Law Reporter* 95, 1–3 (1995):158–177 for a discussion of the earlier decision.
29. Oliver Thomas, "Religious Expression in Public Schools," in *Finding Common Ground,* ed. Charles Haynes, 12.1; Richard N. Ostling, "Is There a Place for God in School?" *Time* (April 11, 1994): 60.
30. See *Religion in the Public Schools: A Joint Statement of Current Events* (April 1995), point 11, available from 15 East 84 St., Suite 501, New York, N.Y., 10028; *R&E* 19, 1 (1992): 9 on an Illinois case and *R&E* 17, 3 (Fall 1990): 297 for a Houston, Texas story. See also, Richard McMillan, "School Prayer: A Problem of Questions and Answers," *R&E* 15, 2 (Spring 1988): 200–203.
31. For a case study of state reaction to the prayer cases, see James R. Durham, *Secular Darkness: Religious Right Involvement in Texas Public Education, 1963–1989* (New York: Peter Lang, 1995), 39–56; Lawrence F. Rossow and Randy Ann Stickney, "*Lee v. Weisman*: Prayer at School Graduation—Another 'Test' for the

Lemon Test," *R&E* 20, 1–3 (1993): 46; for a number of stories about the *Jager* case in Douglas County, Ga., see *R&E* 16, 2 (Spring/Summer 1989): 154–155; and Nat Hentoff, in *R&E* 16, 1 (Winter 1989): 45–46.

32. Thomas, "Religious Expression," in *Finding Common Ground*, ed. Charles Haynes, 12.2–12.4; Whitehead, *Rights of Religious Persons*, 229–253; Michael D. Simpson, "School Prayer Is Back," *NEA Today*, September 15, 1994, 19; and Pamela Coyle, "The Prayer Pendulum," *ABA Journal* 81 (January 1995): 62–66.
33. See *R&E* 19, 2–3 (Spring/Fall 1992) for a series of commentaries on the case. Perry A. Zirkel, "A Bedeviling Message from Providence," *Phi Delta Kappan* 74, 2 (October 1992): 183ff. For more background, read Eugene C. Bjorklun, "The Rites of Spring: Prayers at High School Graduation," *West's Education Law Reporter* 61, 1 (August 30, 1990):1–9.
34. Thomas, "Religious Expression," 12.2–12.3. See Whitehead, *Rights of Religious Persons*, 248–251; "High Court Declines to Clarify Status of Graduation Prayer," *Education Week*, July 12, 1995, 22.
35. See Commentaries section in *R&E* 16, 1 (Winter 1989): 33–44. Many News sections of *R&E* from 1986 through 1990 contain accounts from cases in various states.
36. *Tinker v. Des Moines Independent Community School District*, 393 U.S. 503 (1969). The key finding from this case, which was based on students protesting the Vietnam War being prohibited from wearing arm bands, was that students do not lose their rights "at the schoolhouse gate."
37. *Widmar v. Vincent*, 454 U.S. 263 (1981); *Bender v. Williamsport Area School District*, 476 U.S. 1132 (1983). For a background on these cases and its relation to the Equal Access Act, see Eugene C. Bjorklun, "The Equal Access Act: Recent Court Decisions," *R&E* 16, 2 (Spring/Summer 1989): 217–232.
38. The Equal Access Act is officially cited as 20 U.S.C. Section 4071. The reactions to the Act ranged widely. A *New York Times* headline indicated that worship in schools was now permitted. See *R&E* issues of 11, 3 (Summer 1984) and 4 (Fall 1984) for a survey of what schools did after the passage of the Act. For an excellent summary of the issues as they existed just prior to *Mergens*, see Thayer S. Warshaw, "Equal Access—Further Developments and Continuing Questions," *R&E* 15, 1 (Winter 1988): 67–68.
39. In practice, there are many complex matters related to access. To be helpful, a number of groups have issued guidelines and pamphlets. The first, now widely reprinted, can be found in Charles Haynes, ed., *Finding Common Ground*, chap. 11. Or see *Religion in the Public Schools: Current Law* (April 1995), point 13, or The National Congress of Parents and Teachers (PTA) and The Freedom Forum, *A Parent's Guide to Religion in the Public Schools*, point 11 on student religious clubs.
40. *Board of Education v. Mergens*, 496 U.S. 226 (1990); for analysis of this case, see Eugene C. Bjorklun, "Implications of *Mergens*: The Equal Access Act and State Constitutions," *R&E* 18, 1–3 (1991): 149–160; also Ron Flowers and others in "Commentaries," *R&E* 17, 1 (Winter 1990): 17–25. Eastland, *Religious Liberty*, pp. 417–437; Whitehead, *Rights of Religious Persons*, Chapter 11, pp. 133–146 on "Equal Access," and chap. 12, "Use of Public School Facilities by Churches and Religious Organizations," 147–159. More recent cases include *Gregoire v. Centennial School District*, 907 F.2d 1366 (3d Cir.); *Lamb's Chapel Center v. Moriches Union Free School District*, 112 S. Ct. 2141 (1993) and *Good News/Good Sports Club v. School District of Ladue*, 28 F.3d 1501 (8th Cir. 1994). [Note: The *Ladue* case appears to be an equal access case, but is not; the school involved is not a high school.] The latter cases are discussed in Ralph D. Mawdsley and Melvin Dunn, "Religious Access to Public Schools: Changing the Rules," *R&E* 22, 1 (Spring 1995): 6–9. See also Charles J. Russo, "Religious Groups and Public School Facilities: A Passing Fancy or the Emergence of a New Trend?" *R&E* 17, 3 (Fall 1990): 357–359.

41. See *R&E* 19, 1 (Winter 1992): 11–12 for brief news accounts. For additional stories at the time *Mergens* was being decided, see *R&E* 17, 2 (Spring/Summer 1990): 157–158 and 3 (Fall 1990): 295–296, on cases involving San Diego, Calif.; Ft. Meyers, Fla.; Dallas, Tex.; and Bridgewater, Mass.
42. James J. Benson, "Reflections from a Bible Club Moderator," *R&E* 22, 2 (Fall 1995): 78–83.
43. Kimberlee Wood Colby, "Religious Freedom in the Public School Setting," *Momentum* 24, 4 (November-December 1993): 55–59, speaks to the issue of extracurricular religious groups using schools as does John S. Aldridge, in "Use of Facilities by Outside Religious Groups," in Gittins, ed., *Religion . . . Constitution.* In the same document, see Stephen S. Russell, "The Equal Access Act and Student Groups."
44. Michael J. Woodruff, "Religious Holidays and the Public Schools," *R&E* 16, 1 (Winter 1989): 123.
45. *Religious Holidays in the Public Schools: Questions and Answers* (1989/90). Produced by seventeen organizations. Reprinted in Haynes, ed., *Finding Common Ground.* Sections have been reprinted in the other brochures/statements cited in this chapter: President Clinton's remarks in PTA's *Parent's Guide*, July 1995, and *Religion in the Public Schools: Current Law.* For religious holiday calendars write to National Conference, 71 5th Avenue, New York, NY 10003, or phone (212) 206–0006, and Educational Extension Systems, P.O. Box 259, Clarks Summit, PA 18411, or phone (717) 586–6490.
46. Albert J. Menendez, *The December Wars: Religious Symbols and Ceremonies in the Public Square* (Buffalo: Prometheus Books, 1993), 83–106, and especially 88, where he indicates that the nation's increasing cultural and religious pluralism and efforts of conservative Christianity to promote their perspectives have heightened tensions over this matter. Tom Flynn, *The Trouble with Christmas* (Buffalo; Prometheus Books, 1993), 170, 208, 222. For a more general source, see Leigh Eric Schmidt, *Consumer Rights: The Buying and Selling of American Holidays* (Princeton: Princeton University Press, 1995).
47. Whitehead, *Rights of Religious Persons*, chap. 16 "Religious Holiday Observances," 213–227. In some detail, Whitehead indicates how the judges used the three-component *Lemon* test to evaluate *Florey v. Sioux Falls School District* 49–5, 464 F. Supp. 91 (D.S.D. 2979). Following that discussion, Whitehead treats the subsequently developed "endorsement" test of Justice Sandra Day O'Connor. O'Connor posits that a violation occurs only when it can be demonstrated that there is clear evidence that a religion is endorsed or demeaned. For a further analysis of *Florey* and that district's policy, see Thayer S. Warshaw, "Religious Practices in Public Schools," *R&E* 10, 2 (Spring 1983): 29–31.
48. See News items from the following issues of *Religion and Public Education: R&E* 15, 4 (Fall 1988): 347; Joseph R. McKinney, "Flag Day: It's Not What It Used to Be," *R&E* 17, 2 (Spring/Summer 1990): 265–277; *R&E* 17, 3 (Fall 1990): 301.
49. The Manhasset, New York, school district policy on religious holidays is reprinted in *R&E* 16, 2 (1989): 259–261. See also Oliver Thomas, "Religious Holidays and Public Schools: A Brief Legal Analysis," 10.6 to 10.8 in Haynes, *Finding Common Ground.* On page 8, Thomas comments "Schools are not required to close on a particular religious holiday but may choose to do so as a matter of administrative convenience as, for example, when large numbers of students are likely to be absent."
50. *Metzl v. Leininger* 57 F. 3d 618 (7th Cir. 1995). A 2–1 judges' decision made on June 19, 1995.
51. *Religious Holidays: Questions & Answers*; Fay Hartog-Rapp, Gretchen Winter, and Michele Freedenthal, "Accommodation of Employee's Religious Observances," in Gittins, ed., *Religion . . . Constitution.* See also Eugene T. Connor, "Accommodating Religious Needs: Policies and Procedures," *R&E* 16, 2 (Spring/Summer 1989): 245, 246, 251.

52. Kniker, "State Laws," 447, and 448; See also Whitehead, *Rights of Religious Persons*, 224–225 for a report on another survey.
53. Whitehead, *Rights of Religious Persons*, pp. 97–104, provides a thorough overview of the legal cases; see especially page 103 for a discussion of *Hedges v. Wauconda Community School District.* See also Oliver Thomas, "Religious Expression in Public Schools," 12.4–12.6 in Haynes, *Finding Common Ground.*
54. Eugene C. Bjorklun, "Distribution of Religious Literature in the Public Schools," *West's Education Law Reporter* 68, 1–4 (September 26, 1991): 957–967. See also Jan C. Robbins, *Student Press and the Hazelwood Decision* (Bloomington: Phi Delta Kappa Educational Foundation, 1988).
55. The picture is not clear on whether teachers can distribute materials. See *West's Education Law Reporter* 80, 1–3 (1993): 68–79. In recent years school officials have been prone to deny students the right to distribute religious newspapers, but have relented when challenged. See *R&E* 16, 2 (Spring/Summer 1989): 160. For a pro and con debate on other issues related to distribution of religious materials, see *R&E*, Commentaries section, 20, 1–3 (1993): 21–26.
56. See *Journal of the American Academy of Religion*, LXIII, 3 (Fall 1995). Its theme is "Religion and Food."
57. Jacqueline A. Stefkovich, "Religious Garb in the Schools: A Different Time, a Different Place," *R&E* 19, 1 (Winter 1992): 43–46; Lawrence Rossow and Sheila Barnes, "In Public School, Dress for Success—Not God," *R&E* 19, 1 (Winter 1992): 47–50. In 1987, the U.S. Supreme Court refused to hear a challenge to an Oregon law prohibiting public school teachers from wearing religious dress. In that case a Eugene, Oregon, teacher was fired for wearing Sikh garb on the job. See *Report from the Capital,* May 1987, for an account. Fay Hartog-Rapp, Gretchen Winter, and Michele Freedenthal, "Religious Garb: May Public School Teachers Wear It?" in Gittins, ed., *Religion . . . Constitution.*
58. *Religion in the Public Schools: Current Laws*, 9 point 17; Dallas, Texas, school district statement is found in Haynes, *Finding Common Ground*, 13.2–13.4. See also comments on 13.1.
59. Whitehead, *Rights of Religious Persons*, 223–224, provides a summary of legal cases in this area, including *Stone v. Graham*, regarding the posting of the Ten Commandments. In that ruling, the Supreme Court held that the purpose was "plainly religious in nature." "Display of Religious Art in Michigan Public School Endorses Christianity, Federal Court Rules," *Church & State* 46, 3 (March 1993): 13. For an article which expresses the opinion that the Court has misread the First Amendment, replacing religious pluralism with dogmatic secularism, see Michael McConnell, "Freedom from Religion? (Purging Religious References from the Public Realm)," *The American Enterprise* 4, 1 (January–February 1993): 34ff.
60. See Appendix B of Haynes, ed., *Finding Common Ground.*

Chapter Three
Culture, Religion, and Education

E. Vance Randall

> *In the beginning God gave to every people a cup, a cup of clay, and from this cup they drank their life. They all dipped in the water but their cups were different. Our cup is broken now. It has passed away.*
>
> —*Proverb of the Digger Indians,* Patterns of Culture and Modern Man[1]

Introduction

Every human being belongs to a culture, follows a particular way of life and thus drinks "their life" from their particular "cup of clay." This way of life provides individual and societal identity as well as normative structures for personal and social behavior. Culture furnishes answers to basic ontological and cosmological questions about the nature of human existence and purpose.

As individuals and societies encounter cultures different from their own, they are confronted with competing world views or ways of living and understanding the world. These world views assert different answers to fundamental questions about the nature of being and the moral order of the universe. A different culture, with its competing world view, also poses a potential threat to the social stability and fabric of a culture. Alternative perspectives present alternative norms and social arrangements. These rival viewpoints compete for the allegiance of individuals and argue for a particular social order. The threat of displacement and loss for those with vested interests in the status quo can be immense. The common result is a culture war.[2]

The history of the world is filled with numerous examples of cultural conflict and our modern era is no different. Some cultural battles center on religious differences such as in Bosnia with the Muslims and Christians, the Catholics and Protestants in Northern Ireland, Muslims and Hindus in India or Christian Fundamentalists and Secularists in America. Other clashes are over land: as with Israel and Palestine; or farmers in Brazil with indigenous tribes in the Amazon rain forest. Additional cultural conflicts involve race and ethnicity such as blacks and whites in America, Hutus and Tutsis in Rwanda, Japanese and Koreans in the Far East. Other cultural disputes focus on social class and distribution of wealth as with oligarchies in Mexico, Guatemala and El Salvador and their peasant populations. Further manifestations of cultural conflicts can be seen in the political arena: Republicans and Democrats in America and the Labor and Tory parties in Great Britain.

As if each of these examples of cultural conflicts was not enough to challenge the social harmony of any society, many of these controversies involve other sources of cultural disputes which occur simultaneously. The cascading crescendo of these cultural conflicts threatens to rip apart our social fabric, balkanize nations into ethnic and religious regions, and drown out cries for dialogue, understanding and compassion.

In his book, *Culture Wars: The Struggle to Define America*, James Davison Hunter provides an intriguing analysis of the current cultural conflict in America. Hunter argues that the focal point of the cultural struggle is over which "moral vision" will ultimately prevail in an increasingly pluralistic American society.[3] Serious questions are raised about the fundamental nature of American society and what constitutes core American values. The intense and, at times, violent public debate waged over what is right and wrong, truth and error, moral and immoral, correct and incorrect, strains our sense of community and social civility. Tortuous issues such as abortion, AIDS, multiculturalism, racism and civil rights, affirmative action, sexual orientation, gender, marriage and divorce, spouse abuse, environmental issues, the proper role of government, church and state, haunt our waking hours. At times it seems as though our society and global communities are flying apart with nothing in common to bind us together. Our social glue dissolving under the corroding solvents of social strife and disparate worldviews. The growing sense of cultural chaos seems to be captured in the following lines from "The Second Coming" by William Butler Yeats:

Things fall apart, the centre cannot hold;
Mere anarchy is loosed upon the world. . . .[4]

American education has not escaped the cultural turmoil of the larger society. Indeed, education performs a pivotal role in the social and cultural reproduction of our society. This causes education to function as a cultural flashpoint where many of the underlying social tensions surface and are played out. The cultural battles fought in our schools over curriculum, governance, teaching and learning, which often split neighborhoods and divide communities, are manifestations of a deeper cultural conflict.

The purpose of this chapter is to examine the important interdependent relationship between education and culture, especially in cultural contexts deeply imbued with a religious ethos. An important part of gaining a better understanding of the cultural conflict and working toward a viable resolution is to have a clear idea about the meaning of central concepts such as "culture," "religion," and "education" and their dynamic relationship with each other.

This chapter is divided into six sections. This first section introduced the cultural conflict in which we find ourselves immersed. The next three sections sketch core components of the three key concepts of culture, religion, and education. The fifth section examines how cultural wars might be resolved and the chapter ends with a summary and concluding observations.

Culture

> *For men and women are not only themselves; they are also the region in which they were born, the city apartment or the farm in which they learned to walk, the games they played as children, the old wive's tale they overheard, the food they ate, the schools they attended, the sports they followed, the poems they read, and the God they believed in.*
>
> —*W. Somerset Maugham*[5]

The word culture comes from the Latin word cultura and literally means "cultivation" or "tillage." The German word kultur reflects the most common usage of culture to describe individuals who are civilized and well educated in the arts, literature, music, language, history, philosophy, fashion, cuisine, social graces, and other indications of social sophistication and refined tastes.[6] To be cultured in this sense is to have the finer things of life, to possess that which is the "best" in thought and speech which thus bestows membership in an elite social class.[7]

The notion of culture, however, as simply possessing educated thoughts and genteel tastes is a narrow one. Edward Burnett Tylor conceived of culture as "that complex whole which includes knowledge, belief, art, morals, custom, and any other capabilities and habits acquired by man as a member of society."[8] This classical definition of culture as "that complex whole" embraces not just the "high culture" of an elite social class but all social aspects and human interactions with others and the physical world.[9]

Although the variety of cultures is immense and the "complex whole" is manifested in numerous ways, all cultures share universal features and perform basic functions and purposes.[10] Every culture represents a different way in which meaning is made of the physical and social world, problems are solved, and a society is perpetuated. It teaches individuals about relating to and greeting one another, kinship and courtship, marriage and family, birth and death. Culture provides a reference point for making meaning out of seemingly random phenomena.[11] Culture is a way of imposing order on chaos, of constructing reality, of making sense out of confusion, of finding patterns in clutter, of making meaning out of the human experience.[12] Clifford Geertz sees culture as a

historically transmitted pattern of meanings embodied in symbols, a system of inherited conceptions expressed in symbolic form by means of which men communicate, perpetuate, and develop their knowledge about and attitudes toward life.[13]

In this symbolist view of culture, the thoughts, feelings, values and attitudes about life and reality are communicated to others through the use of symbols. These symbols can take a variety of forms such as stories, myths, legends, rituals, customs, art, music, dance, and technology.[14] Regardless of the particular symbolism, the important tasks they perform are to convey an objective reality and disclose an understanding of what is "real" and "true." Thus culture is a *Weltanschauung* or worldview, and enculturation is the process of "world-building" for the individual.[15]

As a world view, culture takes on nomothetic or normative function. As Geertz observes, "culture is best seen not as complexes of concrete behavior patterns—customs, usages, traditions, habit clusters, as has been the case up to now, but as a set of control mechanisms—plans, recipes, rules, instructions . . .—for governing of behavior."[16] Culture as world view legitimates social arrangements and relationships, political structures, roles of men and women, distributions of resources, punishments and rewards, and social statuses. Culture instructs us on what we should think, what we should believe and how we should act. In a word, culture establishes and imposes boundaries.

Culture also serves as the nurturing medium of personal identity, self-worth, and the forging of a particular image of human nature.[17] Young Pai asserts that the

> *culture to which one belongs, then, becomes the root of the individual's identity, because culture gives us a sense of power and confidence by giving us the basis of achieving our goals, determining what is desirable and undesirable and developing the purpose of our life. Accordingly, to reject or demean a person's cultural heritage is to do psychological and moral violence to the dignity and worth of that individual.*[18]

The critical role that culture plays in the formation of societal and individual identity may explain why foreign cultures are often perceived as a threat to social stability and individual security. Cultural differences are translated as moral deficits and are threatening for at least two reasons. First, a culture engenders feelings of social and individual superiority. A different culture and its members are looked upon as inferior, backward, or even worse. This notion of cultural superiority or ethnocentricity may even call for keeping the superior race "pure" or uncontaminated by an inferior race. Second, different cultures represent competing paradigms or world views. Bound up with these alternative world views are different notions of right and wrong, morality and justice, and the resulting social structures and rewards. By its very presence, another culture questions the hegemonic position of the dominant culture. If there are other cultures, other world views, other social arrangements and norms, just how do we know that we are right and they are wrong?

American history is replete with examples of cultural clashes involving religion, race, political persuasion, gender, ethnic origin, social class, labor and business, war and peace, the environment, sexual orientation, abortion, family configurations, and education. These ubiquitous conflicts raise the question of whether there is an "American" culture, whether there are any core values in American society which all must embrace, and whether there are any "right" answers to these social dilemmas.[19] Whether it is the issue of English as the official American language, national guidelines for history textbooks, the request to establish a gay and lesbian club at a high school, abortion, the National Endowment for the Humanities sponsorship of Robert Mappelthorpe's homoerotic art, driving spikes in trees to preserve original woodlands, AIDS education, the Enola Gay exhibit, affirmative action, film and lyrics filled with sex and violence, political correctness, sexual harassment, school prayer, pornography or college curriculum, the litany of current culture clashes seems endless.

James Davison Hunter distills the current "fields of conflict" in America's culture war into five general categories: "the family, education, media, law, and electoral politics."[20] These areas represent the specific arenas of engagement where the battles of the American culture war are currently being fought.

At the base of any culture war, including the cultural conflict in America, is power and domination. Whose moral vision will prevail? Which world view will become the dominant perspective? Whose private values will be enthroned as public values? Who will provide the definitive substance of American culture? Who will decide what it means to be an American? How will social institutions be configured, social norms constructed and individual lives ordered? There is simply an enormous stake in the outcome of culture wars.

Before moving to a discussion of religion and culture, one parting observation needs to be made about the character of culture. Culture does play a central, dominating, powerful role in all societies and in the life of each individual. Culture shapes and creates society as well as the individual. In painting the concept of culture with such broad brush strokes, however, three important qualifications must be made. First, culture is not a monolithic entity. Within each superordinate culture such as American culture or Zulu culture, there exists a large variety of subcultures. An American not only partakes of the overall national culture, but also participates in an ethnic culture, a regional culture (e.g., West Coast, Midwest, South, New England, etc.), the institutional cultures found in workplace, community organizations, religious groups, the family, and technology to name just a few. In addition, the ease of international travel provides a broad exposure to a great diversity of distinctly different cultures. These regional canopies of cultures within the larger national cultural umbrella also influence the culture which the individual has appropriated as his or her own world view. Second, culture itself changes and adapts to changing times and circumstances. It acts but culture is also acted upon. The America of the 1990s is substantially different from the America of the 1890s. The values, mores, and world view of Americans in the 1950s changed radically with the social revolution that swept through the country a decade later. Culture is a dynamic, evolving phenomenon.

And finally, unless one is a strict behaviorist, individuals are not puppets of some cultural puppet master which simply react to cultural stimuli. Men and women are rational, moral agents who can choose for themselves. If a universal, characteristic feature of all cultures is that culture is learned, then it can be unlearned, or at least, modified or expanded. Otherwise we are haunted by the specter of determinism, a position that would require us not to hold individuals responsible for their actions. However, these three caveats or even the perspective of this entire chapter on culture, religions, and education, are a reflection of my own cultural background and world view.[21] Even in doing cultural meta-analysis, one cannot totally escape his or her own cultural lens. The interpretative lens of culture simply colors everything. There is no escape.

Religion

Religion is the human enterprise by which a sacred cosmos is established.

—*Peter Berger*[22]

Not all cultures have a religious dimension but any religion is part of a larger cultural system. The word "religion" comes from the

Latin *religio*, which literally means "to tie on" or "fasten behind." What, then, does religion "tie on" or add to culture? Religion becomes a particular way in which meaning and understanding about the natural world and society take on a supernatural explanation. This supernatural world view embodies powers and realities that transcend the daily human existence. Ordinary objects and activities, even reality, are divided into spheres of the sacred and the profane.[23] In designating certain objects and activities in a culture as sacred, "any object becomes *something else*, yet it continues to remain *itself*, for it continues to participate in its surrounding cosmic milieu. . . .its immediate reality is transmuted into a supernatural reality."[24] Even the cosmos can take on a sacred character which "both transcends and includes man."[25] James Moseley observes that "if culture is the web of meanings through which humans have personal and social being, then religion may be understood as the way people symbolically express their culture's relation to a primordial, fundamental order of reality, often imaged as a divine being."[26] It provides answers to the profound existential questions about where we come from, why we are here and where we are going.

Religion is more than just imbuing certain objects and events with religious symbolism or even a set of dogmas or series of rituals. It becomes a lived phenomenon, a way of life which gives coherence to existence and integrates the individual with the community and the heavenly cosmos. Religion functions as a cultural bonding agent with the sacred at the center and the source of divine law.

With world view permeated by a religious or supernatural perspective, the boundaries established by culture now become more than just social boundaries but sacred boundaries. The nature of mankind, the normative aspects of interpersonal relationships, social roles, the political order all become part of the larger sacred cosmos. Religion serves to legitimate specific social roles and arrangements by "locating them with a sacred and cosmic frame of reference" of ultimate reality.[27] A culture becomes a reflection of the divine, eternal order of the universe, a sacred micro-cosmos. Transgressing norms of a religiously-oriented culture offends not just social sensibilities but also violates one's true nature and disrupts the divine harmony of the universe.

With roots sunk deep in the Puritan experience, nourished by three major revivals or Great Awakenings, with the fourth one currently in progress, religion has always played an important role in America.[28] The founding leaders of the United States acknowledged the central place of religion and divine influence and wrote this acknowledgment into America's founding documents.[29] The First Amendment in the Bill of Rights gave constitutional protection to religious beliefs but forbade the establishment of a national church or national religion. The American ethos and culture was defined by philosophy of the Enlightenment and theology of Protestant Christianity.[30] The cultural vision of nineteenth-century Protestant America echoed the Puritan motif of a "city on a hill." The United States was looked upon as the "redeemer nation entrusted with a millennial destiny."[31] Until the end of the nineteenth century, America was a Protestant nation, God was Protestant, and Americans were God's chosen people.

The dominance of the "Anglo-Protestant empire" in American culture began to break up by the early part of the twentieth century.[32] America was no longer just a Christian-Protestant nation but a Christian nation. The breaking up of the "Righteous Empire" came as a result of outside forces and pressures from within. The massive immigration dramatically changed the religious and ethnic demographics of America, and consequently, the political dynamics. For example, by 1906 40 percent of American church members were of the Roman Catholic faith. Other indigenous religious groups such as the Mormons, Seventh-Day Adventists, and Christian Scientists also posed a threat to Protestant hegemony.

Internal schisms also weakened the Protestant hold on American culture. Protestants had battled with heretical movements such as Deists, Owenites, and Unitarians. Serious divisions were caused by the Civil War and the war on modernism (e.g., Darwinism, higher biblical criticism) with the "'private party' of fundamentalism and the 'public party' of liberalism."[33] By 1950 Will Herberg could write of Protestants, Catholics, and Jews as Americans, and a Catholic was actually elected president of United States in 1960.[34]

The growth of religious pluralism in America, however, has also been accompanied by an increased secularism in public life. Religious belief and practice have become more privatized. Prayer, Bible reading, and posting the Ten Commandments in public schools have been declared unconstitutional.[35] Stephen Carter refers to this "trend in our political and legal cultures toward treating religious beliefs as arbitrary and unimportant" as a "culture of disbelief."[36] Richard Neuhaus would go even further and claim that political and legal cultures are in fact hostile toward religion.[37] This viewpoint acquired additional credence with the 1990 Supreme Court decision of *Employment Division, Department of Human Resources v. Smith*, which in the opinion of many legal scholars, eviscerated the Free Exercise Clause of any substantive protections of religious practice.[38] However, in response to this key court decision, Congress passed the Religious Freedom Restoration Act of 1991.[39]

In addition to overt legal and political efforts to marginalize religious belief in the formation of public policy, Moseley points to modernity with its "pluralization of social life-worlds" as the primary factor in divorcing religion from the American public life.[40] Modernity with its

technology and bureaucracy, along with urbanization and mass communications, have created many "worlds" for modern individuals. In traditional societies—or, as we have seen, in the vision of American Puritans—all of life's activities and meanings are integrated into a single world of experience. The unifying order of a traditional culture is expressed in its religion, which symbolizes how this world's coherence mirrors or replicates the order of the cosmos itself. When the forces of modernity began to disassociate the world of work from other aspects of life, the authority of religious symbols ceased to be unquestioned.[41]

In a reactionary response to the "godlessness" and secular humanism in our current society, many fundamentalist Protestants and other religious conservatives have worked to infuse religion back into the civic discourse as a legitimate voice in the political and social life of the nation.[42] They have advocated a return to basic Victorian values and fiscal conservatism. They have opposed the teaching of organic evolution in schools, values clarification, outcome based education, abortion, and feminism and requested that offensive books be withdrawn from the school library. They have favored the teaching of traditional family values and creationism in schools. Many have withdrawn their children from public schools and placed them in private schools. These efforts to bring religion back into the "public square" of American life, however, have often been met with determined resistance from those with an opposing viewpoint.

"Opposing moral visions," James Davison Hunter claims, are "at the heart of the culture war."[43] Hunter characterizes these two opposing moral visions as the "*impluse toward orthodoxy*" and "*the impulse toward progressivism.*"[44] The moral vision of orthodoxy is the traditional religious vision based on a belief in a transcendent or divine moral authority, objective reality, eternal truths, and universal values. For example, a Supreme Being exists who created a universe permeated with a moral order. This moral order transcends space, time, and social context. Moral laws of right and wrong exist independent of any specific culture or society. True happiness results when individual and societal behavior is in harmony with these universal moral laws.

On the other hand, the moral vision of progressivism holds that moral authority is a function of a particular cultural context and time. Reality is not something that is "discovered" out there but is "created" and subjectively experienced. Truth, values, social norms, notions of right and wrong are social constructs and products of a specific culture. The origins of this moral vision can be found in the Enlightenment.

The origins of the orthodox moral vision is Protestant Christianity while the progressive moral vision has its roots in Enlightenment philosophy.[45] The orthodox world view is grounded in a sacred cosmos. The progressive world view is guided by the "Enlightenment ideology with its secularism (indifference to religious truth), naturalism (denial of the supernatural), and positivism (limitation of inquiry only to those areas that can be investigated empirically)."[46] These two perspectives or belief systems about human nature, the purpose of life and character of the universe are based on incommensurable premises and principles. Hunter concludes that the current culture war is due to

> two fundamentally different cultural systems. *Each side operates from within its own constellation of values, interests, and assumptions. At the center of each are two distinct conceptions of moral au-*

thority—two different ways of apprehending reality, of ordering experiences, of making moral judgments. Each side of the cultural divide, then, speaks with a different moral vocabulary. Each side operates out of a different mode of debate and persuasion. Each side represents the tendencies of a separate and competing moral galaxy. They are, indeed, "worlds apart."[47]

Hunter's observation that the American culture war has basically two diametrically opposed positions which are "worlds apart" is an important insight. However, the labels he attaches to each world view, orthodox and progressive, connotate a value judgment about the merits of each perspective. The designation, orthodoxy juxtaposed with progressivism, is itself a manifestation of the very culture war he describes in his book: orthodoxy versus progressivism. Orthodoxy with its fundamental beliefs in a transcendental, if not supernatural, reality is contrasted with progressivism, a nontranscendental naturalism. The term "orthodox," as commonly used in American culture, has a pejorative or disparaging meaning. To be orthodox is to be closed-minded, rigid, an unthinking conformist, trapped by tradition and custom in another place and time, blind to changing circumstances, and unwilling to consider new ideas. In a word, old-fashioned and out-of-touch with the real world. On the other hand, the customary understanding of progressivism is just the opposite. Progressivists are just that, progressive, forward looking, constantly moving ahead to something better, open-minded, willing to entertain new ideas and practices, responsive to change and in touch with how things really are. The message behind the juxtaposition of orthodoxy and progressivism is clear. The orthodox moral vision with its transcendental and supernatural or religious worldview is limited, narrow, and backward, if not a little irrational. The worldview of the progressivists, nontranscendental, naturalistic, and nonreligious, however, is the vision of progress, growth, and rationality. These two worldviews might be more aptly designated as religious and secular or, in many instances, theistic and nontheistic. Perhaps supernaturalism better captures the essence of orthodox moral vision while postmodernism with its multiple realities and relativism is probably a more accurate description of the worldview of progressivism.

Education

> *At present opinion is divided about the subjects of education. All do not take the same view about what should be learned by the young, either with a view to plain goodness or with a view to the best life possible . . . Goodness itself, to begin with, has not the same meaning for all the different people who honour it . . . it is hardly surprising there should also be difference about the right methods of practising goodness.*
>
> —*Aristotle,* The Politics

Education is the process by which a culture transmits itself to the next generation. In this process, a society is reproduced and an individual is created. Through education individuals are acculturated or learn their own culture. The particular form or shape in which the educative process takes place can be formal or informal, highly structured and purposeful or simply the unconscious imitation of others. The important point is that education, both in its content and pedagogy, is the cultural furnace where a particular image of mankind and the world is forged and a way of living is passed on.[48]

That education is the crucial focal point of any cultural conflict, then, should not be surprising nor should its inherent political nature be a source of astonishment. The type of education one receives influences how one perceives reality, what meanings are attached to these perceptions, what social arrangements are legitimate, which personal relationships are proper, and what constitutes moral or unethical behavior. A world view with its moral vision defines the individual and specifies his or her proper place in society and the cosmos. The determination of the substance of education and the nature of the world view it propagates is ultimately a political exercise of power to achieve social ends. Whoever controls the education controls the formation of a world view with its particular belief system.[49] The history of American education is no exception.

The first immigrants to the New World sought to replicate the culture and way of life that they had left behind. Whether it was the Puritan Commonwealth in Massachusetts or the lifestyle of English gentry in the South, all colonists sought to preserve and pass on their world view. The first generation of Americans saw education as the means to create an American culture and people and ensure national survival. The common school movement establishing "public" or government schools was a response to social instability of the 1830s and 1840s. The targeted population was those who posed the greatest threat to the American society—the poor, immigrants, and the ethnically and religiously unwashed. These minority groups or cultural outsiders did not fit into the image or mold of the dominant cultural group in nineteenth-century America, those who were white, middle class, Anglo-Saxon, and Protestant.[50] The response of many minority groups was to establish their own system of "private" schools to preserve and perpetuate their ethnic and religious culture.[51] Public schools through the progressive era at the turn of the century and on into our current era have also been asked to solve national crises and social problems. Schools were asked to Americanize and socialize immigrants in the 1920s, "win the cold war in the 1950s, end poverty in the 1960s, . . . solve the problems of unemployment in the 1970s," and restore the nation as the economic and technological leader of the world in the 1980s and 1990s.[52]

The development of American education has important implications for better understanding our cultural conflict and why schools serve as cultural flashpoint. First, schools in America have been used and continue to be used as a mechanism of acculturation and socialization. American schools, public and private, teach particular world views. This observation, however, is but to state the obvious. Any school or education system performs the same basic functions. The second point is that American schools, public schools that is, are tied to the state and nationalism. When these two factors, socialization and the police power of the state, are combined, tortuous political problems present themselves. When government schools are established, whatever world view(s) they present takes on the imprimatur of the state. This presents a real moral and practical dilemma for those individuals with dissenting viewpoints when compulsory education laws accompany state sponsored schools and government monies are severely restricted to this public school system. Most parents

want to raise their children according to their own belief system. The problem arises when other individuals or institutions charged with the responsibility of assisting parents in their child-rearing obligations present ideas and values to the children that are contrary to the fundamental values and beliefs of the parents. This becomes especially problematic when it discredits some beliefs and exalts others in a setting where the children are a captive audience, and parents are financially unable to place their children in an educational environment that is compatible with their personal beliefs.[53]

Although a private education option exists, wealth becomes the determining factor of whether parents and children with different moral vision can exercise their constitutional right of freedom of conscience. Another option open to parents is to try and gain as much control of their neighborhood school as they can. This control is acquired through the democratic process, a highly political process, and the legal machinery of the state, an expensive and cumbersome route.

If schools are the central means of transmitting values and ways of looking at the world, then schools are going to be at the center of cultural conflicts. The battle is over whose private values, beliefs, world views will be elevated to public orthodoxy. The culture war in the educational arena is fought over whose moral vision will prevail, which notions of right and wrong will be approved, which historical account and public policies will be accepted and in whose image the upcoming generation will be created. The contemporary cultural conflict in American education takes on a much sharper edge with the state, with its coercive powers and immense benefits, taking a near monopolistic role in education.

Resolving Cultural Conflict

Culture, with us, ends in headache.

—Ralph Waldo Emerson

As individuals encounter different cultures, different world views, different ways of living, inevitably questions of rightness or wrongness arise. Are differences between cultures deficits, assets, or just plain differences?[54] How should members from various cultures or subcultures treat each other? Can different cultures peacefully coexist, especially when core cultural values may be incommensurable? Is there any "objective" way of sorting out answers to these perplexing questions?

These are not just abstract, impersonal questions and issues about the larger social body or mental gymnastics for those in academia. Cultures do draw normative boundaries and establish who are members and who are outsiders.[55] These outsiders, at least among all primitive tribes, are "summarily denied a place anywhere in the human scheme." For example, among Native Americans the

tribal names in common use, Zuñi, Déné, Kiowa, and the rest, are names by which primitive people know themselves, and are only their native terms for "the human beings," that is, themselves. Outside of the closed group there are no human beings.[56]

More common examples with deeply tragic consequences of defining cultural outsiders as less than human are African blacks pressed into slavery for American slave owners and the extermination of Jews by Germany during World War II.[57] In addition to the issues of social solidarity and control and cultural hegemony, perhaps this process of dehumanization helps explain in part the inhumanity of man. How else can the brutality and butchery witnessed recently in Rwanda and Bosnia be explained?

The two polar positions on this complex question are cultural monism and cultural relativism. Cultural monism holds that there is only one true culture, way of life and world view, namely ours. This ethnocentric position by definition excludes the possibility that other cultures have anything of value to offer. Cultural monism holds that the metaphysical and epistemological stance as well as the axiological values of the one true culture are superior. In this xenophobic perspective, other cultures are inferior and need to be destroyed or the people in these other cultures must be decultured and assimilated into the "right" culture. For example, the dominant culture in America during the nineteenth-century held that Protestantism was the only true religion, Anglo-Saxon the pure ethnic group, and white males inherently superior human beings. If people did not fit this mold or image, they were considered inferior and had to either be changed through education or segregated to an inferior social status, a second class member of the society.

Cultural relativism, on the other hand, considers all cultures of equal value and worth. All cultures are socially constructed as are all social norms. There are no absolute values nor is there any truth with a capital "T." There is no universal standard to evaluate the worth of a specific view of human nature, ethical behavior, family configurations, social arrangements and relationships, political systems, the meaning of life or the universe except within the particular cultural context whence it came. There is no universal moral order. There can be no moral outcry over the immolation of widows in India, child prostitution in Thailand, polygamy in Africa, the KKK and other white supremicist groups or subcultures in the United States, and incestual practices among some aboriginal tribes outside of the particular culture in which these examples occur.[58]

Cultural monism assumes a position of infallibility and omniscience, a most difficult position to prove and defend for it would require only one instance or example of fallibility or ignorance to render a fatal blow. Cultural relativism tries to avoid the indefensible posture of cultural monism by simply avoiding any evaluative posture with its truth claims. Truth claims and value judgments can be evaluated only in a specific cultural context. There are no universals. In making this claim of nonuniversality, it becomes a self-refuting argument and an indefensible position. To claim there are no universals or absolutes is itself a universal, absolute claim, and therefore inherently contradictory. If neither cultural monism nor relativism provide adequate position to anchor our response to cultural diversity, what location will?

Historically, there have been five general types of responses to cultural differences. Such differences have typically been addressed in one of the following ways—accommodation, acculturation, assimilation, segregation, and annihilation.[59] Accommodation is very similar to the idea of pluralistic, multicultural society. Different cultures are accorded equal respect and deference. There are no pressures on any cultural group to modify or abandon cultural elements. The multicultural society in Hawaii probably comes closest to this approach to various cultures existing together in relative harmony.

Acculturation is a second method of dealing with cultural diversity. An individual learns another culture, becomes bi-cultural, able to understand and participate in more than one culture. This "salad bowl" approach is far more characteristic of immigrants to America than the melting pot theory. Hence the proliferation of

American modifiers: African-American, Chinese-American, Japanese-American, etc.

A third approach, assimilation or the "melting pot" approach aims at absorbing or incorporating the foreign culture within the dominant culture until it becomes indistinguishable and loses its cultural identity. The 1909 play written by Israel Zangwill about a Russian Jewish immigrant who falls in love with a Gentile woman captures the spirit of this now abandoned American social policy of deculturalization of "foreigners."

America is God's Crucible, the great Melting Pot where all the races of Europe are melting and reforming! Here you stand, good folk, think I, when I see them at Ellis Island, here you stand in your 50 groups, with your 50 languages and histories, and your 50 blood hatreds and rivalries. But you won't be long like that, brothers, for these are the fires of God you've come to—these are the fires of God. A fig for your feuds and vendettas! Germans and Frenchman, Irishmen and Englishmen, Jews and Russians—into the Crucible with you all! God is making the American.[60]

The fourth strategy in dealing with cultural differences is that of segregation. The minority culture (in terms of power) is tolerated but only if its members stay in self-contained areas. Here we see creation of homelands for tribal blacks in South Africa and the American versions of apartheid with the placement of Native Americans on reservations and in racial ghettos and neighborhoods. The rise of both white and black Protestant churches in the nineteenth century and ethnic enclaves are other examples of segregationist strategies at work in American history.

Finally, the fifth tactic is that of simple annihilation. It is simple only in the fact that the solution is final and irreversible. The Crusades, the Albigensian massacre, the Inquisition, the extermination of the Jewish people in Germany during World War II, the slaughter of Hutus in Rwanda, the massacre of Kurds in Iraq, and the "ethnic cleansing" occurring in Bosnia are but a few examples.

None of the approaches, with the possible exception of the accommodation model in Hawaii, have been very successful in dealing with cultural diversity. Our nation and many parts of the world are still racked with social strife and culture wars. Just how should we handle our cultural differences? This is a tough question and it will probably never be resolved to the satisfaction of every party. There are, however, three perspectives that may be useful in beginning the construction of meta-cultural theory: critical pragmatism,[61] personalism,[62] and pluralism.[63] These three perspectives strive to strike a middle ground between cultural monism and cultural anarchy and chaos.

An adequate presentation of the core elements of these three perspectives is beyond the scope of this chapter. Briefly however, critical pragmatism offers a mode of inquiry to examine cultural diversity and differing world views. Personalism argues that we must go beyond "cultural racism" and see others as possessing basic human rights and deserving "unconditional respect" because of their humanity.[64] Along this line of reasoning, Winfried Böhm reminds us of Immanuel Kant's standard of treatment for those different from ourselves—the foreigners should not be treated as "*hostis*, or enemy, but as *hospes*, or guest."[65] Pluralism argues against government standardization of society and for cultural diversity and accommodation. Pluralism is not anarchy and recognizes the need for some common ground. But "autonomy to direct one's life in a meaningful manner can often engender respect and loyalty toward the state. One is far more willing to give consideration and support when it is reciprocated."[66]

The task of resolving cultural conflicts is a daunting one. However, the degree of difficulty does not excuse us from trying our best and then trying again. The price of the alternative is just too high.

Summary

The concept of culture is complex and perplexing as are religion and education, two of its major components. Culture with all of its dynamic and interactive elements is certainly not a subject for mastery but a study worthy of our best efforts and thought. The power of a religious dimension in a culture and how it orders the universe, society and the life of the individual in significant and profound ways should not be underestimated. Neither should the central role of education be forgotten nor relegated to the cultural fringes.

The difficult dilemma of how to respond to cultural diversity and resolve cultural conflict eludes easy answers and simplistic solutions. The search for common ground, mutual respect and cultural accommodation will require Job-like patience and perseverance in an increasingly pluralistic society. The pathos expressed in the Digger Indian proverb does not need to be repeated with other cultures. People from every culture deserve to drink the water of life with their own cup.

Notes

1. Ruth Benedict, *Patterns of Culture* (Boston: Houghton Mifflin Company, 1934; reprint, New York: The New American Library, 1959), 33 (page reference is to reprint edition).
2. The term "culture wars" was first used in nineteenth-century Germany when Otto von Bismark, the German prime minister used a state-sponsored "Kulturkampf" or "struggle for civilization" to create a unified Germany by attempting to create "a common high culture in which national values, largely synonymous with those of enlightened Protestantism, would be shared." This essentially amounted to an attack on members of the Catholic church and schools in Germany. John L. Snell, *The Democratic Movement in Germany, 1789–1914* (Chapel Hill: The University of Carolina Press, 1976), 179; Helmut Walser Smith, *German Nationalism and Religious Conflict* (Princeton, N.J.: Princeton University Press, 1995), 20.
3. James Davison Hunter, *Culture Wars: The Struggle to Define America* (New York: Basic Books, Inc. 1991), 107.
4. William B. Yeats, "The Second Coming," *The Norton Anthology of English Literature* , ed. M.H. Abrams, 6th ed., vol. 2 (New York: W.W. Norton & Company, Inc., 1993), 1180, lines 3,4.
5. W. Somerset Maugham, *The Razor's Edge* (New York: Penguin Books, 1978), 8.
6. Bennett M. Berger, *An Essay on Culture: Symbolic Structure and Social Structures* (Berkeley: University of California Press, 1995), and Albert Schweitzer, *The Philosophy of Civilization* (New York: Macmillian Company, 1949).
7. Matthew Arnold, *Culture and Anarchy* (London: Smith, Elder and Co., 1869).
8. Edward Burnett Tylor, *Primitive Culture: Researches into the Development of Mythology, Philosophy, Religion, Art, and Custom*, vol. 1 (London: Bradbury, Evans, and Co., 1871), 1.
9. Over 150 definitions of culture are reviewed in the work by Alfred L. Kroeber and Clyde Kluckhohn, *Culture: A Critical Review of Concepts and Definitions* (Cambridge, Mass.: Harvard University Peabody Museum of American Archeology and Ethnology, 1952). Other helpful discussions about the nature of culture can be found in Wendy Griswold, *Culture and Societies in a Changing World* (Thousand Oaks, Calif.: Pine Forge Press, 1994), Jeffrey C. Alexander and Steven Seidman, eds., *Culture and Society: Contemporary Debates* (Cambridge: Cambridge University Press, 1990), and Bennett M. Berger, *An Essay on Culture.*
10. James P. Spradley lists six common elements found in all cultures. First, all cultures organize and classify human experience into categories to help make descriptive sense of the world in which they live. Second, all cultures have a symbolic code or a means whereby meaning is assigned to the various facets of human experience. For example in American culture, a proper and respectful way of greeting someone is to look the other person in the eye while giving a firm handshake. However, for some Native Americans and Asians, respect is shown by not looking directly into the eyes of the other person. Third, all cultures are arbitrary social systems; there is no Platonic cultural ideal. Cultures are socially constructed and are a function of a particular time, place and people. Fourth, culture is learned. A child is not "born" with a particular culture but is enculturated into a

particular way of life. Fifth, culture is a device used to accomplish human objectives. For example, each culture has a moral or legal code to maintain social order. Sixth, awareness of one's culture exists at different levels. Some aspects of culture are explicit and others implicit. James P. Spradley, *Anthropology—The Cultural Perspective* (New York: John Wiley & Sons, 1980), 9–16.

11. Spradley sees a culture as "the acquired knowledge that people use to interpret experience and generate social behavior." James P. Spradley, *The Ethnographic Interview* (Fort Worth: Holt, Rinehart and Winston, Inc., 1979), 5.
12. Ruth Benedict, *Patterns of Culture*; Peter L. Berger, *The Sacred Canopy: Elements of a Sociological Theory of Religion* (New York: Doubleday, 1967; reprint, New York: Doubleday, 1990).
13. Clifford Geertz, *The Interpretation of Culture* (New York: Basic Books Inc., 1973), 89.
14. Mary Douglas, *Natural Symbols: Explorations in Cosmology* (New York: Vintage Books, 1973).
15. Peter L. Berger, *The Sacred Canopy.*
16. Clifford Geertz, *The Interpretation of Culture,* 44.
17. Winfried Böhm, "Multicultural Education and Xenophobia," paper presented at the annual meeting of the Far West Philosophy of Education Society, Provo, Utah, 1–2 December 1995.
18. Young Pai, *Cultural Foundations of Education* (New York: Macmillian Publishing Company, 1990), 24.
19. Pai defines core values as well-defined "patterns of behavior and attitudes that are useful in meeting human needs and resolving conflicts between individuals and groups" accepted by the dominant social group. Young Pai, *Cultural Foundations of Education,* 26. Pai refers to a study by George Spindler which identifies five traditional core values of American culture: "(1) Puritan morality, (2) work-success ethic, (3) individualism, (4) achievement orientation, and (5) future-time orientation." Since the mid-1950s, these traditional values have come under attack from the cultural revolution and social upheavals of the 1960s, the economic and environmental concerns of the 1970s and 1980s, and the technology and cultural diversity issues of the mid-1980s through 1990s. The last forty years have been a time of cultural ambiguity and adjustment. The rapidity of the social change and the degree of cultural turmoil, however, have made it difficult to determine the correct cultural alignment.
20. Hunter, *Culture Wars,* 173.
21. A. Masland, "Organizational Culture in the Study of Higher Education," *Review of Higher Education* 8 (1985):160.
22. Berger, *The Sacred Canopy,* 25.
23. Mircea Eliade, *The Sacred and the Profane: The Nature of Religion* (San Diego: Harcourt Brace Jovanovich, 1959).
24. Ibid., 12.
25. Berger, *The Sacred Canopy,* 26.
26. James G. Moseley, *A Cultural History of Religion in America.* (Westport, Conn.: Greenwood Press, 1981), 84.
27. Berger, *The Sacred Canopy,* 33.
28. Robert P. Fogel, "The Fourth Great Awakening and the Political Realignment of the 1990s," *BYU Studies* 35 (3) 1996: 31–43.
29. "We hold these truths to be self-evident, that all men are created equal, that they are endowed by their Creator with certain unalienable Rights, that among these are Life, Liberty, and the pursuit of Happiness. . . . And for the support of this Declaration, with a firm reliance on the Protection of Divine Providence, we mutually pledge to each other our Lives, our Fortunes and our sacred Honor." *Declaration of Independence.*

    "The fact that the Founding Fathers believed devotedly that there is a God and that the unalienable rights of man were rooted in Him is clearly evidenced in writings from the Mayflower Compact to the Constitution itself." *Abington School District v. Schempp*, 374 U.S. 203, 213 (1963).

30. Donald Meyers, *The Democratic Enlightenment* (New York: G.P. Putnam's Sons, 1976), 213–214.
31. David Tyack and Elisabeth Hansot, *Managers of Virtue: Public School Leadership in America, 1820–1980* (New York: Basic Books, Inc., 1982), 19.
32. Martin E. Marty, *Righteous Empire: The Protestant Experience in America* (New York: The Dial Press, 1970), 155.
33. Moseley, *A Cultural History of Religion in America*, 28.
34. Will Herberg, *Protestant—Catholic—Jew: An Essay in American Religious Sociology* (Garden City, N.Y.: Doubleday & Company, Inc., 1960).
35. Teacher-led or school-sponsored prayers in public schools is unconstitutional, *Engel v. Vitale*, 370 U.S. 421 (1962), *Wallace v. Jaffree*, 472 U.S. 38 (1985) and *Lee v. Weisman*, 112B S.Ct. 2649 (1992); *Abington School District v. Schempp*, 374 U.S. 203 (1963)—cannot read Bible as part of school devotional; *Stone v. Graham*, 449 U.S. 39 (1980)—cannot post Ten Commandments in schools.
36. Stephen L. Carter, *The Culture of Disbelief: How American Law and Politics Trivialize Religious Devotion* (New York: Basic Books, 1993), 6.
37. Richard Neuhaus, *The Naked Public Square* (Grand Rapids, MI.: Eerdmans, 1984).
38. *Employment Division Department of Human Resources* v. *Smith,* 110 S.Ct. 1595 (1990). See K.D. Kelly, "Abandoning the Compelling Interest Test in Free Exercise Cases: *Employment Division, Department of Human Resources v. Smith,*" *Catholic University Law Review*, 40 (1991): 929–965; and Michael W. McConnell, "Free Exercise Revisionism and the Smith Decision," *University of Chicago Law Review* 57 (1990): 1109.
39. Senator Orrin Hatch, R-Utah, and Representative Henry Hyde, R-Ill., are proposing a Religious Equality amendment to the Constitution. Senator Hatch is "concerned that the government not drive religion out of the public square and from our public dialogue on issues confronting our people. And I am concerned that the government not single out persons of faith for worse treatment that their fellow Americans when it comes to enjoying the benefits of public resources." Lee Davidson, "Hatch Promotes 'Religious Equality,'" *Desert News* (23 December 1995): A13.
40. James G. Moseley, *A Cultural History of Religion in America,* 28.
41. Ibid., p 135.
42. See Geroge M. Marsden, *Fundamentalism and American Culture* (Oxford: Oxford University Press, 1980) for an excellent treatment of fundamentalism. Other helpful sources addressing the issue of culture and religion include H. Richard Niebuhr, *Christ and Culture* (New York: Harper Colophon Books, 1951), Harey Cox, *Religion in the Secular City* (New York: Simon & Schuster, 1984), and Robert N. Bellah and Phillip E. Hammond, *Varieties of Civil Religion* (San Francisco: Harper & Row, 1980).
43. Hunter, *Culture Wars*, 290.
44. Ibid., 43.
45. Ibid., 116; Donald Meyer, *The Democratic Enlightenment,* 213.
46. E. Vance Randall, *Private Schools and Public Power: A Case for Pluralism* (New York: Teachers College Press, 1994), 47.
47. Hunter, *Culture Wars*, 128.
48. For additional studies of culture and education, see C. Camilleri, *Cultural Anthropology and Education* (Great Britain: Kogan Page, 1986), Catherine Marshall, Douglas Mitchell, and Frederick Wirt, *Culture and Educational Policy in the American States* (New York: The Falmer Press, 1989), and Mary E. Henry, *School Cultures: Universes of Meanings in Private Schools* (Norwood, N.J.: Ablex Publishing Corporation, 1993).

49. One of the first things a totalitarian regime initiates as part of the effort to gain political and social control is either to eliminate the educated class and/or require uncooperative individuals to enter re-education camps. Examples of where this has happened are China, North Korea, South Vietnam, and Cambodia. Other countries such as Israel attenuate the potential instability of social conflict by providing a highly censored and ideological educational program for the subjugated group, the Palestinians in this case.
50. R. Laurence Moore, *Religious Outsiders and the Making of Americans* (New York: Oxford University Press, 1986) and Randall, *Private Schools and Public Power*, 27–36.
51. David B. Tyack, *Turning Points in American Educational History* (New York: Wiley & Sons, 1967), 231.
52. Joel Spring, *The American Schools 1642–1985* (New York: Longman, 1986), 336. For an examination of the conservative influence on education, see Ira Shor, *Culture Wars: School and Society in the Conservative Restoration, 1969–1984* (Boston: Routledge & Kegan Paul, 1986).
53. Randall, *Private Schools and Public Power*, 125.
54. Young Pai, *Cultural Foundations of Education*, 33–34.
55. Böhm, "Multicultural Education and Xenophobia"; R. Laurence Moore, *Religious Outsiders and the Making of Americans.*
56. Ruth Benedict, *Patterns of Culture*, 21–22.
57. For religious examples in American history, see R. Laurence Moore, *Religious Outsiders and the Making of Americans.*
58. Another recent example illustrating this dilemma is the death of Ibtihaj Hassoun in Israel. She had returned home to her Druse village to reconcile with her family after having left twenty-two years earlier. As she approached the main square, her brother, Amer, confronted her and stabbed her in the stomach with a knife while other villagers looked on and cheered. Ibtihaj's mother said the killing was justified because she had left home, divorced her Druse husband, and remarried outside the faith. "'Honor killings'" are widely accepted by the Druse religious community. Needless to say, her brother was arrested immediately by Israeli police. Scheherazade Faramarzi, "Druse Woman Killed by Brother for Honor," Provo (Utah) *Daily Herald*, 27 December 1995, D6.
59. Böhm describes three approaches: "conversion, segregation, or liquidation" in "Multicultural Education and Xenophobia," 3.
60. Israel Zangwill, *The Melting Pot* (New York: Macmillian, 1909), 37; quoted in Daniel U. Levine and Rayna F. Levine, *Society and Education*, 9th ed. (Boston: Allyn and Bacon, 1996).
61. Catherine Cornbleth and Dexter Waugh, *The Great Speckled Bird: Multicultural Politics and Education Policymaking* (New York: St. Martin's Press, 1995), 28–34.
62. Böhm, "Multicultural Education and Xenophobia."
63. Randall, *Private Schools and Public Power.*
64. Böhm, "Multicultural Education and Xenophobia," 3.
65. Ibid.
66. Randall, *Private Schools and Public Power*, 122.

Chapter Four
Religious Schools in America
Worldviews and Education

E. Vance Randall

Introduction

Few topics generate as much passionate discussion and interest as religion and politics. It should not be surprising then, that education, which is also a political and often a religious endeavor, occupies a perennial and prominent role in public policy debates. This is especially true with American education for three basic reasons. First, education is a process by which an individual is created, a culture transmitted, and a society reproduced. The type of education one receives influences how reality is perceived and which world views are considered as legitimate. It is from these accepted world views or belief systems that social relationships and institutions are justified. Second, the American society has forged an ideological link between a state-sanctioned and -supported school system and the preservation and progress of the nation. One implication suggested by this linkage is the existence of some sort of a majoritarian orthodoxy with respect to values, attitudes, and behavior.

And third, there is a dynamic, if not conflicting, tension in the American republic between the concepts of ideological pluralism and public values. This tension is expressed best in our national motto, *e pluribus unum* (out of many, one). How does a democracy strike a balance between pluralism and social solidarity, between diversity and commonality? How do various religious groups in America with their own sense of truth and reality fit into American society and transmit their particular world views to their children? What is the

A substantial portion of this chapter appeared earlier in "The State and Religious Schools in America: An Overview of a Rocky Relationship," *Journal of Research on Christian Education* (1994) (3): 175–198. Permission to use material from that article was granted by the *Journal of Research on Christian Education* and is gratefully acknowledged.

appropriate relationship between the state and religious schools? These questions become even more acute in a growing pluralistic society with a state-sponsored system of public schools.

The purpose of this article is to present a historical overview of the relationship between the state and religious schools that offer part or all of a K–12 program. This overview will help provide a better understanding of religious schools and their relationship to the state in a society with a government school ethos. This article is subdivided into four major sections. The first three sections correspond to pivotal historical periods—colonial to common school era, progressive school era to 1930, and 1930 to 1996. The fourth section summarizes the article and offers some concluding observations.

Colonial Schools to Common Schools

The majority of American colonists set out to replicate the way of life they had left in England. The Puritans of New England, for example, were determined to establish a Christian commonwealth in Massachusetts. The Anglicans in the southern colonies were content to reproduce the life of English gentry rather than Puritan piety. Those in the middle colonies such as the Quakers in Pennsylvania and the Catholics in Maryland, comprised a socially, religiously and ethnically diverse group, each with their own world views and belief systems. Power was not concentrated in the hands of an aristocratic class nor was there a strong bond between the state and any particular religious group. This fragmentation of power was reflected in their systems of educational governance and structure. Each religious or cultural group decided for themselves the substance and process of their educational endeavors.[1] But what the colonists all had in common was a desire to survive the harshness of the New World and the "barbarism" of the wilderness, with their culture, religion, and ethnic identity intact.[2]

The forms that education took and the means by which it was supervised are evidence of the bewildering variety of schooling in colonial America. Schools were established by village towns, trading companies, religious orders such as the Jesuits, a variety of religious denominations, and individuals such as ministers, women, and town schoolmasters. State involvement with the educational affairs of the colonies was limited primarily to the granting of charters or acts of incorporation, setting governing boards, and approving teachers. There were few regulations to oversee education. Cremin (1970) observes that "virtually anyone could teach and virtually anyone could learn, at least among whites, and the market rather than the church or the legislature governed through multifarious contractual relationships."[3] In the absence of state-sponsored schools and a diminished capacity of the family and community to transmit culture, the individual churches and educational institutions assumed a more prominent role in the transfer of a particular culture, religious belief system, and ethnic identity. By the end of the colonial period,

education no longer was a cohesive force serving one master but was used freely to further the ends of separate ideological entities, both religious and secular. . . . Wishing to preserve their own religious views, individual communities undertook to block any effort that would infringe on their rights to establish school policies. Diversity of belief was protected by law and custom.[4]

The transition from colonial status to a nation-state had little initial impact on education. Education proceeded on as before with its diversity in configuration, content, and control.[5] Federal and state constitutions and legislation, for the most part, merely confirmed or legalized the current state of educational affairs.[6] The involvement of state governments with education was quite modest and was usually limited to the granting of acts of incorporation to private schools, continuing the colonial practice of providing some form of rudimentary education for the poor, and assisting and encouraging various educational institutions such as churches in their efforts to provide opportunities for education.

The most important piece of legislation passed during this period was the First Amendment in (1791) giving constitutional protection to religious belief and mandating a legal separation of church and state. Butts and Cremin correctly point out that

[w]hen church was separated from state, the state retained its legal rights to control education and to authorize private and religious education under a grant of power from the state by charter and legislative enactment. This is of paramount importance in the history of American education.[7]

This also established religious pluralism as a public policy and removed the possible legal threat of religious orthodoxy as a requirement for teachers. The problem this presented, however, was who would be the social integrator, the articulator and guardian of the culture and its norms. Who would replace the church in the performance of these crucial functions and how would that be decided? For Thomas Jefferson the answer would be found in the state, that bastion of rationality and objectivity.

Common Schools to Progressive Schools

The America of the 1830s and 1840s was quite different from that of nascent nation. Sectarian strife, the regional conflict between the North and South, the political conflict between the East and the West, massive immigration, the industrial revolution and urbanization with its accompanying social ills contributed to a state of cultural conflict. It was a time of much social upheaval and unrest which called for new solutions and a significant restructuring of current public policy to address the growing instability.[8]

Led by crusading social reformers and humanitarians, many believed that education, an education provided by a government-sponsored system of "common schools," was the sure foundation of any meaningful social reform. The purpose of the common school was to bring cultural harmony, economic prosperity, and social justice to the American nation. It would perform this role of a social panacea by educating the young in a socially-shared core of practical and cultural knowledge in a common school house that was sponsored, supported and controlled by the state.[9]

The direct and deliberate participation of the state in the provision of educational services on such a wholesale level as in the establishment of common schools constituted the beginnings of a radical restructuring of the roles the individual, the family, the church and the community would fulfill in relation to each other and especially in relation to the state. It also stands as an anomaly in nineteenth-century public policy infused with voluntarism.[10] In terms of control over education, this development marked the inauguration of a profound shift in power and direction away from the family and traditional private agencies such as the church and other community institutions to the state.

That the common school movement appealed to many should not be mistaken as a consensus on American education. It involved a bitter contest over whose private values and ideologies would be elevated to the status of public beliefs. In addition, each interest group supported the common school movement for different and sometimes conflicting reasons. In their efforts to build a majority through a federation of interest groups, the common school advocates had created an unrealistic set of expectations and had made extravagant claims for this new state school that would provide continual fodder for the ubiquitous debate over the end and means of education and the role of schools in our society. A major cost inherent in the establishment of state-sponsored schools in America was an educational program with conflict built into the system. The government school would always be a center of controversy because it had been touted as the universal elixir for individual and social ills and embodied the legitimization of particular values and beliefs. It could not be all things to all people, especially when some of the services demanded of it were conflicting and contradictory in nature and touched on fundamental beliefs about man and society.[11]

Private Schools and State Schools

The effect of the common school movement on private schools was felt in a number of ways. Many private schools were forced to close their doors as middle class parents could no longer afford to pay both tuition and taxes for the state schools. Many others, especially those sponsored by various Protestant denominations, were simply absorbed into the public school system. By 1850 only 138 private schools remained in New York City from the 430 in 1829. In Massachusetts, the private academies declined from 1308 in 1840 to 350 some forty years later.[12] Several Protestant denominations, such as the Calvinists, Lutherans, Episcopalians, Quakers and Dutch Reformed, strengthened or established their own school systems in response to the diluted Protestantism, the perceived "godlessness" in the state school, or as an effort to preserve their culture and language.[13]

Many immigrant groups supported, often at great sacrifice, their own private schools designed to perpetuate their religion and ethnic heritage. Norwegian Lutherans in Minnesota, Polish Catholics in Chicago, Rus-

sian Jews in Boston created their own educational systems, sometimes to supplement the public schools and sometimes to compete with them, but always to preserve their own culture. They juxtaposed their own ethnocentrisms against American ethnocentrism.[14]

In the political arena, a major confrontation between private schools, particularly religious schools, and the government was over the disbursement of state monies. It had been customary in many states to subsidize religious and non-religious educational institutions. With the entrance of the state as a participant and competitor, the reformers argued that the compulsory property tax should be reserved for the common schools. A sharing of tax monies to all interested parties would simply dilute any concentrated efforts of educational reform and would violate the First Amendment in the case of schools sponsored by religious bodies.[15]

The great "school war" in New York between common school advocates and the Catholics provides a good example of how a cultural and religious minority group fought the assimilation process of the state school. In light of the violent anti-Catholic riots and burning of some Catholic churches, the First Plenary Council of Baltimore in 1852 suggested that every parish support its own school to prevent exposure to their children to the Protestant indoctrination of the public school. This policy was made mandatory some thirty years later in the Third Plenary Council.[16] The Catholics viewed the new common schools as anti-Catholic, generic Protestant schools with an innate bias against everything that was not Protestant and Anglo-American, and posing both a religious and ethnic threat since most Catholics were also recent immigrants from Ireland and Germany.[17] The outcome of the political and legislative battles left tax monies firmly in place for state schools. With the loss of state subsidies for their schools, the only alternative in the eyes of many was cultural and religious capitulation or the establishment of a separate but costly private school system.

Clearly, the continued presence of private schools alongside state schools was a source a genuine irritation and concern for common school advocates and social reformers. These private schools represented a threat to their efforts of restructuring society because of the differing visions of man and society that were taught. They were potential, if not actual, sources of educational, ideological, and social heresy.[18]

In institutionalizing much of the nationalistic and Protestant ideology and rhetoric of the preceding sixty years, the common school movement had established, in one sense, a state church. The civil religion of nationalism, Whiggish republicanism, Enlightenment doctrines, capitalism, and generic Protestantism was just as "sectarian" as the beliefs of the traditional religious denominations. The state school assumed more and more functions traditionally performed by the church and "is probably the closest Americans have come toward creating an established church."[19] It became the source, the guardian, and the articulator of social values. Its primary objective was to mold and shape the social misfits, those who were different and did not meet the cultural, religious, and social standards, into acceptable and proper members of society. Those who most often felt the brunt of this forced assimilation and socialization were also those least able to resist—the poor, the immigrant, the member of an ethnic or religious minority.

What had once been the quintessential American institutions—the private school, the church, and the family—were now becoming institutional outsiders in American society. Although the conceptual patterns, educational themes, and institutional foundations for the modern state in education formed during this era would be expanded and refined, one pivotal piece of the structure was missing—the coercive power of the state. This essential element was quick in coming, however, in the form of compulsory schooling laws.

Compulsory Schooling Laws and State Regulations

After the national trauma of the Civil War, the "search for order," the "lure of instant stability-by-statute," thrust the state into areas of personal, family, and community life that had traditionally been untouched or very narrowly restricted.[20] A particular focus of the legislative and regulatory efforts was the child.

In the area of education, the coercive impulses in this "Age of Compulsion" were manifested primarily in the passage of compulsory education and attendance laws. These laws had a profound effect on American education and represented a significant reordering of the relationship between the family and the state. They became a legislative mechanism through which state intervention in education was realized. While recognizing the right of parents to educate their children, the state posited its right, *parens patriae* and *in loco parentis*, to see that the child was educated to ensure the perpetuation of the state. Charles Burgess maintains that

> *[of] all the changes in American education [during the last quarter of the nineteenth century] . . . none was more momentous than the state-by-state endorsement of the arguments that the state could compel children to attend schools, could punish parents and guardians who did not abide by the attendance laws, and, as a final measure, could confine truants along with other delinquent children in appropriate boarding institutions.*[21]

For private schools, the passage of compulsory education laws was of immense importance. Although the government recognized attendance at private schools as fulfilling compulsory attendance laws, these laws became the legislative justification and legal mechanism through which the state could intervene and regulate the activities of the private school. With the attendance at school now required by state law, private schools performed a function mandated by the state. In order to insure that the intent of the legislature was being fulfilled, the state intervention to some degree was necessary to insure compliance with state law.[22]

There were, however, several strict measures passed or proposed before the turn of the century that would have severely restricted or abolished private schools.[23] In 1874 the California compulsory education statute contained a proposed provision making enrollment in a private school a criminal offense unless the local board of education gave specific approval for the child in question. Massachusetts passed a comprehensive provision for the approval of private schools in 1888.[24] Although it did not pass, a bill was submitted to the New York legislature in 1889 which would have required teachers in private schools to take the same qualifying exams as public school teachers.[25]

The Bennett Law in Wisconsin and Edwards Law in Illinois passed in 1889 required that certain subjects be taught in English. While this requirement may appear entirely reasonable and innocuous, the political fallout from this legislation that was later repealed in 1891 affected the political scene in Wisconsin for the next ten years. The large German population saw it as an attack on their language and culture while the Catholics and Lutherans felt it threatened their private school system. Governor William D. Hoard admitted that the legislation was "aimed at sectarian schools."[26] And finally, many states in the South and for a limited period of time, Ohio and Rhode Island, denied private schools a tax exempt status.[27]

The first quarter of the twentieth century found America embroiled in war on two fronts that would have a great impact on both public and private education. The first "war" had been in the making for some time as shocking exposés by muckraking journalists and investigative reporters brought to public attention the extent of political corruption, the capture of government by big business, and the decadence and poverty in America. The second war was World War I.

From these turbulent conditions emerged the Progressive Era bent on reforming society and restoring calm and stability. The major premise of progressive reformers, most of whom were white, middle to upper class, well educated, and Protestant, was that the individualism and *laissez faire* attitude of the state had to be changed. The state had to be purified of special interest groups, that is, big business, and its police powers and resources expanded and brought to bear directly on the ills of society.[28]

The effect of the Progressive Era had a very significant impact on American education that is still with us today. "The most quickened profession, the most altered social institution outside of politics," notes Graham, "was surely education."[29] A new educational philosophy championed by John Dewey emphasized the importance of preparing students to be successful and productive members of society. This more pragmatic orientation for education would also prepare students "hygienically, morally, and politically for what reformers considered responsible behavior in a modern, industrial society."[30] Even though there were important curricular changes, the intent as usual was control rather than liberty.[31]

In keeping with a basic tenet of progressivism, public education was turned over to the educational expert.

Society would control its own evolution through schooling; professional management would replace politics; science would replace religion and custom as sources of authority, and experts would adapt education to the transformed conditions of modern life.[32]

Power in educational matters had largely been transferred to an "interlocking directorate of urban elites," a growing cadre of educational experts and an expanding educational bureaucracy with their own vested interests, their view of the "one best system" of education with their concepts of man and the good society.[33] The earlier ideology of common values or beliefs was exchanged for an ideology of technology and expertise. The "certainties grounded in . . . God's will" were replaced with the "assurance of expert knowledge."[34] Hansot and Tyack conclude that

much of the awesome power to define what was normal and desirable in schooling—the creation of a template of approved practice—fell to non-elected private individuals and groups claiming special competence to judge what is in the public good.[35]

The initial effects of the reforms of the Progressive Era on private elementary and secondary schools were stricter compliance with the provisions of compulsory attendance laws that applied to private schools. Furthermore, there was the spillover effect from increased regulations of public schools for certain required courses. By the middle of the 1920s, the legislative foundation for regulating private schools had been set in place and would receive incremental additions during the succeeding decades.

The most significant effect, however, came in the form of legislation stipulating that only attendance at public schools would satisfy compulsory education laws and prohibiting the teaching of certain subjects. The motivation for such legislation, which essentially outlawed private schools or seriously intervened in their operations, was not the tenets of technological ideology of the educational expert. This would occur later. It was the result of conservative groups reacting to the xenophobia engendered during the war, religious and racial bigotry, and an attempt to force some sense of moral and cultural stability on a rapidly changing, increasingly secular society.

Michigan was one of the first states to try to legally prohibit the existence of private schools. Its first attempt in 1920 to amend the state constitution failed as did a second attempt in 1924.[36] The fanatical nationalistic fervor of its advocates, mixed with the usual doses of nativistic racial, religious, and cultural bigotry, fanned the flames of intolerance and called for the police powers of the state to impose their world view on others.[37]

The next state to legislate against the right of private schools to exist was the state of Oregon in 1922. Unlike efforts in Michigan, the proposed initiative took the form of a change in the state compulsory education law rather than as an amendment to the state constitution. As in the Michigan case, supporters wrapped themselves in the American flag and equated public schools with true patriotism. Conservative and even fascist groups gave their hearty endorsement and support to the measure.[38]

A Catholic parochial school and a military academy filed suit in federal court that the measure was unconstitutional. Their claim of unconstitutionality was upheld by the federal district court in March of 1924, and a restraining order was issued against the state of Oregon. The state governor, Walter M. Pierce, then appealed the decision to the United States Supreme Court. In its landmark decision rendered in 1925, the United States Supreme Court sustained the lower court ruling and declared the Oregon Compulsory Education Law unconstitutional (*Pierce, et al. v. Society of Sisters*, 268 U.S. 510 [1925]; *Pierce, et al. v. Hill Military Academy*, 268 U.S. 510 [1925]). Other states attempting to outlaw private schools with referendums were California and Washington, but they were also unsuccessful.[39]

In addition to legislation that, in effect, prohibited private schools, other statutes were passed regulating the curriculum. In 1919, three states, Nebraska, Iowa, and Ohio, passed analogous acts requiring that instruction in all schools, public and private alike, must be given in the English language.[40]

Ostensibly, these 1919 enactments were designed to assist in the Americanization of immigrants to insure public safety. Their real focus, however, was directed toward the large German-speaking communities in these three states and were a manifestation of postwar xenophobia. For example, Robert T. Meyer, a Lutheran teacher in the Zion Parochial School, was convicted by the state of Nebraska with violating the 1919 Simian Act. He did this by using Bible stories to teach reading in German to Raymond Parpart, a ten-year old boy enrolled in a religious school sponsored by the Zion Evangelical Lutheran Congregation.[41] Meyer's conviction was challenged in the state court as unconstitutional. The Nebraska court ruled, as did the courts in the other two states facing similar constitutional questions, in favor of the state (*Nebraska District of Evangelical Lutheran Synod of Missouri et al. v. McKelvie*, 104 Neb. 93, 175 N.W. 531 [1921]; *Bohning v. State of Ohio*, 102 Ohio St. 474, 132 N.E. 20 [1921]; *Pohl v. State of Ohio*, 102 Ohio St. 474, 132 N.E. 20 [1921]; *Bartels v. Iowa*, 191 Ia. 1060, 181 N.W. 508 [1921]). These state court rulings were appealed in 1923 to the United States Supreme Court where they were overturned on the grounds of violation of liberties protected under the Fourteenth Amendment (*Meyer v. State of Nebraska*, 262 U.S. 390 [1923]).

While the *Pierce* decision firmly established the right of private schools to exist, it also confirmed the right of states to issue reasonable regulations governing the operations of private schools. The *Meyer* decision restricted the state in prescribing what may not be taught in private schools. These two United States Supreme Court decisions are of obvious importance to all religious schools. They guarantee the constitutional right to exist and offer great protection to kinds of subject matter which may be taught, matters of fundamental importance to the schools' purpose and existence.

Although religious schools are sponsored by institutions with a wide range of theological and religious beliefs, these schools hold four things in common. First, they all believe in a transcendent moral order in the universe. Many of these religious schools, be they Jewish, Christian, or Islamic in theological orientation, have definite theistic beliefs, beliefs in a God who intervenes in the affairs of men and who has revealed His will in sacred writings. Second, these theistic world views posit a sacred moral code and a divine order and structure for individual and institutional life. This calls for an integration of religious principles into daily living. Third, the religious belief system and its value base permeate the entire operations of the school, the educational experience, the curriculum, and expectations for staff and student behavior. The Association of Christian Schools International, for example, sees Christian Day Schools as "Christian institutions where Jesus Christ and the Bible are central in the school curriculum and in the lives of teachers and administrators."[42] For the Seventh-Day Adventists, the Bible is "at the focal point of the curriculum" where "all subjects [are taught] within the framework of the biblical world view."[43] And fourth, the religious school teaches its own particular theology and religious doctrines. For the Calvinist Day schools, this means thorough instruction in the "sovereignty of God in the totality of life" which is "the fundamental principle upon which the Calvinist system rests."[44] Despite theological differences, which in some cases are significant, there is much that religious schools have in common.[45]

1930–1996: The Modern Era

Since 1930 the social, religious, and educational landscape of America has changed dramatically. Not only have a Catholic and a born-again Christian been elected president, but racial segregation, prayer and bible reading have been outlawed by the Supreme Court in public schools (*Brown v. Board of Education*, 347 U.S. 483 [1954]; *Engel v. Vitale*, 370 U.S. 421 [1962]; *Abington School District v. Schempp*, 374 U.S. 203 [1963]). Our country has experienced the Great Depression, World War II, the Korean and Vietnam Wars, the cold war, and social upheaval of the 1960s with the rise of a youth counterculture which caused many to question traditional institutions and sources of authority. At the same time education was tied even more closely to the socialization and political goals of government, especially on the federal level, "as schools were asked to win the Cold War in the 1950's, end poverty in the 1960's, . . . solve problems of unemployment in the 1970's" and re-establish the nation as the economic and technological leader of the world in the 1980s.[46]

Since the 1970s, we have witnessed an educational revival in the public schools with waves of innovations and reform with open classrooms, accountability, competency testing, and back-to-basics movements which has only been matched by a burgeoning bureaucracy to administer and implement these new programs. Such action was often justified with the "ideology of professionalism"—the political and educational experts know best.[47]

Free schools or "alternative" schools have been established as educational options to the public school system. Catholic enrollment at parochial schools declined dramatically as Catholics found the public schools "de-Protestantized" by the increased secularity in society and, thus, far more palatable.

Our society has also experienced an evangelical revival, a Fourth Great Awakening, during the past twenty-five years which has impacted the political and educational climate.[48] In a reactionary response to the "godlessness" of the public schools with their growing problems of discipline, drugs, sex, poor educational programs, and crime, all concurrent with instruction in sex education and evolution, many fundamentalist Protestants, other conservative groups, and concerned parents, abandoned the public school system and established their own schools.[49] Many no longer felt a sense of loyalty to an institution involved in practices and beliefs so offensive and alien to their own. Efforts to initiate reforms or to have a meaningful voice in determining the educational environment of their children were unsuccessful. Exit was the only acceptable option left.[50] In 1961–1962 there were only 250–300 private Protestant schools in the entire nation. By 1984 this figure was over 6,000. Between 1971 and 1981 there was a 47 percent increase in the number of Protestant private schools, 91 percent increase in enrollment, and 116 percent increase in the number of teachers.[51] As of 1992, enrollments in these new Christian schools represent "approximately 20 percent of the total private school population and 2–3 percent of the national school population."[52]

The relationship between the state and religious schools since the *Meyer, Pierce*, and *Farrington* cases over sixty years ago has been an unsettled one. This is especially true for the past twenty-five years which has been punctuated at times with abusive behavior by the state.[53] An illustration of this is found in the landmark case of *Wisconsin v. Yoder* in 1972.[54] In the fall of 1968, three Amish parents, Jona Yoder, Adin Yutzy, and Wallace Miller, refused to enroll their children in the local public high school. Their children had attended public schools and had successfully completed the eighth grade. This was in keeping with Amish beliefs in a limited contact with society and to be apart from the world. Exposure to the larger society and its worldly ways, as represented in the high school, would destroy the religious faith of the children. The preservation of the rich Amish heritage and the spiritual salvation of the children were dependent upon following the Amish way of life. However, the Wisconsin compulsory education law required that all children between ages of 7 and 16 attend a public or private school or elsewhere where the instruction was "substantially equivalent" to that found in the public school. In a spirit of cooperation, the Amish parents proposed to provide a two-year vocational education program to comply with the law. The state of Wisconsin then refused this offer. This now placed the Amish in a dilemma: comply with state law or follow one's religious convictions. The Amish parents chose the later and were convicted of breaking the law.

The decision of the trial court was eventually appealed to United States Supreme Court. The Court concluded that the First and Fourteenth Amendments precluded the state of Wisconsin from compelling the three fathers to send their Amish children to a public high school. The two additional years of vocational training would satisfy the demands of the statute.

The uniqueness of *Yoder* is that it combines the rights of parents to direct the education of their children with claims of free exercise of religion against excessive state action. The value of *Yoder* for other similar situations, however, is somewhat limited by the caveats attached to the decision. To receive similar consideration and protection, another religious group would need to be almost identical to the Amish.[55] Another disturbing aspect of the *Yoder* case was the primarily financial interest of the state of Wisconsin in the Amish children. The court record revealed that

> *there is strong evidence that the purpose of this prosecution was not to further the compelling interests of the state in education, but rather the reprehensible objective, under the facts of this case, to force the Amish into [public] school only for the purpose of qualifying for augmented state aids.*[56]

Another major development with religious schools and the state is the refusal of many of the new fundamentalist private schools to comply with few, if any, state regulations on the basis of First Amendment violations. The aversion to any state interference in fundamentalist religious schools is based on the belief that religious schools are an integral part of a church's ministry in helping parents with their divine mandate to educate their children.[57] Education is inherently a religious activity and religious schools are but an indivisible part of the church's larger mission. A pastor of an unapproved fundamentalist Baptist church school explained

We don't want approval, because we feel it's a matter of state control. Jesus said in Matthew, Chapter 16, "I will build my church, and the gates of hell will not prevail against it." We believe the head of the Church is Jesus Christ, and if I let the State become the head of the church, then I will be removing the Lord from His position, and this Church is definitely built on the Lord, Jesus Christ.[58]

Another dimension of the belief driving the position of fundamentalist schools on state regulation is the firm conviction that the world view of modern society is morally and religiously bankrupt. It is because of this very world view that fundamentalist schools, often at great personal cost and sacrifice, were established in the first place, to provide a physical and spiritual refuge from a wicked world. In their view, the insistence of a bureaucratic agency of the state, a member of this fallen society, to exercise any control over a fundamentalist school is to sleep with the enemy. State regulation simply threatens the integrity of the church and its religious beliefs.[59] State and local educational officials, firmly convinced of their expertise, have often been equally determined to enforce these regulations, with the outcome frequently determined in the courts.[60]

Not unlike the *Yoder* case with the Amish, there are some curious aspects in the state's insistence to regulate private schools. In a comprehensive study of state regulation of private schools, Randall did not find a single documented case where a student had been harmed either physically or educationally by attending a private school. What was discovered was undisputed evidence submitted to the court that students receiving education in a private school were making satisfactory progress and in some instances, they were doing better than they had been in the public school.[61] For example, in the *Sheridan Road Baptist Church v. Department of Education*, a religious school had complied with all the state requirements except teacher certification. All the teachers in this church school had college degrees and the school had asked that these degrees be accepted in lieu of teacher certification to avoid submitting to state authority. This request was denied and the school authorities were convicted even though the court record indicated that students in the school had "acceptable and, indeed, above average levels of scholastic achievement."[62] Furthermore, counsel for the state of Michigan even admitted that "there [was] no allegation on [its] part that the children were being deprived of an education or being miseducated."[63] Examples such as this one call into serious question the viability of the state's position and a willingness to make reasonable accommodation for religious convictions.

Court cases involving state regulation of private schools, along with the Amish case (*Yoder*), have turned the issue of appropriate state controls into a policy dilemma. In the context of an increasing pluralistic society, this social controversy has raised anew all of the old but fundamental questions about the nature of man and the good society, who controls the child, the power of the state, and whose values and beliefs will ultimately prevail.[64]

Three events in the past six years, each with important implications for religious schools, demonstrate the continued ambiguity in public policy regarding the importance and place of religious belief. The first deals with protection of religious beliefs previously afforded by the First Amendment. In a stunning decision, the United States Supreme Court in *Employment Division, Department of Human Resources v. Smith*, 110 S.Ct. 1595 (1990), eviscerated the Free Exercise Clause of any substantive protection of religious practice by removing the "compelling interest" test for "neutral, generally applicable regulatory law."[65] With regulatory law that was neutral and had general application, the traditional "compelling interest" test and the "least restrictive means" standard would not be used in those cases where only a free exercise claim was raised. The claim of infringement on free exercise of religious beliefs had to be "in conjunction with other constitutional protections, such as freedom of speech, and of the press . . . or the right of parents . . . to direct the education of their children" to warrant the higher standard of judicial review.[66] The implications of this case were potentially devastating in terms of protecting religious schools from state intervention and control. Violation of religious belief and practice through state action was no longer sufficient by itself to justify the application of the "strict scrutiny" standard of judicial review reserved for cases involving fundamental rights. Clearly, the *Smith* decision had marginalized and trivialized religious belief and convictions.

The second event of importance was a congressional response to the Court's *Smith* decision. In November 1993, Congress passed the Religious Freedom Restoration Act of 1993. The purpose of the Act was to "restore the compelling interest test . . . and to guarantee its application in all cases where free exercise of religion is substantially burdened."[67]

Subsequent court cases, however, revealed that the Religious Freedom Restoration Act (RFRA) did not have the full effect intended by Congress. Senator Orrin Hatch, chairman of the Senate Judiciary Committee, held hearings in 1995 to investigate continued problems with unreasonable governmental burdens on religious beliefs and practices, problems that the RFRA was supposed to eliminate. Senator Hatch expressed the concern that "government not drive religion out of the public square and from our public dialogue on issues confronting our people."[68] As a consequence of the committee hearings, Senator Hatch and Representative Henry Hyde introduced a joint resolution in December 1995 calling for an amendment to the Constitution. The proposed "Religious Equality" amendment would prevent the government from "deny[ing] benefits to or otherwise discriminat[ing] against any private person or group on account of religious, belief, or identity."[69] Passage of this amendment could have dramatic implications for funding of private schools and would give further evidence that the government may be giving religious perspectives equal and nondiscriminatory treatment.

Conclusion

Religious schools have occupied a prominent position in American education. Until the establishment of government schools in the 1830s and 1840s, religious schools were the primary source of education. Since then religious schools have functioned as a social safety valve, a way in which those with world views and religious values different from the majoritarian ideology can find legitimate expression in the education of their children. Their ability to do so, however, is determined by the extent of state intervention into the operations of religious schools and the availability of resources. The centralization of decision making and socialization in the hands of the state has been a gradual process in which the spheres of influence and funds have been wrested away from families, churches, communities, and other nongovernment organizations. The transfer of power from the private to the government sector has been massive.

The relationship between American society and religion and between the state and church schools has been uneven at best. The role religious belief should play in our culture and in education has been and will continue to be problematic. Recent congressional actions, however, provide a cautious optimism that religious perspectives in matters of public policy and education will not be discounted and marginalized as they have in the past.[70]

Notes

1. Lawrence Cremin, *American Education: The National Experience* (New York: Harper & Row, 1980); Merle Curti, *The Social Ideas of American Educators* (Totowa, N.J.: Littlefield & Adams, 1974); and Adolph E. Meyer, *An Educational History of the American People* (New York: McGraw-Hill, 1957).
2. Bernard Bailyn, *Education in the Forming of American Society* (New York: W.W. Norton & Company, Inc., 1960).
3. Lawrence Cremin, *American Education: The Colonial Experience 1607–1783* (New York: Harper & Row, 1970), 559.
4. Bernard Mehl, "Education in American History," *Foundations of Education* (New York: John Wiley & Sons, 1963), 13–14.
5. Carl F. Kaestle, "Common Schools before the 'Common School Revival': New York Schooling in the 1790's," *History of Education Quarterly* 12 (Winter: 1972): 465–500.
6. Bernard Bailyn, "Political Experience and Enlightenment Ideas in Eighteenth-Century America," *The American Historical Review* 52 (January 1962): 339–351; Cremin, *American Education: The National Experience*; and Curti, *The Social Ideas of American Educators.*
7. R. Freeman Butts and Lawrence A. Cremin, *A History of Education in the American Culture* (New York: Henry Holt and Company, 1953), 29.
8. Clarence Karier, *The Individual, Society and Education*, 2nd ed. (Chicago: University of Illinois Press, 1986); Diane Ravitch, *The Great School Wars* (New York: Basic Books, 1974); Stanley K. Schultz, *The Culture Factory—Boston Public Schools 1789–1860* (New York: Oxford University Press, 1973); and Robert H. Wiebe, *The Search for Order—1877–1920* (New York: Hill & Wang, 1967).
9. Joel Spring, *The American School 1642–1985* (New York: Longman, Inc., 1986).
10. David Tyack and Thomas James, "State Government and American Public Education: Exploring the 'Primeval Forest,'" *History of Education Quarterly* 26 (Spring 1986): 39–69.
11. Frank P. Besag and Jack L. Nelson, *The Foundations of Education: Stasis and Change* (New York: Random House, 1934), and Clarence Karier, *The Individual, Society and Education*, 2nd ed. (Chicago: University of Illinois Press, 1986).
12. David Nasaw, *Schooled to Order—A Social History of Public Schooling in the United States* (New York: Oxford University Press, 1979).
13. Lloyd P. Jorgenson, "The Birth of a Tradition" *The World of Education—Selected Readings* (New York: Macmillian, 1968), and Otto F. Kraushaar, *American*

Nonpublic Schools—Patterns of Diversity (Baltimore: Johns Hopkins University Press, 1972).

14. David B. Tyack, *Turning Points in American Educational History* (New York: John Wiley & Sons, 1967), 231.
15. Cremin, *American Education: The National Experience;* and Nasaw, *Schooled to Order.*
16. David Tyack, Thomas, James and Aaron Benavot, *Law and the Shaping of Public Education, 1785–1954* (Madison: University of Wisconsin Press, 1987).
17. Patricia M. Lines, *Treatment of Religion in Public Schools and the Impact on Private Education* (Denver: Education Commission of the States [ERIC Document Reproduction Service No. ED 262 857], 1984, September).
18. Lawrence Cremin, *The American Common School* (New York: Teachers College, Columbia University, 1951), 61–62.
19. David Tyack and Elisabeth Hansot, *Managers of Virtue—Public School Leadership in America, 1820–1920* (New York: Basic Books, 1982), 249; Rockne M. McCarthy, James W. Skillen, and William A. Harper, *Disestablishment a Second Time—Genuine Pluralism for American Schools* (Grand Rapids, Mich.: Christian University Press, 1982); and Rousas John Rushdoony, "The State as an Establishment of Religion," in *Freedom and Education: Pierce v. Society of Sisters Reconsidered,* eds. Donald P. Kommers and Michael J. Wahoske, (South Bend, Ind.: Center for Civil Rights, University of Notre Dame Law School, 1978), 37–46.
20. Charles Burgess, "The Goddess, the School Book, and Compulsion," *Harvard Educational Review* 46 (May 1976): 205, and Wiebe, *The Search for Order—1877–1920.*
21. Burgess, "The Goddess," 212.
22. Raymond McLaughlin, *A History of State Legislation Affecting Private Elementary and Secondary Schools in the United States, 1870–1945* (Washington, D.C.: The Catholic University of America Press, 1946).
23. Kraushaar, *American Nonpublic Schools—Patterns of Diversity.*
24. Lloyd P. Jorgenson, *The State and the Non-Public School, 1825–1925* (Columbia: University of Missouri Press, 1987), and McLaughlin, *A History of State Legislation.*
25. Forest C. Ensign, *Compulsory School Attendance and Child Labor* (Iowa City: Athens Press, 1921).
26. William F. Whyte, "The Bennett Law Campaign in Wisconsin" *Wisconsin Magazine of History* 10 (June 1927): 377; Lloyd P. Jorgenson, *The State and the Nonpublic School, 1825–1925* (Columbia: University of Missouri Press, 1987); J.J. Mapel, "The Repeal of the Compulsory Education Laws in Wisconsin and Illinois," *Educational Review* 1 (1891): 52–57; Roger Wyman, "Wisconsin Ethnic Groups and the Election of 1890," *The Wisconsin Magazine of History* 51 (Summer 1968): 269–293.
27. McLaughlin, *A History of State Legislation.*
28. Grant McConnell, *Private Power and American Democracy* (New York: Random House, Inc., 1970), 30–50; Otis L. Graham Jr., *The Great Campaign: Reform and War in America, 1900–1928* (Englewood Cliffs, N.J.: Prentice-Hall, Inc., 1971); and Arthur S. Link, William A. Link, and William B. Catton, *American Epoch—A History of the United States Since 1900, vol. 1, An Era of Economic and Social Change, Reform, and World Wars 1900–1945* (New York: Alfred A. Knopf, 1986), 44–64.
29. Graham, *The Great Campaign,* 26.
30. Link, Link, and Catton, *American Epoch,* 1: 61.
31. Ibid., 61–62.
32. Tyack and Hansot, *Managers of Virtue,* 107.
33. David B. Tyack, The *One Best System—A History of American Urban Education* (Cambridge, Mass.: Harvard University Press, 1974), 6–7, 126–176.
34. Tyack and Hansot, *Managers of Virtue,* 4.

35. Elisabeth Hansot and David Tyack, "A Usable Past: Using History in Education Policy," in *Policy Making in Education—Eighty-first Yearbook of Education*, ed. Ann Lieberman and Milbrey W. McLaughlin (Chicago: University of Chicago Press, 1982), 7.
36. Ward G. Reeder, "State Control of Private and Parochial Schools," *School and Society* 17, 434 (21 April 1923): 427.
37. McLaughlin, A *History of State Legislation*, 111–113.
38. Jorgenson, *The State and the Non-public School, 1825–1925.*
39. W.E. Belleau, "State Regulation of Private Schools," *School and Society* 34, 874 (26 September 1931): 440; McLaughlin, *A History of State Legislation*, 108; and Tyack, James, and Benavot, *Law and the Shaping of Public Education, 1785–1954*, 246, n. 6.
40. Ensign, *Compulsory School Attendance and Child Labor*, 212–213; David Tyack, "Ways of Seeing: An Essay on the History of Compulsory Schooling," *Harvard Educational Review* 46, 3 (August 1976): 372, and McLaughlin, *A History of State Legislation*, 72–74.
41. Jon Diefenthaler, "Lutheran Schools in America," in *Religious Schooling in America*, ed. James C. Carper and Thomas C. Hunt (Birmingham, Ala.: Religious Education Press, 1984), 49, and E. Vance Randall, *Private Schools and Public Power: A Case for Pluralism* (New York: Teachers College Press, 1994), 58.
42. James C. Carper, "The Christian Day School," in *Religious Schooling in America*, 114.
43. George R. Knight, "Seventh-Day Adventist Education: A Historical Sketch and Profile," in Ibid., 92.
44. Donald Oppewal and Peter P. DeBoer, "Calvinist Day Schools: Roots and Branches," in Ibid., 59.
45. For an excellent treatment of various beliefs of religious schools see James C. Carper and Thomas C. Hunt, eds., *Religious Schooling in America*. In addition, an indispensable guide to additional research on religious schools is Thomas C. Hunt, James C. Carper, and Charles R. Kniker, eds., *Religious Schools in America: A Selected Bibliography* (New York: Garland Publishing Inc., 1986).
46. Spring, *The American School 1642–1985*, 336.
47. Tyack and Hansot, *Managers of Virtue*, 226.
48. Robert P. Fogel, "The Fourth Great Awakening and the Political Realignment of the 1990s." *BYU Studies* 35, 3 (1995–1996): 31–43; Susan D. Rose, "Abandoning the Myth of Equality and Democracy? The Impact of the Religious Right of American Education," paper presented at the annual meeting of the American Education Research Association, Religion and Education Special Interest Group, April 1995, San Francisco, Calif.
49. Carper, "The Christian Day School," in *Religious Schooling in America*, 116; Eugene F. Provenzo Jr., *Religious Fundamentalism and American Education: The Battle for the Public Schools* (Albany: State University of New York Press, 1990); Susan D. Rose, "Abandoning the Myth of Equality and Democracy?" in Susan D. Rose, *Keeping Them out of the Hands of Satan: Evangelical Schooling in America* (New York: Routledge, 1988); George M. Marsden, Fundamentalism and American Culture: *The Shaping of Twentieth-Century Evangelicalism 1870–1925* (New York: Oxford University Press, 1980); and Wade C. Roof and William McKinney, *American Mainline Religion: Its Changing Shape and Future* (New Brunswick: Rutgers University Press, 1987).
50. Donald A. Erickson, "Choice and Private Schools: Dynamics of Supply and Demand," in Daniel C. Levy, ed., *Private Education: Studies in Choice and Public Policy* (New York: Oxford University Press, 1986), 90, and Albert O. Hirschman, *Exit, Voice and Loyalty: Responses to Decline in Firms, Organizations and States* (Cambridge, Mass.: Harvard University Press, 1970).
51. Erickson, "Choice and Private Schools: Dynamics of Supply and Demand," 88–89.
52. Susan D. Rose, "Abandoning the Myth of Equality and Democracy?" 4.

53. Donald A. Erickson, "Showdown at an Amish Schoolhouse: A Description and Analysis of the Iowa Controversy," in Donald A. Erickson, ed., *Public Controls for Nonpublic Schools* (Chicago: University of Chicago Press, 1969), 15–59, and E. Vance Randall, *Private Schools and Public Power: A Case for Pluralism* (New York: Teachers College Press, 1994).
54. *Wisconsin v. Yoder,* 406 U.S. 205 (1972).
55. For additional analysis of *Yoder*, see E. Vance Randall, *Private Schools and Public Power: A Case for Pluralism*, 67–72.
56. *State v. Yoder,* 182 N.W.2d 539, 550 (Wis. 1971), J. Heffernan, dissenting opinion.
57. See Proverbs 22:6, Deuteronomy 6:6–7, Ephesians 6:4.
58. *State v. Shaver,* 294 N.W.2d 883, 887 (N.D. 1980). See similar rationale expressed in *State v. Faith Baptist Church,* 301 N.W.2d 571, 574 (Neb. 1981); *Bangor Baptist Church v. State of Me., Dept. of Educ.,* 576 F. Supp. 1299 (D. Me. 1983); *Johnson v. Charles City Comm. Schools Bd.,* 368 N.W.2d 74, 76–77 (Iowa 1985); *Braintree Baptist Temple v. Holbrook Public Schools,* 616 F.Supp. 81 (D. Mass. 1984); *Fellowship Baptist Church v. Benton,* 620 F.Supp. 308 (1985), 815 F.2d 485 (8th Cir. 1987); and *New Life Baptist Church Academy v. Town of East Longmeadow,* 885 F.2d 940 (1st Cir. 1989), *cert. denied* 110 S.Ct. 1782 (1990).
59. Provenzo, *Religious Fundamentalism and American Education,* 81–85.
60. For example, see *State ex rel. Douglas v. Faith Baptist Church,* 301 N.W.2d 571, *appeal dismissed sub nom. Faith Baptist Church v. Douglas,* 454 U.S. 803 (1981); *New Life Baptist Church Academy v. Town of East Longmeadow,* 885 F.2d 940 (1st Cir. 1989), *cert. denied,* 110 S.Ct. 1782 (1990).
61. Randall, *Private Schools and Public Power.*
62. *Sheridan Road Baptist Church v. Department of Education,* 396 N.W. 2D 373, 418. n. 54 (Mich. 1986).
63. Ibid., 396 N.W. 2D at 417, n. 53.
64. For a representative, though polemical piece, of a fundamentalist position, see Blair Adams, Joel Stein, and Howard Wheeler, *Who Owns the Children? Public Compulsion, Private Responsibility and the Dilemma of Ultimate Authority,* 5th ed. (Waco, Tex.: Truth Forum, 1991).
65. *Employment Division, Department of Human Resources v. Smith,* 110 S.Ct. at 1605 (1990).
66. Ibid., 110 S.Ct. at 1601.
67. *House, Religious Freedom Restoration Act of 1993,* 103rd Cong., H.R. 1308, Sec. 2 (b).
68. Lee Davidson, "Hatch Promotes 'Religious Equality,'" *Desert News,* 23 December 1995, A13. As an example of continued disregard for religion, Senator Hatch referred to a radio station at Fordham University that was denied a government grant for a transmission tower because the station broadcasts a weekly Catholic Mass as part of its program.
69. "Proposing an amendment to the Constitution of the United States . . . ," U.S. Congress. Senate. Religious Equality Amendment, 104th Cong., 1st sess., S.J. 45, *Congressional Record,* vol. 141, no. 207. Daily ed. (22 December 1995), S 19259-19260.

Text of the Religious Equality Amendment
Joint Resolution

Proposing an amendment to the Constitution of the United States in order to secure the unalienable right of the people to acknowledge, worship, and serve their Creator, according to the dictates of conscience.

Resolved by the Senate and House of Representatives of the United States of America in Congress assembled (two-thirds of each House concurring therein), That the following article is proposed as an amendment to the Constitution of the United States, which shall be valid to all intents and purposes as part of the Constitution when ratified by the legislatures of three-fourths of the several States within seven years after the date of its submission for ratification:

Article

Neither the United States nor any State shall deny benefits to or otherwise discriminate against any private person or group on account of religious expression, belief, or identity; nor shall the prohibition on laws respecting an establishment of religion be construed to require such discrimination.

70. Stephen L. Carter, *The Culture of Disbelief: How American Law and Politics Trivialize Religious Devotion* (New York: Basic Books, 1993), and Richard Neuhaus, *The Naked Public Square* (Grand Rapids, Mich.: Eerdmans, 1984).

Chapter Five

Cross-National Analysis of Religious Schools

Institutional Adaptation from Four Perspectives

Bruce S. Cooper and Rita E. Guare

> *Religion and choice can not be separated, for their separation creates a distinction so artificial that the meaning of choice systems is lost. To be sure, it is possible to imagine schools for existentialists, atheists, or agnostics; one can even imagine schools in which "secular humanism" is the dominant philosophy [e.g., some public schools]. But such schools are few among many, they are not the rule in a diverse society. The rule would be schools in which the dominant values flow from the great religious traditions. In the West, for many years, that meant the Judeo-Christian tradition; and even if its dominance is no longer so certain or complete, it is still the dominant tradition.*[1]

Introduction

Religious schools are very special institutions, not only because they teach academic subjects and socialize the young; but also because they are charged with the communal responsibility to inculcate spiritual values, beliefs, and conduct—thus perpetuating the faith.[2] This specialness vividly comes to life when we apply an international perspective, test common definitions, and apply new categories within the context of each separate country.

Since religious schools look very different from nation to nation in their organization, sponsorship, funding, and control, we can conclude that these schools are highly "adaptive" organizations. That is, they appear to adjust and accommodate in unique and complex ways to national constitutional provisions, to legal and political demands, to ethno-cultural and linguistic needs and diversity, to varying public and private funding arrangements, and to overall demands within each society for quality and equitable education for all. Richard F. Elmore concludes, in his book on school restructuring, similarly that adaptive realignment occurs

> *. . . in response to changes in the political and social environment of schooling. . . . But the underlying dynamics of this process are* adaptive *rather than transformational. The formulation of the problems and the array of political interests aligned around these problems will vary significantly from one setting to another*[3]

—and certainly from one nation to another.

Thus, theories of institutional adaptability—the concept that organizations like these sectarian schools must adjust, accommodate and survive in their national and regional contexts—frame our analysis of these elementary and secondary schools for students ages 5 to 18 across nations. "Adaptation theory" captures the real dilemmas faced by many of these schools. They walk a thin line between:

a. Remaining separate, distinct organizations counterpoised against many mainstream beliefs and values and thus drawing criticism as non-egalitarian, divisive, undemocratic and even prejudice-inducing; or
b. Over-identifying with the core culture, joining the state sector, ceasing to be true to their own beliefs, and thus becoming indistinguishable from state-run schools. To use Estelle James's term, these religious schools may become truly "quasi-governmental." And to borrow a Scriptural phrase, religious schools can thus be caught between serving God and serving Caesar.

The separating of our private and public lives, our religious and public discourse, are modernist modes of thought. An alternative, post-modern view is emerging, one of particularism, pluralism, community, artistry, and adaptability. Yet no matter how adaptive, pluralistic, and communal religious schools may appear in their social and political context, they still remain religious in some essential sense, tapping some deeply felt spirituality, reverence, and sense of divinity. The language of post-modernism with its characteristic suspicion and critical force combines a discourse of hope and sympathy with a more unifying vision of life, one in which "people feel a deep desire for a comprehensive and comprehending orientation."[4] To be human is to have a capacity for the sacred, for genuineness and for depth in our encounters, as we search for the soul in living.

The Soul of Religious Education

Is not listening to the pulse of wonder worth silence and abstinence from self-assertion? Why do we not set apart an hour of living for devotion to God by surrendering to stillness? We dwell on the edge of mystery and ignore it, wasting our souls and risking our stake in God.[5]

—*Rabbi Abraham Heschel*

The essence of the human person is to reach out toward incomprehensible Mystery.[6] This human stretch constitutes life's quest and discloses the soul of religious education which is directed toward the More in life, Ultimacy, the Ground of Being, or that "strange, 'Wholly Other' Power that obtrudes into life." [7] Paradoxically, Rabbi Heschel reminds us that we live on the edge of this infinite landscape which many of us fail to explore. The promise of life lies in moving beyond the familiar sounds, the words we expect to hear. As Monika Hellwig describes, "It is a matter of engaging reality in action, allowing it to talk back to us and listening to what is said. It is a constant willingness to be taken by surprise."[8]

At the depth of every interaction of the self with others and with the world, human experience reveals that "we are inescapably related to Mystery which is immanent and transcendent, which issues invitations we must respond to, which is ambiguous about its intentions, and which is real and important beyond all else."[9] The very nature of religious education intuits something solemn, serious and tender about the human relationship to Mystery. Deep within, persons harbor this Mystery, the vital sense of Other in the world, which carries them beyond the surface of the sensible world to the regions of religious truth. Yet, because of what we view as distractions, the sacred-profane rupture in life persists and we risk our stake in God.

In some way, all reality reflects the rhythmic presence of Mystery. Ultimacy appears in human experience as the source, the ground, the origin of meaning.[10] It also manifests itself in relation to an awareness of human limits through religious education. It is precisely because of its persuasiveness and ultimate character that Mystery grounds the deepest of human hopes.

Earthborn, but alive with something of God's own spirit, the human person is called to transcend the narrow limits of self by giving birth to a new order of things. This "always-already not-yet reality of grace"[11] about which David Tracy speaks so compellingly opens the person to the very heart of religious education. Religious education is a way of realizing these deeply spiritual yearnings. In cultures of belief and disbelief, religious education seeks to be real by professing faith and translating knowledge of truths into aims and practices that honor the essence of the human person.

Members of faith communities seek to establish "patterns of formation in faithfulness,"[12] and these patterns are rightly called religious education. In considering Thomas Groome's powerful understanding of religious education, we sense that the engagement of the whole person in real life situations and relationships guides the project of religious education.

> *Education that is intentionally "religious" is clearly a transcendent activity. In attempting to "bring things together again" (a meaning suggested by the Latin roots of religious) in the context of ultimacy, it attempts to nurture to awareness and lived expression, the human capacity for the transcendent. In other words, [religious education] encourages people to interpret their lives, relate to others, and engage in the world in ways that faithfully reflect what they perceive as ultimate in life, that is, from a faith perspective.*[13]

The challenge of religious education is to inspire members of faith communities to live and act faithfully in response to what they experience as ultimate.

The dramatic interplay of life and religion is the vision Gabriel Moran offers in his theory of religious education. Moran's work begins with the conviction that the project of religious education is "one of the most universal, most urgent, and most practical questions"[14] facing us today. In proposing a theory of religion and education, Moran suggests that two things are likely to occur when religions meet education.

First, a transformation of the religious group from within will result in changed institutions and a new way for transmitting the religious life to the faithful. Secondly, a conversation with other religious groups may encourage the pluralistic commitments which religious educators need to make in their efforts toward truth-seeking.

From education's side of the encounter with religion, we may expect to discover an appreciation of religion that might lead to a recovery of those lost forms of learning that call us beyond the rationalistic model that dominates schooling today. If education truly encounters religion, as Moran suggests, education would take on a diversity of forms with qualities he calls "rooted" and "reverent."

Education would have roots in the earth, the body, and the family. Without diminishing its drive toward rational inquiry, education can be conceptualized to include community life, daily work, and contemplative quiet. Education would be centered on how people are living and would be concerned with people to learn the art of living.[15] For Moran, religious education is a way to help people "celebrate life's joys and bear with its sorrows."[16] It is inspired by what is real in people's lives and honors that richness within community.

Religious education understands that the ordinary in life is sacred and the everyday is the primary source of religion. Thus, the soul of religious education rests in both the ultimate and the transcendent; the particular and the pluralistic; the defined and the ambiguous; the rooted and the adaptive. Essentially its story is parable, and its vision is paradox. By attending to the "pulse of wonder" in all life events, religious education discloses its soul and invites the faithful to remember that we have a stake in God.

Cross-National Perspectives on Adaptability

In four related sections, this chapter now applies an international perspective to religious schools, analyzing how they try to adjust to the following key contexts and the dilemmas that often result:

1. *The Ethno-Cultural and Linguistic Context:* Cultural and linguistic heterogeneity is a powerful driver in the demand for religious education across nations. Various religious groups seek to adapt to their surroundings and propagate their religious beliefs. But highly diverse societies also show concerns to create a

"core" or national culture, sometimes threatening the status of separate religious schools.

2. *The Constitutional-Legal Context:* Public laws and policies set the framework within which religious schools exist across the globe, and how they are governed and funded—or not.
3. *The Financial Support Context:* Following from constitutional provision, political action, and legal support, the world's religious schools are affected profoundly by their sources and levels of funding from government and private benefactors. With increased subsidies came greater regulation, and perhaps a concomitant loss of autonomy and distinctness.
4. *The Identity-Equity-Quality Reform Context:* Broader education movements for equity, identity, reform, privatization, restructuring, and improvement all exert influence on religious schools across nations, and ultimately shape these schools' futures. Thus, adaptation within these four "contexts" (cultural, legal, financial, and reform) may help to explain the wide diversity of religious schools across nations, and provide useful lessons.

The Ethno-Cultural Context and Linguistic Context

Religious education is rooted in cultural, historical, political. and linguistic pluralism. From anthropological theory, it is clear that religion provides people with values, attitudes, and beliefs that inform their way of living within social and cultural structures. Through story and ritual, religion and, by extension, religious education, provide people with powerful symbols which shape their way of living faithfully within culture.

Emile Durkheim accounted for the cultural domination in religion through his analysis of society, personality, and the use of symbols. Durkheim wrote:

Thus there is something eternal in religion which is destined to survive all particular symbols in which religious thought has successfully enveloped itself. There can be no society which does not feel the need of upholding and reaffirming at regular intervals the collective sentiments and the collective ideas which make its unity and its personality.[17]

A religious-based education is concerned with presenting cultural symbols of what it means to be a religious person in contemporary society. While Durkheim emphasized the power of religio-cultural symbols in maintaining and promoting the existing social order, the German sociologist Max Weber was concerned with the power of religious symbols, embraced by charismatic leaders, as a way of transforming political, social, and economic structures.[18] These contrasting views are legitimated when religion and culture are seen as two opposing areas of human existence, namely, the sacred and the profane.

Paul Tillich suggests a different kind of relationship through his analysis that "religion is the substance of culture, culture is the form of religion."[19] Tillich understands religion as the Ultimate Concern, the substance of all cultural activity. Without this depth dimension, the ethno-cultural context is meaningless and without foundation. Tillich's conviction that culture is the form of religion is seen when religion expresses itself through the forms of culture. The historical/political context and the language and symbols of a people become the forms through which the ultimate is apprehended. The multiplicity of expressions of each culture's Ultimate Concern will be important as we consider religio-cultural linguistic pluralism across nations.

In his study of Islam, Clifford Geertz captured the foundation of religion and the relationship to the ordinary affairs of culture. The study uncovered the inseparable link between the Islamic world view and an ethic of life. Sacred symbols were found to be the expressive way of uniting the Islamic vision. This study points to the growing importance of contextualization in the meeting of religion, culture and education.[20]

Contextualization consciously situates any group's religious education and mission in the historical, social, political, and economic conditions within which it finds itself. At the same time, contextualization critically assesses the forces that shape and/or distort the particular mission of religious education. In different times and places, different people raise questions of faith. By asking different questions of faith and by participating in the search for understanding, nations have given rise to different forms of religious education.

As the work of Estelle James and others illustrate, religious schools exist and adapt within broad social and religious contexts.

Thus, a highly homogenous society with one official religion would hardly need separate religious schools since the government system would probably embrace the dominant religious values and beliefs. For example, in the United States, the State of Utah has the fewest private and religious schools in the nation because the population is mostly Mormon and the public school personnel are Mormon as well. New York City, on the other hand, is home to 180 ethnic groups and all religions, putting pressure on the public system to remain scrupulously "neutral" and fulfilling no religious needs for any group. The result is the nation's largest, most diverse religious school community.

Across the continents, South Africa presents an interesting case. With its population of 43 million, South Africa is a country of living faiths.[21] Although South Africa claims a Christian heritage, the country has never been mono-religious. A rich and growing culture of religious affiliation and diversity includes Muslims, Jews, Hindus, and Buddhists. The multi-religious culture of South Africa presents a real challenge for religious education. Yet, until the Interim Constitution of 1994, South Africa had chosen a single tradition of religious education in state schools, forcing some minority religious groups to find alternatives for the instruction and practice of their faith. The Constitution cites the discriminatory religious practices in state schools and addresses the violation of human rights. In effect, the Interim Constitution presents serious implications for a new curriculum of religious education in South African public schools. Despite the efforts to respond to religious pluralism in state schools, a number of private religious schools are growing. The challenge for these religious communities in South Africa remains clear: to contextualize the particular faith tradition by honoring the indigenous African cultures.

Embracing cultural pluralism is far more difficult than we ever imagine, and in the case of religious pluralism more tensions arise. In each case and with varying degrees of success, countries with cultures of multi-faiths are contextualizing the mission and the message of diverse faith traditions. Yet, the demand for private religious education is both real and strong especially in those countries where particular religious groups have been marginalized.

Thus, ethno-cultural and linguistic context is a powerful shaper of religious education, in the following complex ways:

- *Cultural Heterogeneity* is "the major determinant of differentiated *demand* for and nonprofit *supply* of private [and religious] education," according to Estelle James.[22] On the demand side of the equation, minority religions may create their own schools to escape discrimination and to perpetuate their beliefs, even when sufficient space is available in state-run schools. On the supply side, she found that "private schools are a convenient institution for diverse non-profit-maximizing religious organizations to use in the competition for a larger market share of 'souls.'"[23] In this race for converts, James found that some religions were more active proselytizers than others, particularly Protestants and Catholics, which she weights more heavily.
- *Excess Demand* is evidently related to national wealth, with poorer countries having less resources to invest in schooling overall, and even less in secondary education—opening the way for the opening of religious schools. In James's words, private and religious school growth are related to following: " . . . excess demand stemming from low public spending is the major explanation for the systematically larger size of the private sector at the secondary level in *developing* countries."[24]
- *Location and Concentration of Religious, Cultural, and Linguistic Groups* is also a determinant of religious schooling, as these communities respond to their immediate environment.
- *Developing v. Developed Nations* also differ in their levels of religious education: it appears that poorer countries have less resources. Thus, James found that "many developing countries restrict access to their public system at the secondary and higher education levels, using non-price mechanisms to ration the limited number of places among the excess demanders."[25] This shortage creates the opportunity both for wealthier people to support private and religious schools for their children and for religious groups from the developed world to open missionary-style high schools to fulfill some unmet demand. As James found,

> *Regression analyses conducted across a pooled primary-secondary sample of 50 countries (100 observations) produced results consistent with these hypotheses. Religious competition and entrepreneurship have highly significant positive effects in all cases. Linguistic heterogeneity*

> *plays a positive (but somewhat lesser) role. These findings have important implications for the behavior of private schools. For example, they suggest that private schools may segment the population along religious, linguistic, nationality, or ideological lines, because of the motivations of their nonprofit producers and consumers.*[26]

In culturally/linguistically diverse societies, religious schools run the risk of being construed as troublesome because they exist outside the public sector. At the center of many faith traditions is a counter-cultural position that seeks to uncover what is oppressive and unjust. Schools of religious education are faithful only when they are troublemaking, that is, only when they are uncovering the structures in the dominant culture that restrict the full flourishing of a people. Religion and religious education provide a place from which to challenge the status quo. Stephen Carter insists that "religion, properly understood, is a very subversive force."[27] Religion, and by extension religious education, possess the moral and ethical imagination to critique existing structures that are stumbling blocks to free and faithful living. Margaret Gorman argues that religious schools can be the leaven in diverse cultures. Acting as biblical yeast, schools of religious education can work to transform cultures rather than oppose or mirror them.[28]

Religious educators who see themselves as "cultural agents," a concept popularized by Henry Giroux, pay close attention to the worlds of meaning and belonging imbedded in cultures. At the same time, religious educators must connect religious education to its context so as to bring about social transformation in the church, the community, and the culture.

Dilemmas of Adaptation to Ethno-Cultural Diversity

Initially, many underdeveloped nations welcomed missionary groups as useful providers of education, particularly at the costly secondary-school level. But as nations developed their own "one best systems" and sought to expand the nationalizing influence of public education, the private religious schools may have posed a threat both ideologically and organizationally.

Even in Canada, which has long been a country with religious diversity and extensive religious schools (mainly Roman Catholic), critics have vigorously objected to public funding of religious schools in Ontario. In effect, the stimulating effects of cultural heterogeneity for religious schools are also the basis of concern that these schools foster discrimination and disunity within the nation state, including the following arguments:

Religious schools are inequitable and discriminatory. Since private religious schools are exclusive in some nations and also charge tuition in others, making them practically unavailable to the poor, detractors have argued that religious schools are "elite" and reinforce the racial and class distinctions in society. Ironically, however, by denying religious schools public subsidies for being "elite," governments are in fact putting denominational education out of the reach of the poor. Furthermore, critics contend that any government support—financial or otherwise—merely exacerbates the social and racial inequalities that already exist. In the United States, for example, Crain and Rossell found that "the Catholic schools in these three cities—Chicago, Cleveland, and Boston—are, on average, much more segregated than the public schools. . . . Thus, these data give us little reason to believe that the impact of private [Catholic] schools is simply benign."[29]

Stephen Arons presents the basis of the argument that private and religious schools are discriminatory, when he wrote that

> *. . . since* Pierce *[the case supporting private, religious education], schooling has increased so much in cost, persuasiveness and importance that what was once a right of meaningful choice abstractly available to all has now become the centerpiece of a profound system of invidious discrimination. . . . More importantly, if those who are the primary, though not the only, victims of unequal access to school choice are members of minority racial, ethnic, and linguistic groups, then these victims of discrimination will be the primary beneficiaries of a properly designed restoration of choice.*[30]

Religious schools are culturally divisive. Religious schools are often opened by and affiliated with a range of ethnic, cultural, linguistic, and doctrinal groups; hence, these institutions are occasionally called divisive, troublesome, and even "undemocratic." Several major books written by supporters of the common, state, or government-run schools have vehemently attacked private and religious education. Henry Levin of Stanford University, a critic of private education, argued that non-government

schools will seek to succeed in particular market niches by specializing in those areas that will attract a particular clientele with similar values and viewpoints. Thus, the very nature of private [religious] school market will tend to undermine the commonalties that spokesmen like Milton Friedman view as necessary for the stable and democratic society."[31]

Religious schools fail to fulfill the "public good." The converse of "private" religious interests are purportedly the "public good," which somehow is the special purview of the "public schools." For some unknown and unsubstantiated reason, religious groups (because they are "different") cannot carry on the public responsibility to produce hardworking, intelligent, moral, informed, democratic people. This argument ends with the false assertion that public education represents the "public good"; private education only the private, individual good.

Private-as-bad in education even extends to the parents, according to Geoffrey Walford, an expert on private and religious schools in Great Britain. He believes that alternatives to the government school sector have yet another negative effect: "The presence of private schools, for example, may harm State schools by taking out from the State sector those parents who are most likely to ensure that high standards of provision and teaching are maintained."[32]

Religious schools teach prejudice and practice indoctrination. Finally, critics such as Bernard J. Shapiro in Canada have stated that students are indoctrinated in the religious schools, and that these children learn to be prejudiced because they are not attending government-run schools where ostensibly the pupils meet and mix with a wider variety of contemporaries. Shapiro and others objected to public funding of religious schools because this would "sanction the isolation of students in homogeneous groups and thereby not only abandon the advantages of a common acculturation but also foster a tendency among the students to think of other people as outsiders—an invitation to prejudice and intolerance."[33] Yet such antagonists of confessional education would themselves isolate and show intolerance of and prejudice toward religious schools—in the name of preventing such negative results in students—an irony somehow lost in the heat of debate.

Constitutional and Legal Rights and Limitations

The constitution first, and then other laws and policies, set the basic framework for analyzing the religious rights of citizens and their doctrinal education. In turn, religious schools—and the communities in which they live—adapt to these legal prescriptions, in part explaining the wide variety of religious school configurations around the world. As Peter Mason, chair of the European Council of National Councils of Independent Schools, explains, "The most obvious and formal controls stem from clauses in written constitutions (where they exist), which define the role of the state, the rights of the individual, the relation of church and state, and the delegation of powers to regional and provincial authorities."[34]

One perspective on the constitutional impact is to analyze the rights of citizens versus the state in religious worship and the education of children. The constitutions of nations range from a total ban on all religion to places that protect the rights of families to participate in religious education but prohibit public financial support, to nations that not only guarantee religious prerogatives of worship and education but publicly fund religious education fully—and even prevent state-subsidized religious schools from charging tuition, thus opening schools to a wide range of socioeconomic groups. Careful analysis shows a wide mix of rights and restrictions:

Banning of Religious Activities

In several nations—and not just the officially atheistic regimes such as the former Soviet bloc, Cuba, or People's Republic of China—religious schools have been banned or severely curtailed. Even in the United States in 1922, the Oregon legislature passed a law requiring "every parent, guardian, or other person having control or charge or custody of a child between 8 and 16 years *to send him to a public school* for the period of time a public school shall be held during the current year."[35] To do otherwise was a misdemeanor. The U.S. Supreme Court, in the landmark 1925 decision, *Pierce* v. *Society of Sisters*, ruled against the Oregon law and in favor of the rights of the family, stating:

The fundamental theory of liberty upon which all governments in this Union repose excludes any general power of the State to standardize its children by forcing them to accept instruction from public teachers only. The child is not the mere creature of the State. Those who nurture him and direct his destiny have the right, coupled with high duty, to recognize they prepare him for additional obligations.[36]

It was this simple statement of principle that was the Magna Carta for religious education in the United States, despite a Bill of Rights that protected religious practices.

Virtually all totalitarian governments, whether of the Left (e.g., Communism, Maoism, Trotskyitsm) or the Right (e.g., Nazism, Fascism), have forcefully outlawed both religion and religious education. These regimes perceive the threat of religious values to the "mind control" required to subjugate the population.

Yet, remarkably, when the ban on religion in the nations of the former Soviet Union was lifted in 1991, the sparks of religious fervor were rekindled and in typical missionary style, religious leaders entered Romania, East Germany, Czechoslovakia, and the Ukraine, and other countries to preach, teach, and importantly, to open religious schools and seminaries for training pastors. The Seventh-Day Adventists, one of the most active Protestant sect internationally in education, devoted major church resources to opening schools and seminaries in these East European countries. Take a few European examples:

Romania. A Seventh-Day Adventist recalls what happened in Romania when the Government closed them down:

Years ago, when the Romanian seminary was confiscated, the leaders retrenched their activities in a small building in Bucharest. There was ample space for the few students the government allowed to come, sometimes only three. Bible teacher, Dezideriu Faluvegi, remembers how pastors organized clandestine tent meetings or traveled two nights in order to have a day of fellowship and study. . . .

During the days when the church was banned and the school was without a seminary building or a library, students assembled in a church on weekends. Many had worked hard all week in coal mines, an assignment deliberately selected for those who wanted to become Christian pastors.[37]

As the Church newsletter reports, once the ban was partially lifted, the North American SDA church cooperated with the Romanian group in sponsoring a three-week seminar of "The Integration of Faith and Learning," attended by over fifty Adventist teachers; a new Sabbath school is under construction using a generous donation from the church in the United States. Already, three secondary schools with 500 students have opened—and American volunteers are serving as English teachers at Prague. The Adventists are even opening a private college (unheard of in the former Communist bloc) to train nurses, which is state-licensed, although the classrooms and laboratories need much renovation.

Czechoslovakia. A new seminary is opening with an international faculty; the hope is to overcome decades of anti-religious policies and to prepare Czechs to become their own ministers and religious school teachers.

Germany. East Germany was more tolerant of religious activities and education than the other Eastern Bloc countries; thus, an Adventist seminary, the Theologische Hochschule Friedensau, has been open with some interruptions since the turn of the century (1899) and is recognized as a university. It is the center of religious training and activity in the former East Germany, holding training institutes for Germany and other nations in Africa and the Middle East (Jordan).

Since the time of the reunification of Germany, we see changes in school preferences. For, according to Mitter and Weiss, "a striking interest in private schools in East Germany appears to be a further significant phenomenon. Currently, this interest can be interpreted as a symptom of aversion to state control and as a corollary a people remembering the collapse of 'democratic centralism'" [as practiced under the Soviet dominated East Germany].[38]

Ukraine. This has been the most difficult nation for religious education since 1990. In Kiev, a new Adventist school has opened with sixty-five students. In Chernovtsky, the church was unable to secure a license to open a school, so a group of "private citizens" filed the request. Rules in the Ukraine prevent even a religious school from calling itself a "church school." In language that sounds somewhat supportive, the Ukrainian law "makes the State responsible for the financial support of any school-age child, the state would, therefore, be helping to sponsor religion, which it has no intention of doing."[39]

After several tries, some "prayer and work," the parent group finally received an official license to open two Adventist schools enrolling 123 pupils, and parent interest is apparently keen. The Director of Education for the Euro-Asia Division, Harry Mayden, reports: "The work is going forward rapidly in spite of the disastrous economic situation in this great land."[40]

Protecting but Limiting Religious Education.

If banning all religious activities is one extreme and supporting all others equally is the other, then most nations fall somewhere in between.

Canada. Here the *Charter of Rights and Freedoms* prevents "discrimination based on race, national or ethnic origin, colour, religion, sex, age, or mental or physical disability" (Section 15:1). It has mainly led, however, to support of the Roman Catholic minority schools (majority in Quebec) but not equally to the support of the education of other religious and ethnic-cultural groups. Stephen B. Lawton, a professor at the Ontario Institute for Studies in Education, wonders whether a true and just interpretation of the *Charter* might extend the right to establish separate, government-supported schools for other ethnic groups. Lawton explains further:

They [supporters] argue that if the Province [of Ontario] is to fund high schools for Roman Catholics, they [the government] must do so for Jews, Anglicans, Hindus, Moslems, evangelical Christians, and, perhaps, Chinese, Italians and so forth. Indeed, some argue that Roman Catholic rights to separate schools at the elementary level ought to be extended to other groups as a result of the new Charter, *even though the rights of Catholics have existed since before Confederation [in 1867] and have therefore been seen as special.*[41]

Thus, Canadian religious schools are treated differentially under the federal constitution, with Catholics receiving better treatment under law than other religious groups. Here is a nation with religious protection and equality for all; it is just that some religions are *more equal* than others, resulting in more resources for Catholic schools.

France. This country experienced radical swings in its attitude toward religious schools, even though the country is fundamentally Roman Catholic. The Jacobeans, leaders of the French Revolution and the Reign of Terror, according to Professor Charles Glenn, "enacted the first educational legislations of modern times based on radical principles: that the child belong to the State [i.e., the "revolution"], that parents were if anything a hindrance to the State's mission of shaping future citizens, and that the Church was a bitter enemy of the State because of its rival claim to educate."[42] As late as 1977, when the recently deceased President François Mitterand (Socialist) met with Church leaders, he found that "the education question is carved into this country as the last symbol of the two Frances; it remains the irritating obstacle that prevents the resolution of the last differences between the Left and the Church."[43] Opponents of Catholic schools do not mince words, as this quote by Jean Cornec, a leader of a parent association, illustrates: "the Catholic hierarchy has never ceased to reduce mankind to a state of slavery, to oppress ideas, and to limit freedom."[44]

Furthermore, in the 1980s the Socialist Party attempted to create one unified, state-run education system by seizing control of the public funding of religious schools—an unpopular notion that helped to defeat the Left in the 1986 national elections. For earlier, under the *Loi Debré* (1959) and the *Loi Guérmeur* (1977), private and religious schools were given (a) the option of receiving public funding and (b) "the power to initiate the hiring of staff who were paid with public funds, subject to government confirmation. This power makes it possible to refuse to consider teachers whose convictions do not correspond to the school's identity."[45]

While religious schools in France have survived the frontal attack from the Socialists and the now moribund Communist Party, Catholic education, according to Glenn, faces the dilemma of being publicly supported and losing its identity and purposes. The French government schools are so centralized and bureaucratic that one proponent of Catholic education warned that real national "unity is fashioned from diversity and not from the totalitarianism of a public system in which we would not be able to express ourselves."[46]

To underscore the depth of French support for Catholic and all religious schools, over a million demonstrators clogged the streets of Paris in 1984—570,000 coming by rail alone—to oppose the Socialist proposal to have the government take control of these schools. (Even the French Jewish community was represented, supporting their religious schools.) This show of power led to the resignation of the Minister of National Education, Alain Savary, in July 1984, and the loss of the national elections by the Socialists in 1986.

United States and *Australia.* These countries provide a most graphic contrast of the effects of constitutional interpretation on the religious schools in their respective nations. While Australia has a constitution modeled consciously after that of the United States, the high courts in the two nations have interpreted the First Amendment on religious freedom differently. As Professor William Lowe Boyd wrote, "In the celebrated DOGS (Defenders of Government Schools) case, the nation's High Court ruled in 1981 that so long as public monies are distributed even-handedly, rather than for the purpose of creating a state-sponsored religion, there is no breach of the Australian Constitution."[47]

In contrast, the U.S. Supreme Court has erected a wall of separation between church and state, presumably to protect the latter from undue influence of the former; however, the net effect has been to deny direct funding to religious schools—the only nation in the modern world to discriminate against all to prevent supporting some. Instead, the United States has minimal subsidy, mainly in the form of indirect aid: tax relief on private and religious school income and property, guaranteed federal aid for low-income students, given through local public schools. Thus, as we shall discuss later, the United States ranks low in the world in percent of students attending religious schools.

Full Support

A number of nations provide equal support to state-run and religiously-affiliated schools in their constitutions.

Holland. Holland has perhaps the most egalitarian constitution for religious schools in the world. The Constitution of 1814, Article 208, revised in 1922, as Mason explains, "establishes the principle of freedom of parental choice and at the same time attempts to secure freedom of access (and therefore equality of opportunity for all) by ordering public funding of both sectors [private-religious and public-state] on equal terms . . .by forbidding private schools to charge fees."[48]

All groups, Marxist, socialist, religious, Montessori, and Steiner schools, are on an even footing, receiving around 80 percent of funds from the government. Again, the laws and Constitution, in conjunction with a strong commitment to a pluralistic and democratic society, have led to wide diversity of private and religious schools available to children regardless of their family income.

Germany. West Germany enacted the Federal Constitution of 1949 which protects the rights of private schools to exist, established religious education as a required subject in all schools, and funded schools for about 70 percent of costs, with churches (e.g., the Catholics in Bavaria) subsidizing further their religious schools. Out of the some 600,000 students in private schools in Germany (5.6 percent of the total pupil population) in 1983, about 310,000 attended Catholic schools and 42,000 Protestant schools (mostly Lutheran), again showing the effects of the federal constitution and the response of religious groups.

Summary

The subtlety of constitutional provision and government policies has a strong effect on the nature of the religious schools in each nation. Where religion is disallowed, religious education nearly disappears. Where freedom of worship is protected constitutionally, some religious schools appear, although they struggle to compete against state-run schools. And the sectarian school sector is largest in those nations that permit or even mandate financial support for religious education. Fully 65 percent of all students in Dutch schools attend private and/or religious schools, among the highest, while the United States at 5 percent is among the lowest.

This constitutional-legal framework sets the stage for sources and levels of funding and the full integration of religious schools into the state system.

Public Funding and Public Control

Funding of religious schools is perhaps the "make or break" issue in sectarian education across the world. Money is both the cause of some changes in religious schools, and the effect of other conditions: for example, legal rights, political power, history and tradition, and the role of the church in society. The nations of the world appear to fall into four categories where funding is concerned. First, those nations that ban religion refuse all concessions to private, religious schools. Where non-government schools do exist, they must pay taxes and are treated like any other business.

Second, nations like the United States that protect religious liberty but refuse direct aid have limited public support to tax-free status for nonprofit schools and some forms of indirect help to children—with nothing to schools themselves. Religious schools adapt to this condition by charging tuition (as high as the market will bear), engaging in extensive fund-raising and endowment efforts, and keeping costs at a minimum, which means paying teachers nearly half what public- or state-employed teachers receive. Thus, important effects of little or no state aid to U.S. religious schools are smaller numbers, smaller schools, a fairly elite pupil group in some locations (since the poor may not be able to afford the tuition), and high levels of voluntarism from parents, parish, and community. Donald A. Erickson calls this effect *gemeinschaft,* a strong, immediate human interaction similar to a family.

Australia. This country provides an example of how funding private religious schools has grown from a small, insignificant issue to one of fundamental differences. In Australia, private schools grew up alongside the public system, as D.S. Anderson explains: "In the 1830s the colonial government established state schools at the same time as maintaining support for existing denominational schools. This created Australia's first dual system."[49] And when the Catholics arrived, they felt challenged by the Protestant-dominated state system and opened schools of their own. Anderson explains:

It was against these public initiatives that the Catholic systems were built in the latter part of the 19th century, at enormous cost, by a church which felt itself to be a threatened and beleaguered minority in an intolerant, Protestant-dominated society. . . . Today, about half of the Catholic children in Australia attend that church's schools, a fraction claimed to be higher than any other country.[50]

At first, the national government aided religious schools only modestly, to help them out of a fiscal crisis, starting in 1964 under Prime Minister Menzies. By the 1980s, however, the funding had grown to a point where the government applied a "needs principle" to direct funds to the neediest schools and even to take all funds away from the forty-one wealthiest private schools in the country that failed.

Denmark. Its national system of schools was created under the national religion, Danish Evangelical Lutheranism; but the nation also was concerned about the rights of other denominations. So, as part of the national law instituting a national system of education, the Danes also agreed to subsidize any group wishing to start its own school, as the law reads: "Today, various kinds of 'free' or independent schools exist, all of them subsidized by up to 85 percent of their operational expenditures."[51] As Denis P. Doyle explained concerning religious rights:

Ever concerned about the rights of minorities, however, the Danes developed a system to preserve religious freedom of non-Lutherans—Jews, Catholics, free thinkers. They were given the right to start their own schools at public expense. Any group of parents—to this day—who among them have 28 children is permitted to claim government funding for their own private school. . . .

To most American observers, it is a fine bit of irony that the Danes assert that the way to preserve religious freedom is to provide public funds for religious (and non-religious) schools. At the same time, and with the same enthusiasm, many Americans argue that religious free-

dom is best preserved by not providing public aid to students who attend religious schools.[52]

The Dilemma of Full Government Involvement

Adapting to legal and financial conditions has a major effect on religious schools, as this section illustrates. In nations with constitutional and policy protections, religious schools in large numbers have joined the "maintained" sector. The effect, as predicted, has been two-fold: first, religious schools run the risk of coming under the direct control of the government, of being heavily regulated, and of thus losing their distinct religious tone and identity.

A leading expert on international analysis of private and religious education, economist Estelle James, captures the irony of government treatment of these schools. If religious schools wish to expand, they often welcome public subsidies. . . . "but they [the subsidies] also enable the government to extract concessions in return, in the form of regulation over inputs, outputs, and other characteristics which satisfy diverse constituencies."[53] And as James continues:

The subsidy and regulation, taken together, have the net effect of raising production costs, increasing paperwork, bureaucratization and depersonalization. While this development is not inevitable, it certainly is common. Thus, the very factors that originally create the demand for a private [religious] sector also set in motion forces making the private sector more like the public. Ironically, as the private sector grows, with public funding and regulation, it becomes quasi-governmental.[54]

Second, religious schools that are heavily subsidized are sometimes blamed for draining public resources and middle-class parents away from the state-run schools. As William L. Boyd concluded about the effects of public support for Australia's private, religious schools:

The great defect of the Australian approach is that, despite the needs-based principle, in practice significant portions of state aid nevertheless continue to subsidize and encourage an elitist sorting dynamic. This dynamic creams off upper-middle-class students and weakens government schools which still must serve three-quarters of the student popula-

tion. Thus, at the heart of the continuing tensions over state aid to private schools in Australia are divisive issues of social class, privilege, and elitism versus social justice and the maintenance of quality of schools for the masses.[55]

It is interesting how religious schools in Australia, as they have grown in size, cost, and political power, have become a contested institution, are held responsible for the health of the public system, and are somehow blamed for the perceived failures of state schools. Thus, as these Canadian and Australian examples show, religious education has moved from the margins to the center of political debate, making it all the more important that we come to understand these schools in a cross-national context.

Education Movements for Reform and Restructuring

International analysis of religious schools presents another important context for explaining their diversity: the nature of national concerns, values, and school reform efforts, including movements for education equity, quality, privatization, and other forms of restructuring. Each of these reform movements has an impact on religious schools, since they often get swept up in the conflicts surrounding these restructurings.

Equity Pressures

Virtually every nation has made an effort to extend education opportunity "equally" and equitably. To the degree that religious schools are seen as hampering these efforts, they are attacked and even disadvantaged. Peter Mason examined this issue across several nations, seeking to see if the "inherited inequalities" were compatible with private and religious education. Interestingly, Mason concluded that,

As in some European countries and in North America, the combination of subsidy with a broad spectrum of types and affiliations of schools has so far ensured in both countries [New Zealand and Australia] a considerable variety of choice with a fair though still inevitably incomplete degree of equality of opportunity, which has been further strengthened since very few schools in either country are overtly selective in terms of ability and even the most 'élite' schools cater for a very wide spectrum.[56]

Quality Pressures

As nations compete in the world for production and for markets for their goods and services, issues of quality education arise. In the United States in 1983, at the peak of Japanese and German competition, the federal government issued a document with as strong a "quality" language as has ever been produced: *A Nation at Risk*, as this report was called, challenged the country to reverse a "rising tide of mediocrity" and even compared the poor condition of education to mortal combat. The report stated, "that if a foreign power had imposed an education system like ours upon us, we would have considered it an act of war."[57]

Movements to raise standards and improve quality often point to the accomplishments of the private religious sector; however, as government schools improve, the reverse pressure on religious schools increases, because many parents wonder why they need to use and pay for (even moderately) private provision when the public schools are improved.

Reform and Privatization

The net effect of these pressures to improve quality were national movements toward choice, competition, vouchers, and even "selling the state" (transferring schools from direct government control to private or quasi-private auspices), as with:

City Technology Colleges (CTCs) and Grant Maintained (GM) Schools in England and Wales. These schools are privatized, in that they receive full Government and private support, but are independently "owned and managed." In several Local Education Authorities in Britain, these CTCs and GM schools are in full competition with more traditional private/religious schools.

Chartered Schools and "contracting out" public schools in Baltimore and Hartford, Connecticut. It is too early to tell just how these new U.S. schools ("chartered" and "outsourced") will affect local religious schools; however, these direct-grant schools will have a distinct advantage over religious schools because of their public funding and support.

Per-capita Funding to Schools. Granting schools per-capita funding is a form of voucher, since the money "follows the student" to the school. Since Holland has the most liberal policy on per-capita funding to parent-organized private and religious schools, nearly 65 percent of all Dutch children attend non-state schools, many of which are religiously affiliated.

Ironically for some private and religious schools, the more the state-run schools became "private-like" with open enrollment, magnet programs, greater parental choice, and real efforts to improve quality, the more students abandoned the religious schools for the much-improved public ones. Hence, the reward for being the paragon of education quality, private initiative, and strong values orientations, was a net reduction in attendance. In England, as one example, chief education officer Donald Naismith in the London Borough of Wandsworth, instituted many reforms resembling the private and religious sector (greater choice, more competition, magnet schools, even CTCs).

Identity. The real question of this cross-national study is: Can religious schools survive, remain true to their God, their values, their communities and congregations, and their beliefs and practices, where pressures to compete may force these schools to join the government sector? Where pressures to be "equitable" undercut many differences among schools? Where pressures for national standards cause more and more schools to conform?

Conclusions

This analysis of religious education across nations and cultures shows just how adaptable these schools are to their environment, being sensitive to their cultural context, where various religions seek to educate their children in the values and beliefs of their denomination or sect; to respond to legal rights and strictures that range from total national prohibition to near total liberty and support; to the sources and levels of funding from government; and to changes in their competitive advantage compared to government-run schools. The complex interrelationships among these four "contexts" in part explain the enormous diversity in religious school provision, structures and characteristics around the globe.

In all these nations and contexts, we see a renewed interest in matters religious. In underdeveloped nations, as James and others found, religious schools fill a gap in public systems which are usually under-funded and where "excess demand" exists, particularly for high school places. In the wealthier, more developed countries, where tax resources have made free, state-run "public" schools universally available, we see an increased demand for religious schooling to fill a spiritual and moral need. Ironically, the post-industrial, post-modernist societies have wealth and material goods aplenty but find the temptations of drugs, pop-culture, and "loose morals" a strong reason to return to religious life—and doctrinal schools are increasing.

Religion proved a most powerful, plentiful, and persistent explanatory variable in the existence of private education across the world. Even in nations that are egalitarian and where religious groups are in the majority, researchers have found that confessional groups are critical. James concludes that "in all cases, the religious variable turned out to be positive and highly significant, . . . and perhaps most important, the role of religious entrepreneurship in determining the relative size of the private sector in education."[58]

Religions, thus, possess the need (to perpetuate the faith), the coherence, the institutions, and the "social capital" to be a driving force behind schooling, as research by James determined:

Universally, across countries, religious groups are the major founders of non-profit service institutions. We see this in the origin of many private schools and voluntary hospitals in the US and England, Catholic schools in France and Latin America, Calvinist schools in Holland, missionary activities in developing countries, services provided by Moslem waqfs *(trusts), etc. Usually, these are proselytizing religions, but other religious/ideological groups often start their own schools as a defensive reaction (for example, the "independence schools" in Kenya and the caste dominated schools in India were started partly to provide an alternative to Western mission schools).*[59]

Further, in most modern countries, pockets of poverty (often in the so-called inner-cities) have challenged the myth of universal and equal opportunity through public or state-run education. In these problem areas, some societies have turned to religious schools to provide the structure and responsiveness, the "social capital" and the commitment to improve education. The research of James S.

Coleman and Thomas Hoffer[60] has shown the effectiveness of religious schools in meeting the special needs of poor children and children of color.

Challenges to Religious Education World-Wide

The major issues that confront religious education across nations, as raised in this chapter, are the following:

Surviving Anti-Religious Societies

From an international perspective, religious schools have long confronted regimes hostile to all religions or just particular ones—and will undoubtedly continue to face such threats. Our analysis on adaptability presents real hope, however, that once the religious prohibitions are weakened significantly or lifted altogether, religious life begins again and religious schools are opened (or reopened). Thus, a deeply-felt need for religious affiliation and the spark of spirituality appear universal and virtually impervious to long-term government attack and persecution.

Recent events in the former Soviet Union are living examples, where religion survived a long period of Communist persecution (1919–1990) and has been reawakened in recent years, along with a rebirth of private religious schools. And the unexpected defeat of the Socialists in the French national elections in the late 1980s is further evidence of a strong commitment to religious education. When Mitterand and his Socialist Party proposed fully regulating Catholic schools and eventually taking them over as regular government institutions, the idea was roundly rejected by French voters in 1986.

Surviving Competition with Government-Run Schools

In nations where state (public) schools receive full funding and religious schools little or none, the latter must compete unfairly with the former. Yet, even in the United States where private religious schools receive very few public funds, and then only indirectly (tax breaks), we are seeing significant adaptation to being in the "private sector" (e.g., active fund-raising, more efficiency, and increased recruitment), and a renaissance in a wide variety of nonpublic confessional schools. Close to a million children are "learning at home," and the majority of these home schoolers are from Christian families who prefer to keep their children away from the avowedly nonreligious public system. Christian schools, run by communities of evangelistic and fundamentalist congregations, are the fastest growing religious schools. And other religious groups (Jewish, Quaker, Lutheran, Greek Orthodox, Episcopalian, and even Roman Catholic) are increasing, although not as dramatically.[61]

Surviving the Restructuring of Public Education

Another challenge to religious school adaptability is the rapid "reform" of public or state schooling, particularly moves to "privatize" and even "voucherize." As state schools become more like private schools, competition increases. Already in the United States and England and Wales, as "public" schools become more "private" in structure and style, we are seeing the improved, restructured public schools attracting students away from the religious schools, an irony that somehow escapes opponents of religious education.[62]

Surviving Inclusion in the State Sector

Finally, in most societies other than the United States, religious schools are given nearly the same status and support as are nonsectarian, government schools. This embrace (a "golden handshake") by government carries its own challenges, however. These include: (a) how to remain somewhat autonomous from state regulation; (b) how to hold fast to the religious mission while fulfilling the public mandates and pressures; (c) how to keep control over hiring practices, so as to recruit teachers and administrators who share the confessional beliefs of the religious school; and (d) how to prepare students to live and compete in the mainstream culture while "keeping the faith."

Donald A. Erickson and others have testified to the deadening effects of being just another public or government-supported school. Erickson's research showed, for example, that when the provincial government in British Columbia, Canada, offered major funding to private, religious schools, these institutions witnessed a precipitous decline in parental involvement and loyalty, in voluntary support, communal feelings, and the special mission of these schools.[63] In other countries, becoming part of the government or "maintained" sector has obliterated much that is religious or special about these schools. In fact, when asked, observers in England, France, Australia, and Canada often overlook religious schools in the government sector—seeing them as just another public or state-run school. This loss of identity may endanger the special mission of religious education.

France presents a case in point. Roman Catholic leaders were well aware of the dangers of Catholic schools being fully absorbed into the system and the concomitant loss of their "Christian character," particularly if the government selected teaching staff and administrators. In Charles Glenn's words,

The specific identity (caractére propre) *of Catholic schools was clearly at the heart of the issue. The National Committee for Catholic Education (CNEC) insisted that this identity must mark all aspects of life of the school, including the development of skills and knowledge. This insistence required free choice for families, real autonomy for each school, collaboration by the staff in a common education enterprise, choice of principal and staff, and special training for teachers.*[64]

The challenge, then, is for religious schools to be legal and acceptable, to receive needed financial support without sacrificing identity, autonomy, and specialness. One can conceive of such a society, one where religious education is valued, protected, and where necessary, even subsidized. Such a nation would respect religion as one of society's greatest expressions of liberty, spirituality, trust, caring, and love—yet would give religious groups the room to be themselves.

As shown in this chapter, however, religious schools and their societies are forever struggling to find the right mix of: (1) liberty and conformity, (2) being of this world or being concerned about the soul and "other worlds," (3) and being able to pursue one's religious practices and education freely, while still participating in mainstream economic and political life. What better measure, across nations, of human liberty and our immediate dedication to the future of our children than a major role for religion in education? Or, as Alfred North Whitehead explained in *The Aims of Education,*

The essence of education is that it is religious. Pray, what is religious education? A religious education is an education which inculcates duty

and reverence. Duty arises from our potential control over the course of events. Where attainable knowledge could have changed the issue, ignorance has the guilt of vice. And the foundation of reverence is this perception, that the present holds within itself the complete sum of existence, backward and forward, that whole amplitude of time, which is eternity.[65]

Notes

1. Denis P. Doyle, "Family Choice in Education: The Case of Denmark, Holland, and Australia," in *Private Schools and Public Policy: International Perspectives,* ed. William Lowe Boyd and James G. Cibulka (New York, Falmer Press, 1989), 57.
2. E.G. West, *Education and the State: A Study in Political Economy,* 2nd ed., (London: Institute for Economic Affairs, 1967).
3. Richard F. Elmore, *Restructuring Schools: The Next Generation of Educational Reform* (San Francisco: Jossey-Bass, 1990), 294.
4. Albert Borgmann, *Crossing the Postmodern Divide* (Chicago: University of Chicago Press, 1992), 144.
5. Abraham J. Heschel, *I Asked for Wonder* (New York: Crossroads, 1991), 21.
6. Karl Rahner, "The Theological Problems Entailed in the Idea of the New Earth," D. Bourke, trans., *Theological Investigations,* vol. 10 (London: Darton, Longman & Todd), 260–280.
7. G. van der Leeuw, *Religion in Essence and Manifestation,* J.E. Turner, trans., (New York: Harper & Row, 1963), 681.
8. Quoted in Mary C. Boys, *Educating in Faith* (New York: Harper & Row, 1981), 209.
9. John Shea, *Stories of God* (Chicago: Thomas Moore Press, 1978), 89.
10. Langdon Gilkey, *Naming the Whirlwind: The Renewal of God-Language,* (New York: Bobbs-Merrill, 1969), chaps. 1–3.
11. David Tracy, *The Analogical Imagination* (New York: Crossroads, 1981), chap. 1.
12. Padraic O'Hare, *The Way of Faithfulness* (Valley Forge, Penn.: Trinity Press, 1993), 23.
13. Thomas H. Groome, *Sharing Faith* (San Francisco: Harper & Row, 1991), 11.
14. Gabriel Moran, *Interplay: A Theory of Religion and Education.* (Winona, Minn: St. Mary's, 1981), 9.
15. Ibid., 162.
16. Ibid., 143.
17. Emile Durkheim, *Elementary Forms of the Religious Life: A Study in Religious Sociology* (New York: The Free Press, 1965), especially 415–447.
18. Max Weber, *The Sociology of Religion.* 1922. Reprint (Boston: Beacon Press, 1964), 3–22.
19. Paul Tillich, "Religion as a Dimension in Man's Spiritual Life," in *Theology of Culture,* ed. Robert C. Kimball (New York: Oxford University Press, 1964), 42.
20. Clifford Geertz, *Islam Observed: Religious Development in Morocco and Indonesia* (Chicago: University of Chicago Press, 1971), 97.
21. Mike C. Kitshoff, "Religious Education in State School in a Multi-Traditional and Democratic South Africa." Paper presented at the Association of Professors of Research and Religious Education, Chicago, November 1995.
22. Estelle James, "Why Do Different Countries Choose a Different Public-Private Mix of Educational Services?" *Journal of Human Resources* 28, 3 (Summer 1993): 579.
23. Ibid., 574.
24. Ibid., 589.
25. Ibid., 580.

26. Ibid., 589.
27. Stephen L. Carter, *The Culture of Disbelief: How American Law and Politics Trivialize Religious Devotions* (New York: Basic Books, 1993), 50.
28. Margaret Gorman, "Catholic Schools: Mirror or Leaven in the 21st Century?" *Momentum*, 24, 1, 42–45.
29. Robert L. Crain and Christine H. Rossell, "Catholic Schools and Racial Segregation," in *Public Values, Private Schools*, ed. Neal E. Devins (New York: Falmer Press, 1989), 209.
30. Stephen Arons, "Educational Choice as a Civil Rights Strategy," in *Public Values, Private Schools*, 274.
31. Henry M. Levin, "Education as a Public and Private Good," in *Public Values, Private Schools*, 217.
32. Geoffrey Walford, "The Reluctant Private Sector: Of Small Schools, People, and Politics, in *Private Schooling: Tradition, Change, and Diversity*, ed. Geoffrey Walford (London: Paul Chapman, 1991), 129.
33. Bernard J. Shapiro, "The Public Funding of Private Schools in Ontario: The Setting, Some Arguments, and Some Matters of Belief," *The Canadian Journal of Education* 11 (1986): 267; and Shapiro, *Report of the Commission on Private Schools in Ontario* (Toronto: Provincial Government of Ontario, 1985).
34. Peter Mason, "Elitism and Patterns of Independent Education," in *Private Schools and Public Policy*, 318.
35. *Pierce v. Society of Sisters*, 268 U.S. 510 (1925). For an excellent analysis of private and religious school laws in the United States, see Lyndon G. Furst and Charles J. Russo, *The Legal Aspects of Nonpublic Schools: A Casebook* (Barrien Springs, Mich.: Andrews University Press, 1993).
36. *Pierce v. Society of Sisters*, 268 U.S. 510 (1925), 14.
37. Ronald Stasdowsky, "Serving Europe and the World through Education," *Adventist Education* (Summer 1995): 28.
38. Wolfgang Mitter and Manfred Weiss, "Educational Transformations in a 'United' Germany," in *Reforming Education: The Emerging Systemic Approach*, ed. Stephen L. Jacobson and Robert Berne (Thousand Oaks, Calif.: Corwin Press, 1993), 218.
39. Harry Mayden, "From Humble Beginnings," *Adventist Education* (Summer, 1995): 35.
40. Ibid., 36.
41. Stephen B. Lawton, "Public, Private, and Separate Schools in Ontario," in *Private Schools and Public Policy*, 177.
42. Glenn, "Parent Choice, 64. See also, Alain Savery, with Catherine Arditti, *En Toute Liberté* (Paris: Hachette, 1985), 64.
43. Gérard Leclerc, *La Bataille de l'école: 15 siécles d'histoire, 3 ans de combat* (Paris: Denoel, 1985), 15.
44. Quoted in Leclerc, ibid., 27.
45. Ibid., 65.
46. Ibid., 68.
47. William Lowe Boyd, "Balancing Public and Private Schools: The Australian Experience and American Implications," in *Private Schools and Public Policy*, 150. See also Joel D. Sherman, "A New Perspective on Aid to Public Education: The Australian Experience," *Phi Delta Kappan* (May 1983): 654–655.
48. Mason, "Elitism and Patterns of Independent Education," 317.
49. D.S. Anderson, "Public Schools in Decline: Implications of the Privatization of Schools in Australia," in *Restructuring Schools: An International Perspective on the Movement to Transform the Control and Performance of Schools*, ed. Headley Beare and William Lowe Boyd (Washington, D.C.: The Falmer Press), 185.
50. Ibid., 185.
51. Denis P. Doyle, "Family Choices in Education," 49–50.
52. Ibid., 50.

53. Estelle James, "Public and Private Education in International Perspective," in *Private Schools and Public Policy*, 233–234.
54. Ibid.
55. Boyd, "Balancing Public and Private Schools," 152.
56. Mason, "Elitism and Patterns of Independent Education," 328.
57. The National Commission on Excellence in Education, *A Nation at Risk* (Washington, D.C.: U.S. Government Printing Office, 1983), 11.
58. James, "Public and Private Education in International Perspectives," 223.
59. Ibid., 220.
60. James S. Coleman and Thomas Hoffer, *Public and Private High Schools* (New York: Basic Books), 1987.
61. Bruce S. Cooper, "The Politics of Privatization: Policy-Making and Private Schools in the USA and Great Britain," in *Private Schools and Public Policy*, 213–236.
62. See Bruce S. Cooper and Grace Dondero, "Survival, Change, and Demands on America's Private Schools: Trends and Policies," *Educational Foundations* 5, 1 (Winter 1991): 51–75.
63. See Donald A. Erickson, "Choice and Private Schools: Dynamics of Supply and Demand," in *Private Education: Studies in Choice and Public Policy*, ed. Daniel C. Levy (New York: Oxford University Press, 1986). See also, Patricia A. Bauch, "Can Poor Parents Make Wise Educational Choices," in *Private Schools and Public Policy*, 285–313.
64. Glenn, "Parent Choice," 64.
65. Alfred North Whitehead, *The Aims of Education and Other Essays* (New York: The Free Press, 1929), 14.

Chapter Six
Law and Church-Related Schools

Mary Angela Shaughnessy, S.C.N.

The topic of the law and church-related schools is a legal infant. While the law relating to public schools has been in an almost constant state of development since 1960, there have been relatively few cases arising from church-related and other private schools. The United States Supreme Court has never heard a private school case involving student dismissal. *Rendell-Baker v. Kohn*,[1] heard in 1982, is the only private school case involving teacher dismissal to have reached the United States Supreme Court.

Prior to 1960 courts were reluctant to interfere in school cases, public or private, to any great degree. Practicing the doctrine of judicial restraint, courts decided very few cases against the educational institution. The 1961 landmark case *Dixon v. Alabama*[2] broke that restraint and won procedural due process protections for students at public colleges and universities. By 1974, secondary school teachers and students had firmly established their rights through such cases as *Tinker v. Des Moines Independent School District* (1969),[3] *Goss v. Lopez* (1975),[4] and *Wood v. Strickland* (1975).[5] But no such protection existed then or exists now in the church-related or other private schools. Because the church-related school is not an extension of the state, students and teachers cannot generally claim Constitutional protections.

Relatively few cases involving the dismissal of students and/or teachers from church-related schools have been brought in any court. However, the last two decades have seen a rise in the number of cases brought by students and teachers in church-related schools. The reticence that once seemed to preclude a church member suing a church authority has largely disappeared. In the past, the doctrines of separation of church and state and charitable immunity protected church-related schools from being successfully sued. These doctrines provide little or no protection today.

Thus, a growing body of case law is emerging in the area of church-related school law. Administrators and others responsible for the operation of church-related schools need to understand this area of law so that they can be more knowledgeable about the rights of students, parents, and teachers in their institutions and more cognizant of their own responsibilities to protect those rights.

The Beginning of Church-Related School Law

The right of the church-related school to exist and of parents to send their children to such schools was established by the 1925 landmark case of *Pierce v. Society of Sisters.*[6] The state of Oregon had passed a law which would have required all parents to send children to public schools in the state. In rejecting the permissibility of the law, the court stated:

The fundamental theory of liberty upon which all governments in this Union repose excludes any general power of the State to standardize its children by forcing them to accept instruction from public teachers only. The child is not the mere creature of the State; those who nurture him and direct his destiny have the right, coupled with the high duty, to recognize and prepare him for additional obligations.[7]

In order to understand which rights are protected in church-related schools and which are not, it is helpful to review the law concerning the rights of school students and teachers, both public and private.

Generally, there are four types of law governing schools: (1) Constitutional law; (2) statutes and regulations; (3) common law; and (4) contract law. As stated above, Constitutional law does not apply to the church-related school. The other three types of law can apply to both public and church-related schools.

Constitutional Law

Students and teachers in public schools are protected by the United States Constitution. In particular, the First Amendment guards the freedoms of speech, press, and assembly; the doctrine of separation of church and state enjoins government from promoting or interfering with religion.

The Fourth Amendment protects persons from unlawful search and seizure. The Fifth Amendment guarantees "due process of law" before a person can be deprived of life, liberty, or property. The Fourteenth Amendment to the Constitution made the Fifth Amendment applicable to the states. The Civil Rights Act of 1871 (Title 42 of the United States Code, Section 1983)[8] further protects persons whose individual Constitutional rights are denied by state authorities.

Prior to 1960, public school officials were generally protected in their actions by the doctrine of *in loco parentis*, that is school officials were considered to be acting in the place of parents. With the previously mentioned landmark college case of *Dixon v. Alabama*,[9] the days of *in loco parentis* began to crumble, and students were seen as having the same Constitutional protections as adults. However, it was nine years before the reasoning in *Dixon* would be extended to cases involving public elementary and secondary schools.

Perhaps the most well-known public school case is *Tinker v. Des Moines Independent School District*, decided in 1969. *Tinker* established the right of public school students to express themselves freely so long as such expression did not interfere with reasonable order in the school: "It can hardly be argued that either students or teachers shed their constitutional rights to freedom of speech or expression at the [public] schoolhouse gate" (p. 506).[10] The First and Fourteenth Amendments' protections thus were extended to public school students facing suspension and/or expulsion.

State Action

Before a church-related institution can be required to grant Constitutional protections to teachers and/or students, the substantial presence of state action must be demonstrated: the state has to be significantly involved in the church-related school or in the contested activity. The court determines whether the involvement is significant.

Three 1970s cases involving private school students are significant because of allegations that state action was present in the schools. The first case was heard in 1970; dismissed students in the Indiana case of *Bright v. Isenbarger*[11] alleged that state action was present because of state regulation of the school and the school's tax exempt status. The court rejected the claim: "Accordingly, . . . this court holds that because the state of Indiana was in no way involved in the challenged actions, defendants' expulsion of plaintiffs was not state action."[12]

In a 1976 expulsion case, *Wisch v. Sanford School, Inc.*,[13] a dismissed student maintained that the federal funding present in the private school through various governmental programs constituted state action. The court, however, disagreed:

> *Plaintiff must show that there was more than "some" state action in this case; not every involvement by the state in the affairs of a private individual or organization, whether through funding or regulation may be used as a basis for a [Section] 1983 claim. The involvement must be "substantial."*[14]

In 1978, a student and his father brought suit against a Catholic high school which had expelled him in the case, *Geraci v. St. Xavier High School,*[15] and alleged the presence of state action. The court found that, even if state action were present, it would have to be so entwined with the contested activity (dismissal of the student) that a symbiotic relationship could be held to exist between the state and the dismissal of the student. If no such relationship exists, state action is not present and Constitutional protections do not apply.

The one Supreme Court case involving a private school teacher contesting dismissal is *Rendell-Baker v. Kohn,*[16] decided in 1982. This case is significant because, although the school received over 90% of its funds from the state, the Supreme Court declined to find the presence of state action significant enough to warrant Constitutional protections. Previous lower courts' decisions had indicated the difficulty of proving significant state action present in teacher dismissals in church-related schools. (See *Lorentzen v. Boston College.*[17]) *Rendell-Baker* indicates that, unless the state can somehow be shown to be involved in the contested activity, the court will not intervene in the action.

To date, no court has found state action present in the dismissal decisions of church-related schools. Indeed, *Rendell-Baker* appears to have rendered the state action argument moot.

Statutes and Regulations

Federal and state statutes and regulations govern the public school and may govern the church-related school as well. Failure to comply with reasonable regulations can result in the imposition of sanctions. Discrimination presents one such situation.

The 1983 case of *Bob Jones University v. United States*[18] illustrates this point. When Bob Jones University, a church-related institution, was found to employ racially discriminatory admissions and disciplinary policies, the Internal Revenue Service withdrew the university's tax-exempt status based on an Internal Revenue Service regulation denying such status to any institution which discriminates on the basis of race. Before a church-related school will be forced to comply with a law or regulation, the state generally must demonstrate a *compelling interest* in the enforcement of the regulation. In *Bob Jones*, the government's compelling interest in racial equality was sufficient for the court to order Bob Jones University to comply with the anti-discrimination regulation or lose its tax-exempt status.

Other examples of compelling state interests in educational regulations might be curriculum or graduation requirements, teacher certification, and school certification requirements. In these cases the state could very possibly prove a compelling state interest in the proper education of the public. The state cannot pass laws so restrictive that a school's existence is placed in jeopardy, however. The right of the church-related school to exist was firmly established in the previously mentioned *Pierce* case.

Common Law

The third type of law which applies to both public and private education is the common law, that law which is found largely in previous court decisions.

Common law principles may also be considered to be derived from God's law, especially by persons in church-related schools. Many common law principles are founded in basic morality such as that found in the Ten Commandments and in other religious writings.

Prior judicial decisions comprise an important part of common law. These decisions are often referred to as "precedents." When a lawsuit is begun, attorneys on both sides begin searching for precedents, prior cases that will support their arguments. In the United States these prior decisions can be found in courts of record for all cases heard since the beginnings of our country, and prior to that time, for all cases heard in England. It is not unusual to find old English cases cited in modern cases.

Common law provides the basis for the idea of fairness, how reasonable people should treat each other. When two parties disagree as to the appropriate treatment, case law is one way of finding support for each party's position.

Contract Law

The fourth type of law which governs both public and church-related school cases is contract law. Public schools are bound by contract law in the governance of their contractual relationships with teachers who sign contracts of employment. Public school students generally are not involved in contractual situations; in the event of disputes between parents, students, and public schools, Constitutional arguments are generally made since such arguments trigger a higher degree of judicial scrutiny than do breach of contract arguments.

In the church-related school, contract law is the predominant law. A contract may be defined as: an agreement between two parties. Generally, the five basic elements of a contract are: (1) mutual assent (2) by legally competent parties (3) for consideration (4) to subject matter that is legal and (5) in a form of agreement which is legal.

Mutual assent implies that two parties entering into a contract agree to its provisions. A church-related school agrees to provide an education to a student and, in return his or her parents accept that offer. A church-related school offers a teacher a contract and the teacher accepts the contractual offer of employment. It is a basic premise of contract law that a binding contract must have both an offer and an acceptance.

Consideration is what the first party agrees to do for the other party in exchange for something from the second party. Thus, each incurs a detriment and a benefit when entering into a contract. A parent enrolls a child in school (a benefit) and agrees to pay tuition (a detriment); the school receives tuition money (a benefit) and agrees to educate the child (a detriment in terms of accepting other children in that child's place and in terms of commitment to providing staff and services for the child's education). The church-related school hires a teacher (a benefit) and must pay a salary (a financial detriment). The teacher receives a salary (a benefit) but must be available to teach on days school is in session (a detriment in terms of personal control of time, etc.).

Legally competent parties implies that the parties entering into the contract (the offeror who makes the offer and the offeree who accepts the offer) are lawfully qualified to make the agreement. Thus, a person who is under the age of eighteen cannot enter into a contract. A person who is not certified as a teacher but misrepresents qualifications and is hired, is not a legally competent party for the purposes of a teaching contract, and the contract can be considered void.

Legal subject matter assumes that what is agreed to is legal. For example, an agreement that a teacher would not marry a person of another race as a condition of employment would not be legal, as such a condition would be construed as a violation of anti-discrimination laws and other freedoms as well.

Legal form may vary from state to state or from school system to school system. In some states, an oral contract may be binding. Generally, it is not a good idea to depend on oral contracts as one person's memory of exactly what was agreed to may not match the second party's recollection. Other factors may be requirements for legal form. If, for example, a contract calls for witnesses, and no witnesses' signatures are found on the contract, the document is probably not in legal form.

If any one of the five elements of a contract is missing, the contract may be held to be null and void.

Breach of Contract

A breach of contract occurs when one party does not do that which was promised, and there are no justifiable reasons for the non-performance.

Breach of contract can be committed by either party to a contract (the school/administrator or the teacher or student). It is generally conceded, however, that it is futile for a church-related or other private school to bring breach of contract charges against a teacher who wants to terminate a contract. A contract for the rendition of personal services will not be enforced; the remedy for breach of contract is damages, not performance of the contract. While teachers can generally break their contracts without severe consequences, schools and administrators cannot lawfully terminate a teacher's employment during a contract term without just cause. Neither can a school terminate a student's enrollment without just cause. Should a school act in such a manner, the wronged teacher or student can seek damages as a remedy.

Some teacher cases arising in church-related schools will illustrate the concept of breach of contract. A 1973 case, *Weithoff v. St. Veronica's School*,[19] is one such example. A teacher was dismissed from a Catholic school for marrying a priest without proper dispensation, thus placing herself outside legitimate church membership. There was a board-adopted rule about observing the teachings of the Catholic Church, but the rule had never been disseminated to the teachers. The teaching contract bound the teacher to "observe the promulgated policies" of the school. Since the policy was never promulgated, the teacher maintained that she could not be bound by it. The court agreed with the teacher and found the school in breach of the contract; the court did not order the teacher's reinstatement, but it did award her the amount of her contractual wages for the contract year.

In a case, the facts of which are similar to *Weithoff*, *Steeber v. Benilde-St. Margaret's High School*,[20] involving a teacher whose contract was not renewed after her remarriage without an annulment, the court found for the school because the school did have a rule that had been promulgated. *Weithoff* and *Steeber* illustrate that courts will look to the provisions of contracts in breach of contract cases and will base their decisions on what the parties involved have agreed to do, and not on what they should have agreed to do or on any other factor.

Courts have upheld the right of church-related schools to make rules of conduct for teachers and students which would not be permissible in the public school. However, those rules of conduct have to be made known to those affected by them.

The case of *Holy Name School of the Congregation of the Holy Name of Jesus of Kimberly v. Department of Industry, Labor and Human Relations*, and *Mary P. Retlick*[21] illustrates this. Retlick's contract was not renewed because she married a divorced man who had not yet received his annulment. The school sought to prove that she was not entitled to unemployment benefits because she willfully violated her contract. However, Retlick was able to demonstrate that the only policy the school had regarding divorced and remarried teachers had to do with religion teachers. Further, the principal had encouraged the teacher to live with her intended husband rather than marry him if she could not marry him within the Catholic Church; so, the school's defense that the marriage was immoral could not withstand judicial scrutiny.

Courts will consider the characteristics and behavior of the parties involved in a contract. Just as the principal's behavior in the *Holy Name* case led the court to discredit the allegation of immoral behavior in the teacher's action, in a different case a teacher's behavior led the court to find that the teacher knew or should have known that his conduct did not meet the norms of the sponsoring school. In *Bischoff v. Brothers of the Sacred Heart*,[22] a Louisiana case, a former Catholic seminarian, who had been divorced and remarried without church approval, was held to have been responsible for knowing that a Catholic school would not accept such an applicant in the religion department. Since plaintiff did not reveal his marital history in applying for a position as a religion teacher, he acted in bad faith and the contract was void *ab initio* (from the beginning.)

Historically, courts have been reluctant to intervene in disputes involving church-related schools because of the doctrine of separation of church and state. A 1982 case proved very significant in changing that reluctance. In *Reardon et al. v. LeMoyne et al.*,[23] four Roman Catholic nuns whose contracts were not renewed after five to twelve years of employment sued the parish school board, the superintendent of schools, and the bishop. The nuns alleged that their contracts had been violated. They had signed the same contracts as lay personnel and statements in the contract and in the school's handbook gave the right of a hearing and an appeal to dismissed teachers. Further, one section of the contract indicated that a person's employment would end "during the summer following one's seventieth birthday." None of the teachers were seventy years of age, and none were granted a hearing. On appeal, the state supreme court held that the nuns' rights had been violated, and, at the very least, they were entitled to a hearing. Thus, in a dramatic departure from legal tradition, the court declined to follow the doctrine of separation of church and state in a matter that was employment, not doctrine, related.

While courts will accept jurisdiction over non-doctrinal issues in church-related schools, they will nonetheless uphold the right of the church-related schools to make and enforce rules for teacher conduct. In the 1990 case, *Little v. St. Mary Magdalene Parish*,[24] a non-Catholic teacher married a Catholic man after obtaining a civil divorce and without an annulment of her first marriage. Such an action was acceptable in her religion. The school terminated her employment. Ms. Little alleged that the school's action was violation of her rights under both Title VII of the Civil Rights Act of 1964 and state law, as well as a breach of contract. Church-related schools are exempt from claims of religious discrimination under Title VII. Ms. Little argued that, by employing a non-Catholic, the parish waived its right to the exemption. The court declined to find such a waiver.

Ms. Little had signed a contract containing a "Cardinal's Clause" which allowed the parish to terminate a teacher's employment for "public rejection of the official teachings, doctrines or laws of the Roman Catholic church." The parish maintained that her conduct, though permissible in her religion, was grounds to terminate her employment in the Catholic school because of the terms of her contract. Thus, it appears that church-related schools can establish standards of conduct for all employees, even those who are not members of the sponsoring religion, so long as those standards are clearly articulated in the employment contract.

Student cases in church-related schools tend to follow similar judicial reasoning. The three cases mentioned earlier, *Bright, Geraci*, and *Wisch*, all dealt with state action issues, but also made secondary breach of contract arguments which were rejected. For example, in *Geraci*,[25] a student helped another young man gain access to the school to throw a pie in the face of a teacher during a final exam. The court found that the student had breached his contract with the school by his actions, and that the school did not breach its contract with the student by expelling him.

Sometimes, a church-related school expulsion can seem unfair. In the case of *Bloch v. Hillel Torah North Suburban Day School*,[26] a first grader was expelled from a Jewish day school for excessive absences and tardiness. Her mother introduced evidence indicating that the real reason for the dismissal was that she had contacted the health department about an epidemic of head lice in the school. The court ruled that, if the expulsion was a retaliation against the mother's actions, it could be a breach of contract; however, the mother's sole remedy would be money damages.

Thus, breach of contract allegations constitute the type of lawsuit that is filed when students or teachers believe that they have been treated unfairly in the church-related school since Constitutional remedies, including reinstatement, are not available.

Torts

While breach of contract cases deal with most situations in which students or teachers are contesting dismissal or some other disciplinary action, tort cases are the most common form of litigation in both the public and private sectors. A tort is defined as a civil or a private wrong other than breach of contract. Torts generally fall into one of the following categories: corporal punishment, search and seizure, defamation of character, and negligence.

Corporal Punishment

Corporal punishment is one of the most controversial issues in education today. Approximately as many states outlaw the administration of corporal punishment in public schools as permit it. Some relatively few states prohibit corporal punishment in both the public and private school.

In 1977 the United States Supreme Court in *Ingraham v. Wright*[27] ruled that students in public schools do not have the same Eighth Amendment protections against cruel and unusual punishment that criminals have. *Ingraham* remains a controversial case today.

Some church-related schools, relying on biblical injunctions to use corporal punishment, may permit it. Its application remains problematic whenever it is applied, as the following cases illustrate.

In a 1987 case, *Illinois v. Burdette Wehmeyer*,[28] the court, using an accountability theory, found a principal guilty of battery of a student who had received a teacher-administered paddling witnessed by the principal. This case illustrates the doctrine of *respondeat superior*, the superior is responsible for the actions of subordinates. If corporal punishment is allowed, the administrator must establish and implement careful guidelines to ensure that abuse is avoided.

Corporal punishment is a broad term that encompasses more than "traditional" types of bodily punishment. Any punitive touching that results in harm to the student can be corporal punishment. Even in the absence of Constitutional protections, both public and private school staff members can be held liable for assault and battery of a student if the student sustains an injury as a result of receiving corporal punishment.

In a 1990 case, *Thrasher v. General Casualty Company of Wisconsin*,[29] the court had to decide whether throwing a student into a blackboard exceeded acceptable limits on corporal punishment. The court declined to find any Fourth or Eighth Amendment Constitutional protections. However, the court refused to dismiss the action against the teacher and remanded it to a lower court for a determination of whether other rights had been violated.

Thrasher illustrates the notion that corporal punishment can be any punitive touching. Thus, developing case law raises the possibility that corporal punishment in all schools will become too risky as a means of discipline, in terms of potential legal liability for educators. The church-related school is generally not governed by the same rules as the public school in regard to corporal punishment. However, the cases cited indicate that all educators should be very careful in any consideration of corporal punishment. Church-related schools are not immune to civil tort cases or criminal charges of assault and battery if a student is injured during the application of corporal punishment.

Church-related school principals, like public school officials, might be well advised to propose other means of discipline than physical ones, both from the standpoint of avoiding lawsuits and from the standpoint of good psychology.

Search and Seizure

The Fourth Amendment to the Constitution protects persons' rights to privacy and requires that a search warrant, granted on a showing of probable cause, be obtained before a search can be conducted. In 1985, however, the U.S. Supreme Court declined to require public schools to obtain search warrants and/or to have probable cause before conducting a search. In *New Jersey v. T.L.O.*,[30] the court ruled that public school officials only have to have reasonable cause before conducting a search.

The church-related school educator does not even have to have reasonable cause to conduct a search. Nonetheless, justice and common sense require that church-related schools should have some kind of policy for searching students and/or seizing their possessions. Searching a student should require "more" cause than searching a locker. Lockers and desks are school property and the school has a right to examine them and their contents. A school strengthens its position by including a phrase such as the following in handbooks, "The school is co-tenant of lockers and desks and reserves the right to search them at any time without notice."

Defamation of Character

Defamation is an unprivileged communication that harms the reputation of another. Defamation can be either written, *libel*, or spoken, *slander*. The truth is an absolute defense in most cases; however, educators are often held to a higher standard. Teachers and administrators should exercise great care in keeping records, and in conversations. Educators should strive to be as factual as possible in written documents and in conversations and to refrain from "editorial" comments. Whatever is written should follow three criteria: (1) it should be specific; (2) it should be behaviorally oriented; and (3) it should be verifiable.

Negligence

By far, the most often litigated tort is negligence. Negligence is the unintentional act or omission that harms another. Before one can be found liable for legal negligence, four elements must be present. If even one of these elements is missing, legal negligence does not exist.

The first element is *duty*. A person charged with negligence must have had a duty in the situation. If a teacher is taking a personal trip to a museum on Saturday afternoon and sees two students engaged in an altercation, the teacher has no legal duty to intervene since he or she is not supervising the students or the museum. Thus, if the student altercation results in injury, the teacher cannot be held responsible in any way since no duty was present.

The second element is *violation of duty*. A person charged with negligence must have had a clear duty which he or she violated. One case which illustrates this concept is the 1982 case, *Smith v. Archbishop of St. Louis.*[31] In this case, a second grade teacher in a Catholic school kept a lighted candle on her desk all day. A student walked too close to the candle and her clothing caught fire, and she sustained serious burns. Clearly, the teacher violated her duty when she kept a lighted candle on her desk for such a long period of time.

The third element is *proximate cause*. There must be a causal relationship between the violation of duty and the fourth element, *injury*. In the *Smith* case, the keeping of the candle contributed greatly to the student's sustaining an injury. Had there been no lighted candle, there would have been no injury.

Courts generally follow the principle, the younger the child, chronologically or mentally, the greater the standard of care required. It might be acceptable to leave a group of high school seniors alone for ten minutes when it would not be acceptable to leave a group of first graders alone.

Most negligence cases occur in the classroom because that is where students spend most of their time. However, there are other areas that are potentially more dangerous than the classroom and, hence, a greater standard of care will be expected from teachers and administrators.

Shop and lab classes contain greater potential for injury than do classrooms, and cases indicate that courts expect teachers to exercise greater caution than they would in ordinary classrooms. Teachers and administrators are also expected to keep equipment in working order and to keep the area free of unnecessary hazards.

Athletics present very real potential for injury. Even if every possible precaution were taken, the possibility for student injury is high. Administrators have very real duties to ensure that: competent, properly trained personnel serve as coaches for teams; clear procedures are followed when accidents occur; there is no delay in seeking medical attention when needed; equipment and playing areas are as hazard-free as possible. Church-related schools have a long history of relying on volunteers to coach; the administrator must ensure that no one coaches who is not qualified.

The best defense for an administrator in a negligence suit is a reasonable attempt to provide for the safety of all through appropriate rules and regulations. The best defense for a teacher is a reasonable effort to implement rules.

Field Trips

Field trips pose special risks in the area of negligence. Administrators would be well advised to require that field trips have some educational or programmatic purpose. Parents should be required to sign permission slips that have been reviewed by an attorney with some experience in school law, before their children are permitted to go on a field trip.

Child Abuse Reporting

Another area of possible negligence results from the failure to report suspected child abuse and/or neglect. Educators who fail to report can incur both civil and criminal penalties. Every state has a law mandating that educators report suspected abuse and neglect. Administrators must ensure that staff members understand the requirements of the child abuse reporting laws and comply with them.

Employment Policies

Another area of special concern to the church-related school administrator is that of employment policies. Administrators are responsible for developing and implementing policies that protect the contractual rights of both the school community and the individual employee. Contracts place certain obligations upon teachers, but they also place obligations upon the employer. It is important that the school's policies be in line with those of the sponsoring church, especially in view of the fact that many contracts bind teachers to observe church rules and regulations.

Policies become extremely important in the area of hiring procedures. These procedures must be in line with the requirements of civil law. Pre-employment inquiries carry the potential for violation of rights. Inquiries into marital status, number of dependents, disabilities, and irrelevant matters should be avoided. When in doubt, the school attorney should be contacted. Many employment applications developed in the past may violate the rights of potential employees, and should be revised to reflect compliance with current law.

Administrators may have legitimate concerns about providing for stability on faculties and about ensuring that persons who are hired will have good attendance. Administrators may not, however, ask a woman if she intends to have children or whether child care will be a problem.

In church-related schools, it is permissible to inquire about church affiliation and about the candidate's willingness to uphold the teachings of the sponsoring church. It is permissible to ask if the person is in good standing in his or her church community. A candidate can be required to produce recommendations from a pastor or rabbi.

Applicants should be asked to sign a statement giving permission for background checks. Many states now have laws requiring that all persons who work in schools be fingerprinted and the fingerprints checked against records of criminals convicted of felonies and/or misdemeanors. In the absence of such a law, a school may wish to set its own policy regarding fingerprinting.

Documentation: Creating a Paper Trail

While it is difficult to discipline employees and to make decisions regarding non-renewal of contract, the principal is charged with these responsibilities. While tenure is a job protection in the public sector, it does not often exist in the church-related sector. The concept of *de facto* tenure, tenure in fact, does not appear to be accepted by many courts today. Most church-related schools have yearly contracts. One way to avoid a *de facto* tenure problem is to insert a clause in the employment contract such as, "Both parties agree there is no tenure." While seeking to protect the school through such a policy, the administrator must also be mindful of the need to act fairly, particularly in a church-related school.

Student Discipline

Student discipline is, of necessity, a major concern for administrators in church-related schools. Without rules and a reasonable implementation of the rules by administration and faculty, order would cease to exist and schools would be unable to perform their function of education. Common law and common sense indicate that persons and institutions responsible for the education of youth are expected to hold students to standards of behavior.

As indicated earlier, what is considered an acceptable procedure in a church-related school may not be deemed constitutional in a public school. Yet *Geraci* hints that the lines between acceptable private school procedures are not completely clear cut; the *Geraci*[32] court discussed *fundamental fairness* as analogous to Constitutional due process. In a consideration of church-related school discipline, it may be important to keep the *Geraci* findings in mind. It is much easier to make and implement fair rules from the outset than to try and undo damages resulting from poorly thought out and/or unfairly implemented rules.

Most school officials and lawyers would agree that the best school law is, like medicine, preventive. The best defense is having tried to follow the right course in the first place. School officials must realize that despite their best efforts in any and all areas of school life, they may well face legal action. School administrators should look carefully at their rules and procedures to ensure that they are reasonable, fair and consistent.

Although a church-related school is not bound to protect the Constitutional freedoms of its students, administrators would be well advised to know what those freedoms are in the public sector and to be prepared to offer some reasonable rationale for rules adopted that are not protective of those freedoms. For example, church-related schools may have dress codes that would not be allowed in a public school today. Church-related schools may demand that students participate in religious exercises and refrain from speech that is critical of the sponsoring religious denomination.

It is the responsibility of the administrator to develop rules, to promulgate rules, and to supervise their implementation. An administrator must be sure that students and their parents know of a rule ("uniforms must be worn") and must ensure that the staff is enforcing the rule. If a student honestly doesn't know of the existence of a rule, through the negligence of staff and/or administration, he or she can hardly be held accountable for not following the rule. If teachers are responsible for implementation of rules, it is important that administrators supervise that implementation. Administrators should strive for consistent enforcement of rules.

Conclusion

Church-related schools are not bound by the strictures of the United States Constitution. Thus, they may forbid behaviors that the public school has no choice but to accept. While granted greater latitude in the administration of their schools than are their public sector counterparts, church-related school officials should seek to be faithful to both the demands of civil law and the directives of the sponsoring church.

Notes

1. *Rendell-Baker v. Kohn*, 102 S. Ct. 2764 (1982).
2. *Dixon v. Alabama State Board of Education*, 186 F. Supp. 945 (1960); *rev.* at 294 F. 2d 150 (U.S.C.A. Fifth Circuit, 1961); *cert. den.* 368 U.S. 930 (1961).
3. *Tinker v. Des Moines Independent School District et al.*, 393 U.S. 503 (1969).
4. *Goss v. Lopez*, 419 U.S. 565 (1975).
5. *Wood v. Strickland*, 420 U.S. 308 (1975).
6. *Pierce v. Society of Sisters*, 268 U.S. 510 (1925).
7. *Id.* at 535.
8. Civil Rights Act of 1871 (Title 42 of the United States Code, Section 1983).
9. *Dixon, supra* note 2.
10. *Tinker, supra* note 3, at 506.
11. *Bright v. Isenbarger*, 314 F. Supp. 1382 (N.D. Ind. 1970).
12. *Id.* at 1395.
13. *Wisch v. Sanford School, Inc.*, 420 F. Supp. 1310 (D. Del. 1976).
14. *Id.* at 1313.
15. *Geraci v. St. Xavier High School*, 13 Ohio Op. 3d 146 (Ohio 1978).
16. *Rendell-Baker, supra* note 1.
17. *Lorentzen v. Boston College*, 440 F. Supp. 464 (1977).
18. *Bob Jones University v. United States*, 103 S. Ct. 2017 (1983).
19. *Weithoff v. St. Veronica's School*, 210 N.W. 2d 108 (Mich. 1973).
20. *Steeber v. Benilde-St. Margaret's High School*, (No. D.C. 739 378, Hennepin County, Minnesota, 1978).
21. *Holy Name School of the Congregation of the Holy Name of Jesus of Kimberly v. Department of Industry, Labor and Human Relations, and Mary P. Retlick*, 326 N.W. 2d 121 (Wis. App. 1982).
22. *Bischoff v. Brothers of the Sacred Heart*, 416 So. 2d 348 (La. App. 1982).
23. *Reardon et al. v. LeMoyne et al.*, 454 A. 2d 428 (N.H. 1982).
24. *Little v. St. Mary Magdalene Parish*, 739 F. Supp. 1003 (1990).
25. *Geraci, supra* note 15.
26. *Bloch v. Hillel Torah North Suburban Day School*, 438 N.E. 2d 976 (1981).
27. *Ingraham v. Wright*, 430 U.S. 65 (1977).
28. *Illinois v. Burdette Wehmeyer*, 509 N.E. 2d 605 (1987).
29. *Thrasher v. General Casualty Company of Wisconsin*, 732 F. Supp. 966 (W.D. Wisc. 1990).
30. *New Jersey v. T.L.O.*, 105 S. Ct. 733 (1985).
31. *Smith v. Archbishop of St. Louis*, 632 S.W. 2d 516 (Mo. Ct. App. 1982).
32. *Geraci, supra* note 15.

Cases Cited

Bischoff v. Brothers of the Sacred Heart, 416 So. 2d 348 (La. App. 1982).
Bloch v. Hillel Torah North Suburban Day School, 438 N.E. 2d 976 (1981).
Bright v. Isenbarger, 314 F. Supp. 1382 (N.D. Ind. 1970).
Civil Rights Act of 1871 (Title 42 of the United States Code, Section 1983).
Dixon v. Alabama State Board of Education, 186 F. Supp. 945 (1960); *rev.* at 294 F. 2d 150 (U.S.C.A. Fifth Circuit, 1961; *cert. den.* 368 U.S. 930 (1961).
Geraci v. St. Xavier High School, 13 Ohio Op. 3d 146 (Ohio 1978).
Goss v. Lopez, 419 U.S. 565 (1975).
Bob Jones University v. United States, 103 S. Ct. 2017 (1983).
Holy Name School of the Congregation of the Holy Name of Jesus of Kimberly v. Department of Industry, Labor and Human Relations, and Mary P. Retlick, 326 N.W. 2d 121 (Wis. App. 1982).
Illinois v. Burdette Wehmeyer, 509 N.E. 2d 605 (1987).
Ingraham v. Wright, 430 U.S. 65 (1977).
Little v. St. Mary Magdalene Parish, 739 F. Supp. 1003 (1990).
Lorentzen v. Boston College, 440 F. Supp. 464 (1977).
New Jersey v. T.L.O., 105 S. Ct. 733 (1985).
Pierce v. Society of Sisters, 268 U.S. 510 (1925).
Reardon et al. v. LeMoyne et al., 454 A. 2d 428 (N.H. 1982).
Rendell-Baker v. Kohn, 102 S. Ct. 2764 (1982).
Smith v. Archbishop of St. Louis, 632 S.W. 2d 516 (Mo. Ct. App. 1982).
Steeber v. Benilde-St. Margaret's High School, (No. D.C. 739 378, Hennepin County, Minnesota, 1978).
Thrasher v. General Casualty Company of Wisconsin, 732 F. Supp. 966 (W.D. Wisc. 1990).
Tinker v. Des Moines Independent School District et al., 393 U.S. 503 (1969).
Weithoff v. St. Veronica's School, 210 N.W. 2d 108 (Mich. 1973).
Wisch v. Sanford School, Inc., 420 F. Supp. 1310 (D. Del. 1976).
Wood v. Strickland, 420 U.S. 308 (1975).

Chapter Seven
Public Policy, Religion, and Education in the United States

William F. Davis, O.S.F.S.

General Background

Any study of education and schooling in the United States will reveal evidence showing that schools, from the earliest days of the first colonies to the present, reflected the wide religious, cultural, and ethnic diversity of the people who came to these shores. From the beginning, the vari ous structures, goals, curriculum, and especially their long-term degree of success in delivering both secular and denominational instruction could be found in each area of this new territory, no matter where the immigrants came from, because that education was basically modeled on the schools and culture found in the colonists' mother country. The greatest degree of permanence and influence in the colonial educational endeavors seems to be most clearly found in the original English colonies.[1]

Almost from the arrival of the first colonists on the North American continent, whether they were Spanish, English, French, or Dutch, there is evidence that public policy, religious, and educational decisions were interacting. Harold Buetow makes reference to a Spanish document issued about the year 1516, in which explorers and missionaries, who were regularly the paid agents of the state, were instructed to be sure that "each village . . . was to have its own school and church, and it was the duty of the missionaries to see that each individual was taught and instructed . . . in the Catholic faith."[2] Later in the English Massachusetts Bay Colony, when civil leaders, many of whom were also church leaders, adopted the first colonial compulsory school attendance law in the year 1642, it stated that the reason was so that parents could be assured that their children would learn to "read and understand the principles of religion."[3]

As time went by, the increase in the desire for a system of schooling throughout the colonies was greatly influenced by the diversity of religious concerns found in each geographic area, whether that was in the New England, Middle Atlantic, or Southern colonies. It was commonly held, that any program of complete education had to include some form of religious training. Furthermore, education and schooling were regarded widely as major functions of church agencies. Even when such programs were held under church-related auspices, public financial support for the variety of existing denominational schools, and later, as the idea of a public common school grew in favor, for religious instruction in the common school was to be more the rule than the exception.[4]

With the birth of the United States, and the adoption of the First Amendment and Bill of Rights at the close of the eighteenth century, religion continued to remain a fixture in the schools found in the various states. It is important to note that every member of the Constitutional Convention came from a colony that before and after ratification of the Constitution and Bill of Rights, levied taxes, collected those taxes, and distributed the funds to church agencies in order to establish and run elementary and secondary schools.[5] Public tax support for church-related schools continued and even increased until about 1820. At that time, such tax support began to experience a slow decline but could still be found in numerous localities after the conclusion of the Civil War.[6] In this early period of the nation's existence, any distinct line between what we now commonly refer to as public and private schools was significantly blurred. This blurring of roles or identity was to last well into the nineteenth century when state and local political control of public education and schooling was to become the established norm.

The new nation came into being attempting to overcome the dilemma of how the policy makers could build a secular governmental structure out of a society made up of a people deeply attached to their various religious faiths. The government they envisioned was not to ". . . prefer, discriminate against or oppress any particular religion."[7] Such an approach led the policy makers into a situation that was in fact a sort of informal establishment of mainstream Protestantism. As the nation entered the nineteenth century, the existing schools were clearly used to transmit the dominant Protestant culture and ethic. Such an approach in the homogeneous Protestant civic society, before the first large influx of Catholic immigrants, was due to a rather informal agreement among the leadership of civil and church groups to end Protestant sectarian quarrels and develop a "non-sectarian" consensus on the structure of the common school curriculum.[8]

Historians of early education and schooling in the United States show that the earliest public "common schools" were, for the most part, operated and controlled by diverse Protestant groups and that their philosophy, administration, staffing, and curriculum structure stressed a common Protestant Establishment set of values.[9] Horace Mann, a leader behind the development of the common school movement and a Unitarian minister, believed that these common schools could be all things to all kinds of children, and could teach secular subjects and a religious value system without having to be specifically sectarian in nature.[10] The use of specific curriculum materials such as the King James Bible and the famous McGuffey Reader, among others, created the clear impression that these schools and the support of a basic nondenominational set of Protestant values were intimately bound together. A number of studies clearly show that church-affiliated schools would continue to be designated as the local public school in many states and were recipients of government financial support well through the nineteenth century.[11]

As the new nation began to show significant expansion both territorially and in population, other forces and fears began to affect public policy decisions and especially the delivery of educational services in many of the established schools. Waves of new immigrants with different religious, ethnic, and cultural backgrounds began to enter the country and pressure built politically and socially to provide an educational system for these new residents that would help preserve what was considered by the older generation of citizens to be a very distinct American form of democracy, civil order, and social principles. The increasing growth of industry and the pressure under Manifest Destiny to move the population westward also added to this increasingly volatile situation. This new national context began to strain the ability of existing voluntary church agencies to provide educational services to all those who now required them in this rapidly expanding nation. In addition, there was a growing suspicion of and even hostility toward private programs of schooling, especially religious, and more specifically Catholic programs, and moves to provide for the exclusive civil control of education and schooling became more prevalent.

In light of this new reality, many Catholics, including both church leaders and the laity, began to view the emerging public common school as a hostile Protestant threat to the faith of Catholic young people. Efforts to maintain or expand church-related schools and at the same time to retain or obtain a share of civil tax monies for such schools were for the most part rejected, though some local compromises were worked out in a number of places for a period of time. In addition, those Protestants who were affiliated with the more evangelical wing of the Protestant community also began to express concern over the public schools, with their less sectarian and more nondenominational set of Protestant values. This evangelical group saw schools that were, from their perspective, increasingly "godless" and secular.[12]

Such feelings of hostility toward a common school for all children increased the pressure that was to lead to the creation of a private school movement, where the overwhelming majority of these schools would be religiously oriented and in particular Catholic. It is argued by some that in the long term minority sects, especially Catholic and evangelical Protestants, were instrumental in helping to remove basic Protestant religion and values from the public school and thus the "triumph of secularization of the public school was in no small measure due to the persistence of . . . parents in refusing to sacrifice their claims of conscience by yielding to a settlement that was entirely satisfactory to the Protestant majority."[13]

Thus, during the first century of the nation's history, we can identify the source of a number of public policy and, specifically, education-oriented controversies on both the federal and state levels that created strains in the relationship between religious and governmental agencies, as well as the professional educators. These strains would grow and carry over into the twentieth century and threaten to remain with us into the next century.

Overview of Private Religious Schools

Beginning with the second half of the nineteenth century and lasting into the early 1970s, private education in the United States was almost synonymous with Catholic schools and certainly with religiously oriented schools. While the Catholic school enrollment showed a significant decline in the 1970s and into the early 1990s, these schools continue to be a major part of the private school community, enrolling more than half of all private school students. Religiously oriented schools currently enroll better than eight out of every ten private school students.

The Catholic community, led by the bishops, debated the school issue over a significant period of the nineteenth century. The debate over the desirability of and the need for Catholic schools can be found recorded in the three Plenary Councils of Baltimore as well as in exchanges between leading church clerics and laity. While not all church leaders supported Catholic schools, the majority did and the effort became a major endeavor during the last part of the nineteenth century and most of the twentieth century, especially the period up to the Second Vatican Council.

Other religious groups, at almost the same time, began to see a need to open schools to serve the particular needs of their church's young people, including Lutheran, especially the Missouri Synod; Calvinist or Dutch and Christian Reformed churches; Seventh Day Adventist; Quaker; Episcopalian; and the more Orthodox part of the Jewish community. In the 1960s and 1970s a new group of religiously oriented Christian Day schools began to grow rapidly and today form a major part of the total private and religious school community. While often not attached to or operated by a specific denomination or church, these schools can generally be associated with the more evangelical wing of Protestantism.

Two new groups that have also begun to show growth over the last decade are schools affiliated with Muslim communities and individual parents who have chosen to school their children at home. The Muslim schools stress a particular religious faith orientation as the basis for their establishment and operation. The home school group is clearly more diverse. While there are a significant number of parents who home school that identify themselves as either Protestant or Catholic and home school for a religious reason, others do not home school for any particular religious reason.

While each of these religious groups opened schools that sought to include some form of denominational religious program in the daily school curriculum and the broader life of the students and staff, many of these groups today, as did those of the nineteenth century, are opening schools in response to what they perceive as threats to a particular cultural heritage or what they view as the secular nature of the existing public schools, a decline in discipline and social values, and an opposition to what they see as excessive meddling by various levels of government in the education of their children.[14]

Public Policy, Religion, and Schools

Public Policy and Political Responsibility

The issue of public policy and the responsibility of the individual citizen, and more especially the religious community leadership and membership, as presented here, reflects the attitude of the Catholic Church's leadership and the membership of the Catholic school community. In such a diverse country, within the diverse private and religious school community, there may be disagreement with one or more of the approaches and policy initiatives outlined here.

Public life in our country should allow for a time and place where basic issues of importance and interest can be debated in a civil manner with the broadest possible public participation, in order that our citizens can work more effectively to attain the common good of all those involved—the basic goal of any good public policy decision. We can easily blame politics and politicians for being part of our public policy problems, but all members of society, and in this case the general educational policy community, needs to enter into an informed and responsible policy debate on the issues involved in the provision of a true quality education. A quality education is one that affects the development of the intellectual, physical, and moral attributes of all of our nation's children, regardless of what type of school they attend, public, private or religious. Catholic church leaders believe that they have a right to engage in such a debate, to try to educate the faithful on their responsibilities, to analyze the impact of issues, and to inspire the members of the church to speak out on the moral and social dimensions of issues that affect the social order.

The participation of the church leaders and members in such a debate is regrettably often misunderstood. These efforts pose no real threat to the political structure or to the diversity found in the country, nor do they diminish the right of other groups to join in the discussion—this includes the responsibility of government officials to intervene in a legitimate and autonomous way. The intent is not to develop a block of voters but to analyze the impact of public policy decisions. With this in mind, and against a background where the role of religion in the public life of the nation has been very visible and almost constant in our history and where issues affecting religion have become more common in the recent political life of the nation, the United States Catholic Conference (USCC), the public policy agency of the Catholic Bishops of the United States, has recently issued two documents outlining in great detail its basic approach to such a public dialogue on public policy issues. These documents are: *Political Responsibility: Proclaiming the Gospel of Life, Protecting the Least among Us, and Pursuing the Common Good,* which deals with a broad range of public policy issues, and *Principles for Educational Reform in the United States,* which is specifically aimed at education issues as they affect all of the children in our schools, public, private, and religious.[15]

The approach outlined in some detail in these documents is an attempt to develop impartial public policy decisions which provide positive benefits for all and in the specific sphere of education to improve the educational situation for all parents, children, and teachers. That educational public policy approach seeks, as a right and a matter of justice, a fair share of financial benefits for all parents, children, and staff engaged in the educational activities of the nation without sacrificing the unique nature of the private and religious schools and their curriculum.

One difficulty in addressing these educational issues may be the current popular terminology—the common use of the terms "public" and "private" to describe educational communities. The use of these terms tends to create a false dichotomy and adds a pejorative tone to the debate as some attempt to paint private schools as elitist, divisive, undemocratic, and serving no public good. A second concern is the concept that tax monies are "public" funds only to be used for "public" entities and endeavors. In our opinion, tax funds are to be used to attain the common good and can be used for a variety of endeavors that benefit the society in which we live. All parents who are taxed and are required to obey the mandatory school attendance laws should be able to receive the benefit of those taxes and not be excluded because of the false assumption that the choice they made is purely private and not serving the public good in any way.

The reality is that a true public education and system of schooling embraces any school that serves the common good of children and the nation as a whole. Private and religious schools are a vital part of our nation's history, serving the public good, and fulfilling legitimate requirements set down by government and educational leaders. Religious schools add a dimension that millions of parents see as a necessary part of a developing child's life and which they see as being absent from the current public school curriculum.[16] Private schools differ from public schools only in the way that they are administered, in how they are currently funded, and that some have a religious focus. The contribution of private and religious schools to our nation's educational, social, and political life is evident and the diversity of the nation's make-up is not served well by demanding a universal "one size fits all" approach to education. As the Catholic bishops say in their document on educational reform, "No single model or means of education is appropriate to the needs and desires of all persons. Therefore, our nation should make available the broadest variety of quality educational opportunities for each individual to choose from, including public, private and religious schools."[17] It seems clear that parents who have the first and principal right to educate their children ". . . should not be burdened economically for choosing a private or religious school in the exercise of this fundamental right."[18]

Public Policy Issues in United States Education

Historically, the federal government has been the junior partner in educational policy making and funding in the United States. The federal Constitution makes no mention of education, thereby leaving the states the responsibility for education under the Tenth Amendment of the Constitution. Currently, every state constitution provides for an established system of public schools and for school funding. The problem raised is how the federal and state governments deal with any kind of financial assistance to private and religious schools. This is further complicated by the fact that attempts to gain such assistance must be made in fifty-one different ways because of the need to deal with the federal Constitution as well as fifty state constitutions.

Furthermore, the First and Fourteenth Amendments to the federal Constitution also come into play. The First includes the religion clauses dealing with the issues of establishment and free exercise of religion. Supreme Court rulings relating to the Fourteenth extend the First Amendment Establishment Clause to the States.

Beginning in the 1840s with the growth of the clearly anti-immigration, anti-Catholic Know-Nothing Party and nourished by the national Republican party, the school policy debate intensified on both the federal and state levels. This led to legislative action to bar public funding to and even eliminate the right of private and religious schools to exist. In 1875, President Grant suggested an amendment to the Constitution to make free public schools mandatory throughout the country, to tax all church property, and to forbid the use of any public funds for religiously affiliated schools. In 1876, the Republican Party platform called for a Constitutional amendment to prohibit the use of tax funds for religiously affiliated schools. This proposal would remain in the national party platform for a decade.[19] Again in 1876, U.S. Representative James Blaine of Maine introduced such an amendment in the federal Congress where it passed the House but was unable to pass in the Senate. It seems clear that Grant, Blaine, and the Republican policy makers did not believe that such financial assistance was prohibited by the First Amendment.[20] In addition, the United States Supreme Court would not come to agree with that constitutional interpretation until the middle of the twentieth century.

In the closing years of the nineteenth century, about forty states adopted amendments to their state constitutions which were similar in intent and structure to Representative Blaine's federal proposal, and these amendments are still commonly referred to as "Blaine Amendments." These amendments or revisions of them, remain in about thirty state constitutions at this time and make the separation of church and state explicit in those state constitutions, whereas it is only implicit in the federal Constitution. In the intervening years a number of states have modified these amendments or adopted some form of statutory provision permitting some form of financial assistance to private and religious schools and their students and staff. These most commonly include assistance to students in the form of transportation, loan of textbooks, provision of health, diagnostic, and remedial services, and some form of reimbursement for state mandated services. A valuable resource for such state regulation and assistance affecting private and religious schools can be found in the 1995 publication of the United States Department of Education's Office for Nonpublic Education: The Regulation of *Private Schools in America: A State-by-State Analysis.*

State policy decision makers continued their efforts to heavily regulate or even eliminate private and religious schools into the twentieth century. In 1923, the United States Supreme Court, in the case of *Meyer v. State of Nebraska*, overturned a Nebraska law that banned teaching in German as an unreasonable regulation of the curriculum of a private school. In 1925, the Supreme Court, in the landmark school case of *Pierce v. Society of Sisters*, overturned an Oregon state law which attempted to make it mandatory for children to attend public schools, thus establishing the right of private and religious schools to exist and of parents to select them if they so desired.[21]

General and Categorical Education Assistance

Beginning in the 1940s, a new era of controversy arose as numerous attempts were made to enact federal legislation to provide general financial assistance to elementary and secondary education. For almost twenty years these efforts, in 1949, 1950, 1961, and 1963, failed to pass in Congress, mainly because of two key issues: (1) whether aid should go to all schools or only public schools, and (2) how to deal with segregated schools. The USCC, and some other interested private school groups, used their influence during each of these debates to oppose all legislation excluding religious schools. A broad coalition of public school groups and the champions of absolute separation of church and state opposed all attempts to provide any such assistance. With that combination of forces, each of these attempts ended in defeat in Congress.

At the same time these general aid proposals were being defeated by these two major coalitions, each holding firmly to their position on assistance, some limited programs of educational assistance such as the National School Lunch Act of 1946 and the National Defense Education Act of 1958, did pass in Congress, and some other forms of limited or categorical assistance (already mentioned) were passed in some state legislatures. The two basic principles that led to the passage of these bills were: (1) to serve the broadest class of beneficiaries possible, without reference to religious affiliation, and (2) to examine the effects, so that the recipient of the assistance would be clearly identified, producing a situation where any benefit accruing to religious entities would result only from the private choice of the recipient.[22] Thus programs providing specific benefits to a specifically designated group of children, for example, educationally, economically, or physically disadvantaged—irrespective of the school he or she attended—would generally have a better chance of passing in the federal or state legislature and even more importantly, surviving an almost inevitable court challenge. This approach has been commonly identified as the "child benefit theory."

Members of Congress who supported this method sponsored by the USCC and other supporters of government assistance generally represented districts or states with large concentrations of Catholic school children and also represented areas with a strong union presence, other than the public education unions, where ethnic membership was high, as well as other religious groups interested in such funding. These members also generally held key positions of leadership in Congress and thus had the power to kill legislation or broker compromises that ensured fair treatment for students and teachers in Catholic and other private and religious schools.[23]

This coalition reached its full potential and success with the passage of the Elementary and Secondary Education Act of 1965 (ESEA), which was a major part of President Johnson's "Great Society." The compromise that the USCC and its allies worked out during this debate, against significant opposition from most of the public school and church separationist groups, included the requirement that the assistance given be focused on a specific group of eligible children, the educationally disadvantaged; that Congress was acting to address unmet national needs which could not be met by states and local agencies; and final control and responsibility for administration of the program of services and funding was placed in the public sector.[24] This program and the basic compromise that forged it has lasted due to a generally bipartisan base of support in the numerous revisions and extensions over almost thirty years. This was clearly evident in the 1988 reauthorization of ESEA, where Congress added provisions aimed at helping to restore program participation levels and quality of services to religious school children after the 1985 Supreme Court decision of *Aguilar v. Felton* that removed public school teachers under Title I of ESEA from delivering remedial services on the premises of religious schools.[25] The most recent reauthorization in 1994 showed for the first time some significant shifting in the coalition support, when some public school groups struggled to shift the delivery of services from students who were educationally disadvantaged to those who were poor.

Parental Choice Options

Beginning in the 1960s, the policy issue that would dominate the educational public policy debate for the foreseeable future focused on how to provide financial assistance to parents so that they would be better able to choose the education they believed to be best suited to the needs of their children, including the option of private and religious schools, as a matter of justice. These efforts initially focused on tuition tax credits or deductions, later on some form of voucher initiative.

Tuition Tax Credits/Deductions

Initially the tuition tax credit proposals put forward were aimed at benefiting parents with children in higher education. Each time these proposals were made, an attempt was made by USCC to add parents with children in elementary and secondary schools to the list of beneficiaries, but none of these attempts were successful. Again, as in the case of attempts to pass general education assistance, the failure to include parents of elementary and secondary school parents would produce a final vote in each case that was a defeat for the tax credit proposal. Beginning in the 1970s, a series of tuition tax credit bills including parents of children in private and religious elementary and secondary schools were introduced in the Congress. The opposition to these attempts would focus on issues of the danger to the principles of separation of church and state, that no "public" funds should be used for "private" and especially religious schools that were elitist and did not serve all the children, the serious threat that such aid would pose to the future funding and ultimate long-range security of the public schools, and finally the disastrous effect this expenditure would have on the condition of the federal budget.

Both President Nixon and the Democratic candidate, Senator McGovern, endorsed this aid concept in the 1972 Presidential campaign. In 1976, the Republican platform supported tax credits for colleges and "consideration of tax benefits for private elementary schools" while the Democratic platform stated that the party "Renews its commitment to the support of a constitutionally acceptable method of providing tax aid for the education of all pupils in non-segregated schools."[26] Similar statements would remain in the platforms of the two major parties in the next three presidential election years. In 1980, candidate Reagan openly supported tuition tax credit aid to private school parents while President Carter did not. Reagan clearly sought support from those groups, especially the Catholic education community, who supported such endeavors. But all efforts to enact such legislation during the Reagan Administration was unsuccessful. Opposition continued from the groups consistently opposed to any such aid, but major factors contributing to the failure of this effort were political naiveté on the part of the tax credit supporters, who took the Reagan Administration's verbal support as firm and consistent when there was no total commitment to the proposal; the inability of the supporters to mobilize a consistent lobbying effort to overcome the opposition, even though the USCC established an office specifically aimed at such an effort (after convening a broad-based committee to address this and similar public policy issues affecting Catholic schools); and finally, the poor condition of the economy in the early years of the new administration, which highlighted budget problems that might be exacerbated by the passage of such proposals. In the 1992 Democratic platform, all references to aid to private schools were eliminated and the language clearly expressed opposition to the concept of such assistance. Language was inserted that endorsed the support of public education only, a clear sign of the increasing power of the public school lobby within that party.

The history of the decades-long federal tuition tax credit battles, all of which ended in defeat, is covered extensively in Sister Dale McDonald's 1995 doctoral dissertation: "Toward Full and Fair

Choice: An Historical Analysis of the Lobbying Efforts of the Catholic School Community in Pursuing Federal Tax-Supported Choice in Education, 1972–1992."[27]

During this same time the Minnesota legislature considered and passed legislation that allowed taxpayers in the state to deduct from their gross incomes expenses, including but not limited to tuition, incurred in the education of their children. This tax deduction legislation was challenged in the courts and in 1983, the United States Supreme Court, in the case of *Mueller v. Allen*, issued a ruling that upheld the constitutionality of the law based on the fact that the benefit was available to all taxpayers who had such expenses, thus providing a constitutionally acceptable blueprint for obtaining tax assistance for parents of children in private and religious schools in the future.[28] After this decision it might have been expected that a rash of such legislation would be proposed and enacted across the country, but the reality is that only Iowa was successful in pursuing this approach to financial assistance, and their legislative success was in the form of a tax credit for education-related expenses. The opponents of a tax-based form of assistance for parents of children in private and religious schools did not disappear even when the benefit was extended to all parents, public, private and religious.

The state of Vermont allows for state aid to be used to pay tuition by parents who have children in approved independent schools. Generally, if the school district does not maintain an elementary or high school, the voters may allow the school board to pay tuition at approved independent schools or at a public school in another jurisdiction. The benefit on the high school level can even be applied to schools located out of state. Vermont also allows for tuition reimbursement to sectarian schools.

In addition to these forms of tuition reimbursement, there are a number of other proposals to revise the tax code, especially on the federal level, that have been discussed and submitted to Congress. These include the children's tax credit proposed in the Republicans' "Contract with America," a bipartisan group of proposals that would create a significant increase in the deduction that can be taken for each dependent; President Clinton's proposed higher education tuition tax credit, which once again the USCC has suggested be expanded to include elementary and secondary school children; and, of course, the general education tax credit or deduction. Some of these proposals are specifically aimed at an education-related expense (tuition tax credit/deduction or education tax credit) while others are more general in nature (general child tax credit or general increase in the dependent deduction). It seems most important that each would provide a broad based tax benefit irregardless of the school a child attends and the benefits to varying degrees would provide a financial benefit that would allow parents more freedom to choose an educational option for their children which they might otherwise not be able to make.

Parental Educational Choice Vouchers/Scholarships

In the 1980s, the attempt to obtain some form of federal or state assistance for parents with children in private and religious schools shifted to some form of educational choice voucher or scholarship. The concept of using a voucher to cover educational expenses is not an idea new to this age or country. It can be found in the writings of a number of major thinkers over the last 200 years, including Adam Smith, Thomas Paine, John Stuart Mill and Milton Friedman. The basic idea behind these proposals is to help make the option of educational choice more affordable for all parents wherever they choose to send their children to school.

One of the initial voucher proposals put forward was a USCC suggestion, after the *Aguilar v. Felton* decision, to have local educational agencies offer parents of Title I students a voucher equal to the cost of the Title I services so that they could purchase the services from a public, private, or religious provider and receive the services in the religious school. This proposal was rejected by voucher opponents and the compromise was the creation of the "Capital Expense" funding procedure. Success finally came when Congress passed the Child Care Development and Block Grant Act of 1990, and for the first time the Congress provided a form of direct assistance to parents in the form of a "certificate" which could be used to pay for child care services in a variety of agencies including those that might be found in a church or religiously affiliated educational institution. This service is really a mixed education and social service approach. As has happened so many times before in major pieces of legislation, in order to obtain final passage for such a significant and precedent setting approach to funding, a compromise had to be found. The basis for this compromise was that a major percentage of child care providers were to be found only in a center-based provider system historically dominated by religiously affiliated agencies of a wide variety of denominations and the overall success of any child-care proposal could not be obtained if the religiously affiliated agencies were going to be eliminated. Therefore, religiously affiliated child care programs that could meet minimal state standards related to health and safety would be eligible to participate in the program.

In the 1990s the United States Senate has had the opportunity to debate and vote on the proposal to provide a limited educational voucher demonstration program in order to test the viability of such a proposal. On three different occasions these demonstration proposals were introduced and defeated in votes in the U.S. Senate. The public school lobby in Washington has engaged in a long and often acrimonious attack on the voucher concept in a major political effort to defeat each of these proposals. Over the course of these debates and votes, the number of votes cast in the Senate in favor of the proposals rose from an initial 36 votes to the most recent vote of 46 in the 103rd Congress. The House of Representatives had never had the opportunity to vote on any type of voucher demonstration project until the 104th Congress. During the long debate over the federal budget, the House Republican leadership developed an educational reform proposal for the District of Columbia which included, among other things, a low income tuition scholarship proposal. This proposal would have allowed low income parents with children in the D.C. public schools to use the scholarships, worth up to a possible $3,000, to move to other public or private and religious schools. This proposal also required a report on the impact of the scholarship program, a part of the bill similar to the earlier Senate demonstration proposals. The proposal was attached to a D.C. appropriations bill and it passed the House toward the end of the first session in late 1995. The Senate version of the D.C. appropriations bill did not contain a similar proposal, so the bill was referred to a Senate/House conference committee where it underwent some modifications. The conference committee report went back to the House where it was acted upon on the day it was received, and the revised bill passed. After some weeks delay, the Senate conference leadership moved to end the debate with a cloture vote and that cloture attempt failed to get the necessary three-fifths majority (i.e., 60 votes) on a vote of 54 to 44. The future of the D.C. reform proposal, the educational scholarship proposal, and the total D.C. appropriations bill is still undecided. Again the public school lobby vigorously opposed the passage of any proposal that included a parental choice proposal, even one limited to the poor in one district and one where the District of Columbia City Council had a veto right over the implementation of the scholarship program. Opponents of the voucher concept regard the passage of any voucher proposal as a major threat, the impact of which will be felt far beyond the single case in question, since it might open the way to additional voucher proposals on the federal and/or state level.

The 104th Congress has other educational choice demonstration projects pending before it. A similarly worded choice demonstration project has been introduced in the Senate by Senators Coats and Lieberman, and in the House by Representatives Weldon and Riggs. A second demonstration proposal with a larger dollar authorization has been introduced in the Senate by Senator Abraham. None of these proposals has yet been scheduled for a vote in either house of Congress but they may become part of the education debate leading up to and through the 1996 presidential election campaign.

Educational voucher proposals have been introduced in a number of state legislatures and in the form of statewide ballot initiatives over the last decade. At the present time such voucher proposals have been adopted in only two states, Wisconsin and Ohio, and in the territory of Puerto Rico. The first voucher proposal to pass a state legislature was in Wisconsin; this was limited to one section of the Milwaukee school district and vouchers could be redeemed only in nonsectarian private schools. The law was challenged in court and its constitutionality was upheld. In 1995, the Wisconsin legislature amended the law increasing the number of vouchers available and, beginning with the 1995–1996 school year, allowing the redemption of the voucher in sectarian schools in Milwaukee. Once again the law has been challenged in Court. The Wisconsin State Supreme Court issued an injunction staying implementation of the law as it affects sectarian schools. Since the injunction was issued after children had been accepted into schools a group of business leaders and charitable trusts raised sufficient funds to pay the tuition of those children who had anticipated receiving educational vouchers to cover their tuition. The hearing on that injunction was scheduled for February 27, 1996.

The second voucher bill to pass was in Puerto Rico and this allowed students to use vouchers to move from public to private, private to public, public to public, and also to newly established charter schools. The law was challenged under the Puerto Rico Constitution with regard to use of vouchers in religious schools and the Supreme Court of Puerto Rico ruled the law unconstitutional. It is not clear as to whether further voucher attempts will be made in Puerto Rico.

The third voucher bill was passed in 1995 in Ohio and applies only to the Cleveland school district. The law was scheduled to go into effect at the beginning of the 1996–1997 school year. Shortly after the process was initiated to accept applications for this program, the teachers unions and others filed suit to stop implementation of the law. No court decision has been issued on the status of this law.

In these voucher debates, the opposition has focused on many of the same arguments that they have used against other attempts to provide financial assistance to parents with children in private and religious schools. The opposition in this case seems to view the voucher proposal as a greater threat than earlier tax-based proposals. This may be a product of the current political atmosphere where the concern over the general state of public education has raised numerous questions and legislative proposals to reform this system of education. This may also be the time that opponents feel that the votes to pass such a proposal are present on the federal and/or state level, where new Republican majorities may be found, although this is not necessarily a given fact. Another factor may be a perception that a positive decision on a voucher proposal is possible if a case gets to the current Supreme Court. This fear has been heightened by comments from some more liberal legal experts that a carefully worded voucher proposal may well be constitutional. Another general fear of many of the opponents of such legislation is that, with the increasing trend toward educational privatization, the voucher movement may get carried along with it. All of these considerations help to explain the presence of vigorous and often increasingly hostile opposition to any proposal on the federal or state level to initiate a voucher form of assistance to parents. The tone of the opposition's rhetoric in any jurisdiction from the east coast to the west coast that has considered such a proposal has become increasing heated. Major public campaigns to defeat voucher legislation and voter initiatives have been launched by opponents, most especially the National Education Association and other public school groups, in places as diverse as California, Oregon, Pennsylvania, Connecticut, and New Jersey.

Other Public Policy Issues

Two other public policy issues that are raising serious education questions are the condition of the economy and, most specifically, the pressures on the federal and state level of budget restraints, and the not-so-totally-new concept being advanced in the Republican dominated Congress to "Block Grant"numerous federal programs, including many education-related programs.

The budget/deficit problem raises questions about how viable any proposal is that suggests that funds be set aside to provide assistance to parents with children in private and religious schools. This situation also raises the question of how much funding will be available to continue existing programs and services to needy students, including those in public, private, or religious schools. In some of these situations the public and private school communities which share the benefits of such programs, whether the benefits are remedial or in the form of curriculum enhancement materials or professional development, have formed temporary coalitions to retain such benefits. This is the type of dialogue and cooperation that ought to bind these groups more closely together. Once the perception is given that someone will lose something that the other group might not lose, the cooperation can easily fall apart.

The concept of using Block Grants to fund federal programs which deliver services to students, including those who attend private and religious schools, carries some major problems with it. Beginning with the school lunch legislation which was passed in the 1940s, and through the passage of ESEA in 1965 to the Improving America's Schools Act of 1994, Congress has followed the suggestions of the USCC and other involved private school groups to provide explicit statutory language to assure the equitable participation of private and religious school children and staff in legislation offering benefits to students. This language is necessary to address the delivery of services to students and staff residing in states with "Blaine Amendments," as well as to deal with the opponents of this assistance who will use the restrictive state law provisions in court challenges. The explicit statutory language needs to assure: (1) the equitable participation of private and religious school students and staff; (2) that assistance goes to the students and staff, not to schools; (3) that funds should supplement and not be commingled with state funds; (4) that federal pre-exemption of state laws limiting the participation of students and staff in religiously oriented schools is provided; and (5) that provision is made for by-pass language that allows the appropriate secretary to provide the required services to private and religious school students where state and local governmental agencies fail or are unwilling to provide such services made available under the law.

Conclusion

Public policy decisions and the debates that lead to them, whether they take place on the federal or state level, have and will continue to have impact on more than just the public school community. It is clear from our history and from the current social and political reality that these decisions also impact on private and religious schools. This has been a consistent lesson of our history. These policy decisions include, but are not limited to, such questions as: whether private and religious schools can exist; whether parents have the freedom and the financial wherewithal to choose them; how those schools, their students, and staff are regulated; the number of days a school must function in a given year; and whether students and staff in private and religious schools will receive benefits and services that they would receive without question if they were in a public school. It is not accurate to say that only public schools are accountable to the government and society. Federal and state regulation of private and religious schools can readily be documented. Education reform efforts in our country have an effect, intended or not, on all schools, including private and religious schools.

Private and religious schools clearly add to the history, tone, and texture of our diverse society and serve the common good. Many private and religious schools, especially in the inner cities of our nation, offer significant financial and educational benefits to those who are the most disadvantaged, and this is often done at a significant human and economic cost to the supporting private and religious communities.

Public policy decisions affecting educational institutions should always be made with the participation of all the school communities that will be affected. Those communities include the parents and the professional staff members. When committees and commissions are established to review issues of interest relating to the education of our children, these communities should be included, with a representation reflective of their presence in and contribution to the well-being of the community. Such an approach seems only a matter of common sense and justice.

The entire educational community in the United States, public, private, and religious, can best address its challenges if all its segments join with government policymakers in a collaborative and constructive dialogue aimed at attaining the common goal of a quality education for all of our nation's children and maintaining the unique diversity and the special nature of our respective educational and school communities. The country cannot afford to see that project negatively affected by an approach that limits the input to public policymaking in education to only one segment of the educational community.

Notes

1. Harold A. Buetow, *Of Singular Benefit: The Story of U.S. Catholic Education* (New York: Macmillan, Co.), 43.
2. Ibid., 3.
3. Martha M. McCarthy, *A Delicate Balance: Church, State and Schools* (Bloomington, Ind.: Phil Delta Kappa Educational Foundation), 5.
4. Otto F. Kraushaar, *American Nonpublic Schools: Patterns of Diversity* (Baltimore: Johns Hopkins University Press), 20.
5. Harold A. Buetow, *A History of United States Catholic Schooling* (Washington, D.C.: National Catholic Educational Association), 14.
6. Kraushaar, *American Nonpublic Schools,* 20.
7. Dale McDonald, "Toward Full and Fair Choice: An Historical Analysis of the Lobbying Efforts of the Catholic School Community in Pursuing Federal Tax-Supported Choice in Education, 1972–1992" (Ph.D. diss., Boston College, 1995), 1.
8. Ibid., 3.

9. Amy S. Wells and Stuart Biegel, "Public Funds for Private Schools: Political and First Amendment Consideration," *American Journal of Education,* May 1993, 3.
10. Kraushaar, *American Nonpublic Schools,* 21.
11. Jay P. Dolan, *The American Catholic Experience* (Garden City, N.Y.: Image Books), 226.
12. Kraushaar, *American Nonpublic Schools,* 21.
13. McCarthy, *A Delicate Balance,* 7.
14. James C. Carper, "The Christian Day School," in *Religious Schooling in America,* ed. James C. Carper and Thomas C. Hunt (Birmingham, Ala.: Religious Education Press), 115.
15. United States Catholic Conference, *Political Responsibility: Proclaiming the Gospel of Life, Protecting the Least among Us, and Pursuing the Common Good* (Washington, D.C.: United States Catholic Conference, 1995); United States Catholic Conference, *Principles for Educational Reform in the United States* (Washington, D.C.: United States Catholic Conference, 1995).
16. Edward McGlynn Gaffney, ed., *Private Schools and the Common Good* (Notre Dame, Ind.: University of Notre Dame Press), xxv.
17. United States Catholic Conference, *Principles for Educational Reform in the United States* (Washington, D.C.: United States Catholic Conference), 3.
18. Ibid., 3.
19. Dolan, *The American Catholic Experience,* 270.
20. James Hennessey, *American Catholic: A History of the Roman Catholic Community in the United States* (New York: Oxford University Press), 185.
21. *Meyer* v. *State of Nebraska,* 262 U.S. 390 (1923); *Pierce v. Society of Sisters,* 268 U.S. 510 (1925).
22. Wells and Biegel, "Public Funds," 6.
23. Frank J. Monahan, "Political Climate in the United States," Unpublished speech delivered at the meeting of the National Association of Catholic School Parents and Alumni, New York, May 23, 1987, 3.
24. Ibid., 5.
25. *Aguilar v. Felton,* 105 S. Ct. 3232 (1985).
26. McDonald, "Toward Full and Fair Choice," 127.
27. Ibid., 1.
28. Frank J. Monahan, *Non-Public Schools and Public Policy: The Past, Present and Perhaps the Future* (Washington, D.C.: National Catholic Educational Association), 25.

Chapter Eight
Mission and Money
Religious Schools and Their Finances

Michael J. Guerra

I. Introduction

"Mission is more important than money, but—no money, no mission." A Catholic high school president offered this justification for the substantial time and effort he gave to financial management and fund-raising on behalf of his school. Like many of his colleagues in other religious schools, he saw his work as an integral part of his church's mission, in effect, as God's business. But he also believed he was called to do God's business in a businesslike way, and he made no apology for linking his institution's spiritual mission to his responsibility to provide material resources.

There are important differences among religious educators in their understanding of how their particular religious communities relate to the larger society. Historically, one barometer of relationships between church and civic communities has been the involvement of the church in building and supporting its own schools. The initial impulse to provide religious schools is often driven by a conviction that passing on the religious community's faith and culture to succeeding generations would be difficult if not impossible without schools that articulate and honor its values. Arguably, the greater the perceived gap between the values of the religious community and the values of the larger civic community, the stronger the commitment to provide religious schools. When Catholics felt especially threatened by a hostile nativist America in the mid-nineteenth century, their bishops endorsed an ambitious effort to provide Catholic schools.[1] While that effort never reached its goal of a school for every parish and a seat in the school for every Catholic child, it did produce an extensive network of schools that currently educates more than 2.5 million students in some 8,000 Catholic elementary and secondary schools.

Even without the benefit of the documented national consensus developed by the Catholic bishops' Council of Baltimore in 1884, the recent growth of new religious schools suggests that during the last half of the twentieth century other religious communities were responding to an increasingly secular culture which they perceived to be hostile to their religious values by opening schools. Data collected by the National Center for Educational Statistics (NCES) show that half or more Catholic schools, Lutheran schools of the Missouri Synod, and Friends schools have been operating for more than forty-five years. On the other hand, most Hebrew schools and conservative Christian schools were established after 1960.

Perceptions of a culture that is unsympathetic to religious faith and values may play a significant role in motivating churches to open schools, but the history of religious schooling suggests a more complex set of

Table 8.1. Percentage of Private Schools in Existence in 1990–1991 Established Prior to Dates from 1900 to 1990 by Affiliation

	Before 1900	Before 1910	Before 1920	Before 1930	Before 1940	Before 1950	Before 1960	Before 1970	Before 1980
Total Private	11.9	16.7	20.8	28.7	31.7	37.6	52.4	68.9	88.1
Catholic	17.1	25.5	31.6	46.1	50.5	58.7	78.9	94.3	97.6
Episcopal	14.3	15.5	16.1	20.8	21.3	28.2	47.9	74.9	91.3
Friends	44.2	48.3	48.3	48.3	48.3	50.2	54.3	64.4	78.0
Seventh Day Adventist	3.8	9.2	15.7	19.5	23.4	26.8	47.4	58.3	62.9
Hebrew Day	0.0	0.0	0.0	1.0	1.0	13.5	26.7	54.4	90.0
Solomon Schechter	0.0	0.0	0.0	0.0	0.0	11.0	21.5	47.7	79.1
Other Jewish	0.7	0.7	0.7	1.9	1.9	13.2	26.1	56.7	74.9
Christian Schools Int'l.	4.9	9.2	22.4	29.3	30.7	42.0	52.2	64.3	87.1
Assoc. of Christian Schools Int'l	0.0	0.5	0.5	2.4	2.4	5.1	9.5	18.8	65.6
Lutheran, Missouri Synod	31.8	35.8	40.9	45.8	49.8	57.6	68.7	76.7	88.5
Lutheran, Wisconsin Synod	28.6	33.2	33.7	39.0	39.9	48.6	55.8	64.8	97.2
Evangelical Lutheran	8.5	9.4	9.4	11.2	11.2	19.7	31.0	57.9	85.6
Other Lutheran	—	—	—	—	—	—	—	—	97.8
Other religious	7.8	10.0	12.2	14.6	15.9	20.7	32.1	45.3	77.4
Conservative Christian	0.0	0.7	0.9	2.3	2.5	4.4	7.3	18.0	68.4
Affiliated	15.0	18.3	22.5	26.1	27.6	34.8	47.5	60.6	81.0
Unaffiliated	3.8	5.5	6.7	7.4	10.5	14.4	36.8	54.4	83.9

Source: United States Department of Education, Office of Educational Research and Improvement. *Private Schools in the United States: A Statistical Profile, 1990–91*. (National Center for Educational Statistics, Statistical Analysis Report, January 1995), p. 13.

Table 8.2. High School Seniors Reporting Community Service, 1990–1991

	Percent of All Seniors Performing Service			Of Seniors with No Required Service
		Any Service Required?		Percent Performing Some Service
School Type	*Total*	*Yes*	*No*	*Some Service*
Public	42.0	13.2	28.8	33.1
Catholic	66.7	45.1	21.4	39.0
Other private	56.7	21.1	35.0	44.3

Source: United States Department of Education, Office of Educational Research and Improvement, *Education Daily,* November 30, 1995, p. 6.

interests may sustain their educational efforts over time. If most religious communities share a common concern for passing their own faith and culture on to succeeding generations, many churches also incorporate an explicit commitment of service to the larger community as an integral part of their educational mission. Student service activities are honored in many religious schools, required in some, and many church-sponsored schools welcome students from other faiths.

While religious schools are often founded to protect a religious community's children from the larger community's values, in time these schools may come to see their mission in terms of serving the larger community precisely by challenging and transforming its values. The shift from protection to engagement described in the documents of a recent national symposium on Catholic schools contrasts sharply with the pastoral vision of the Catholic bishops who saw themselves as shepherds of an endangered flock a century earlier.

Catholic schools are deeply rooted in the life of the church, the body of Jesus Christ, who is the source of all life. Catholic schools draw their life's breath from their roots in the Catholic community and they, in turn, breathe new life into the church.[2]

Catholic schools are proud and productive partners in American education. At this moment in history, Catholic schools are no longer a small number of outposts offering separation and security in a hostile culture, but a vast network of institutions lighting the lives of the communities they serve in every corner of the land.[3]

Although leaders of religious schools are not driven by visions of increased profits or larger market-share, their schools represent a major business activity, educating more than 4 million students in more than 20,000 institutions. Using the current average per pupil cost of $6,084 in public education,[4] it would cost taxpayers more than $24 billion to educate these students in the nation's public schools. In addition to academic, civic, and moral contributions to the common good, religious schools also make a rather substantial financial contribution to the American educational enterprise.

Table 8.3. Percentage of Private Schools Charging Tuition, Percentage Allowing Tuition Reductions, and Average Tuitions in 1987–1988 and 1990–1991, by Level and Affiliation

	% Charging Tuition	% Allowing Reductions	Average Tuition					
			Elementary		Secondary		Combined	
	90–91	*90–91*	*87–88*	*90–91*	*87–88*	*90–91*	*87–88*	*90–91*
Total Private	94.5	85.6	$1,423	$1,780	$3,054	$4,395	$2,622	$3,524
Catholic	98.9	94.4	$981	$1,243	$2,026	$2,878	—	—
Episcopal	100.0	89.3	$2,615	$2,686	$6,088	$9,368	$5,022	$5,503
Friends	100.0	89.9	$3,379	$4,093	—	—	$6,207	$7,811
Seventh Day Adventist	98.9	95.2	$1,069	$1,280	$3,075	$3,557	$1,553	$1,989
Hebrew Day	100.0	96.9	$3,119	$3,895	$3,026	$4,730	$3,331	—
Solomon Schechter	100.0	95.5	$3,594	$4,419	—	—	—	—
Other Jewish	100.0	95.4	—	$4,200	—	$4,681	—	#,928
Christian Schools Int'l.	100.0	99.0	$1,762	$2,116	$2,488	$3,008	$2,224	$2,862
Assoc. of Christian Schools Int'l	99.9	93.7	$1,427	$1,866	$2,483	$2,831	$1,532	$1,827
Lutheran, Missouri Synod	98.1	93.5	$1,139	$1,824	—	$2,912	—	—
Lutheran, Wisconsin Synod	94.5	89.0	—	$1,020	—	—	—	—
Evangelical Lutheran	96.9	88.8	$1,293	$1,795	—	—	—	—
Other Lutheran	92.5	83.8	$713	$1,283	—	—	—	—
Catholic								
Parochial	98.6	94.3	$941	$1,210	$1,583	$2,944	—	—
Diocesan	99.5	97.2	$922	$1,213	$1,777	$2,364	—	—
Private Order	99.0	87.3	—	$1,995	$2,369	$3,378	—	—
Other religious								
Conservative Christian	95.4	92.0	$1,338	$1,738	$3,418	$4,039	$1,506	$2,037
Affiliated	98.2	93.2	$1,399	$1,932	$3,618	$4,215	$2,122	$2,295
Unaffiliated	84.2	70.6	$1,377	$1,326	—	$4,365	$1,688	$2,625

Source: United States Department of Education, Office of Educational Research and Improvement. *Private Schools in the United States: A Statistical Profile, 1990–91.* (National Center for Educational Statistics, Statistical Analysis Report, January 1995), p. 17.

Table 8.4. Average Percentage of School Revenue from Various Sources

Source	% Total Revenue
Tuition and Fees	52.0
School Fund-raising	10.0
Endowment	2.0
Parish Subsidy	35.0
Other	2.0

Source: Robert Kealey, Balance Sheet for Catholic Elementary Schools: 1993 Income and Expenses, (National Catholic Educational Association, 1994), p. 15.

Income

Tuition is the primary source of income for virtually all religious schools. There are significant variations in tuition rates among religious schools, and between elementary and secondary schools within religious communities. Generally, Episcopal and Friends schools have the highest tuitions, while Catholic elementary, Seventh Day Adventist and Lutheran schools have the lowest tuitions. The latest comprehensive figures collected and published by the U.S. Department of Education are provided in Table 8.3.

More recent data from national associations of religious schools provide little or no evidence of substantial increases in tuition levels since 1991 and offer additional information about other sources of revenue for church sponsored schools. Some churches provide substantial congregational support for schools, while others expect schools to pay their own way. Most schools generate additional non-tuition income through fund-raising and development efforts.

In 1993 the average tuition for a Catholic elementary school was $1,152, and represented about half of the school's operating income. Direct parish support provided about one third of the school's income, with the balance generated by school-based development and fund-raising activity.

For Catholic high schools, the average tuition in 1994 was $3,316. During the past ten years tuition revenue in Catholic high schools has remained around 75 percent of total operating income. The balance of school income was generated by a growing development and fund-raising effort (15 percent), and a diminishing subsidy, a portion of which represented the contributed services of sisters, priests, and brothers whose compensation remained marginally lower than lay teachers. Staffing the classrooms of Catholic schools with religious personnel who were given housing and other non-cash support in addition to modest stipends paid to their religious communities, once the norm, is now the exception. In 1965, religious personnel represented a majority of all Catholic school teachers. Today lay teachers represent 90 percent of the more than 164,000 men and women teaching in Catholic elementary and secondary schools. As a result, contributed services no longer represent a substantial source of support for most Catholic schools. While the shift to lay teachers had significant economic consequences for Catholic schools, at this point virtually all Catholic schools have substantially reduced their dependence on contributed services to balance their operating budgets. The transition to lay staffing represented a major fiscal challenge for Catholic schools, but it is a challenge that is largely behind them.

For Seventh Day Adventist schools, relatively low tuitions are supplemented by relatively high levels of church support at both the local and regional conference levels. The church encourages its members to tithe, and commits 21 percent of all tithing income to support church-sponsored educational institutions at all levels.[5]

Lutheran schools vary in the levels of support provided to schools by congregations. For schools sponsored by congregations affiliated with the Lutheran Church-Missouri Synod, tuition represents half the income of a typical elementary school, with the balance coming from congregational support. For high schools, tuition and fees represent about 60 percent of income, and congregational support 15 percent. The balance, 25 percent, is generated from other sources.[6] Schools associated with the Evangelical Lutheran Church in America draw about 95 percent of their income from tuition and fees, with the balance coming largely from development and fund-raising activities. Subsidies from congregations are relatively uncommon.[7]

Many of the newly formed evangelical Christian schools are funded almost entirely by relatively modest tuitions. These schools vary substantially in enrollments, and annual tuitions vary from about $1,500 in the newer and smaller schools that constitute the majority to about $4,000 in older and larger schools.[8]

Christian Schools International, representing an older community of Christian schools, describes 90 percent of its member schools as private, governed by boards elected by associations of Christian parents; 10 percent are parochial schools in which church boards typically appoint the school boards that run the schools. Virtually all schools charge a tuition that often matches full per pupil cost. Non-tuition revenues which stood at 25 percent of total income a generation earlier are at 15 percent and slipping, as tuitions increase. Non-tuition income is generated by each school's development efforts, which include annual drives, auctions, and appeals to foundations and businesses.[9]

Expenses

Per Pupil Costs

Like all schools, the operating costs of religiously sponsored schools are driven largely by the levels of compensation provided for teachers and administrators. For example, personnel costs represent about 75 percent of the total operating expenses of the average Catholic high school. The average per pupil cost for a Catholic secondary school was $4,541 in 1994.[10] A year earlier, the average per pupil cost for a Catholic elementary school was $2,044.[11]

Reports available from other church groups reflect similar cost structures. Schools sponsored by congregations of the Lutheran Church-Missouri Synod reported per pupil costs that averaged $2,100 for elementary schools and $4,500 for secondary schools. Evangelical Lutheran schools reported average per pupil costs of $2,200 for elementary schools, $3,800 for high schools. Given their higher tuitions, it is reasonable to assume that operating costs also run substantially higher in Episcopal, Friends, and Hebrew schools, but their combined enrollments represent a relatively small portion of the religious school sector (cf. Table 8.3). On average, current per pupil costs for all religiously affiliated elementary schools fall between $2,000 and $2,500; the average for secondary schools, between $4,500 and $5,000.

Compensation

The importance of the teaching staff could hardly be understated in schools that have a religious as well as an academic mission. If teachers are the heart of every school, teachers are surely the heart and soul of the religiously sponsored school. Church groups differ in their approaches to teacher recruitment and certification. While only a handful of states have explicit certification requirements for private school teachers, three quarters of the teachers in Catholic schools are certified in their main field.[12] Many Christian educators see teaching as a special ministry within the church and provide their own licensing procedures to certify those who will function in a ministerial capacity as teachers and administrators. Seventh Day Adventists have developed a ceremony for teachers that is similar to their ordination rites for pastors. Interestingly, salaries for pastors and teachers in the Seventh Day Adventist community are essentially the same. Although the church accepts students from non-member families who acknowledge and accept the school's religious identity, only members of the church may serve as teachers.

Compensation for teachers in religiously sponsored schools typically follows the patterns found in other schools. Salaries are based largely on academic preparation and years of teaching experience. In most settings, teachers' salaries in religious schools lag behind public school teachers' salaries by margins ranging from 10 percent to 50 percent. Greater gaps at median and maximum salaries reflect relatively higher turnover rates in these schools. Variations in years of teaching experience and movement of teachers between private and public schools was summarized by a U.S. Department of Education report in 1995.

> *. . . 53 percent of private school teachers had fewer than 10 years' experience, compared to 36 percent for public school teachers. Substantial amounts of movement between public and private teaching markets occur, and it would appear that teachers are more likely to take jobs in private schools early in their careers than late. In 1988, about 9,500 private school teachers transferred to public schools, and about 5,800 teachers transferred from public to private schools (Rollefson 1993). Conservative Christian and other religiously oriented but unaffiliated schools are especially open to new and inexperienced teachers, employing teachers in 1990—almost a quarter of whom had less than 3 years' teaching experience and two-thirds of whom had fewer than 10 years' experience. On average, teachers at Catholic private-order and Missouri Synod Lutheran schools, at the other extreme, had amounts of teaching experiences similar to public school teachers.*[13]

The same report provides salary data for 1988 and 1991. To put the 1991 numbers in perspective, the average public school teacher's salary that year was $30,751.

More recent data from several national organizations make it possible to see some of the differences between elementary and secondary school salaries, and to describe the range of salaries within particular religiously sponsored school groups. In spite of the variations in reporting formats and schedules, the data provide a basis for some general comparisons.

Catholic elementary schools reported an average teacher's salary of $19,132 in 1993. During that year the average starting salary

Table 8.5. Teachers' Salaries and Job Satisfaction Ratings in 1987–1988 and 1990–1991, by Affiliation

	Base Salary		Extra Salary		Rating on Teach Again?		Rating on Satisfaction
	87–88	*90–91*	*87–88*	*90–91*	*87–88*	*90–91*	*90–91*
Catholic	$14,415	$18,347	$352	$1,629	6.7	7.1	8.4
Episcopal	$17,415	$21,522	$174	$3,503	6.6	6.9	8.7
Friends	$16,870	$23,499	$765	—	7.5	6.8	8.3
Seventh Day Adventist	$19,946	$22,287	$223	—	6.3	6.2	7.9
Hebrew Day	$17,383	$19,273	$728	—	6.0	6.4	8.3
Solomon Schechter	$17,769	$19,354	$292	—	4.9	6.5	8.4
Other Jewish	—	$15,911	—	—	—	7.1	8.7
Christian Schools Int'l.	$18,026	$18,293	$403	$1,086	6.8	7.9	8.8
Assoc. of Christian Schools Int'l	$11,402	$14,699	$522	$1,247	7.9	8.4	8.8
Lutheran, Missouri Synod	$15,491	$17,751	$388	$1,571	7.0	7.4	8.3
Lutheran, Wisconsin Synod	—	$17,330	—	—	7.5	8.2	
Evangelical Lutheran	$10,988	$18,734	—	$1,074	8.9	7.8	8.7
Other Lutheran	$13,590	$16,569	$314	—	7.3	8.8	9.2
Catholic	$14,437	$18,347	$353	$1,629	6.7	7.1	8.4
Parochial	$13,614	$16,324	$186	$1,636	6.9	7.3	8.5
Diocesan	$14,386	$17,994	$454	$1,363	6.3	7.3	8.4
Private Order	$17,342	$24,359	$811	$1,907	6.7	6.6	8.3
Other religious	$13,956	$16,431	$361	$1,748	7.3	7.5	8.5
Conservative Christian	$10,981	$14,048	$384	$1,684	7.8	8.0	8.7
Affiliated	$16,229	$18,160	$355	$1,898	7.0	7.2	8.4
Unaffiliated	$13,657	$16,674	$339	$1,371	6.9	7.4	8.3

Source: United States Department of Education, Office of Educational Research and Improvement. *Private Schools in the United States: A Statistical Profile, 1990–91.* (National Center for Educational Statistics, Statistical Analysis Report, January 1995), p. 69.

was $15,676, and the average lay principal's salary was $32,160.[14] Catholic secondary schools reported the median teacher's salary was $26,800 in 1994. In the same year starting salaries for teachers in Catholic high schools averaged $19,000, and maximum salaries averaged $34,400. The average lay principal's salary was $51,000.[15]

Schools sponsored by the Lutheran Church-Missouri Synod reported the average salary for all teachers in 1995 was $21,027, and the average for all administrators was $25,146. When high school teachers are considered separately, their average salary increases to $23,733, revealing a much smaller gap between Lutheran elementary and secondary teachers than the 40 percent gap between Catholic elementary and secondary school teachers. Catholic and Lutheran parochial schools are largely decentralized, and salaries vary by region and congregation. The $21,000 average reported for Lutheran school teachers in 1995 includes wide variations that range from a low of $59 (a volunteer?) to a high of $51,000.[16]

Seventh Day Adventist Conferences set wage scales for all school personnel within a region. The Columbia Union Conference, which includes Delaware, the District of Columbia, Maryland, New Jersey, Ohio, Pennsylvania, Virginia, and West Virginia, set 1995 salaries for new teachers at $22,008 for a ten-month commitment. Underscoring their vision of the central importance of the teacher, these schools will pay a new principal $22,212 for a ten-month commitment. In the same region a teacher with an M.A., appropriate certification and six years' experience earned $32,136. Seventh Day Adventists are also committed to a strong benefits package for all their teachers. The package includes a fully-funded medical plan, a non-contributory retirement plan, and substantial tuition reductions for faculty children attending a Seventh Day Adventist college.[17]

Christian Schools International (CSI) reports that salary levels are recommended by the national organization and set by the local church groups. In 1995, CSI recommended a starting salary of $24,171, and a maximum of $41,000. Local salaries averaged $20,164 to start, with $32,312 as the average maximum.[18]

The Association of Christian Schools International (ACSI), representing about 3,000 conservative evangelical schools, reports average starting salaries for teachers fall generally between $15,000 and

$18,000. Administrators in the smaller schools that constitute the majority are offered starting salaries in the $25,000 range.[19]

The evidence over time suggests that school leaders recognize that a committed and stable faculty is the key to the successful accomplishment of the school's mission, and they are making the improvement of teachers' salaries a priority. Acknowledging differences in the timing and format of the financial data generated by these national organizations, the salaries they report leave little doubt that most teachers in religious schools are not motivated by the promise of a handsome compensation package.

Since the majority of religious schools are parochial, that is, sponsored by a particular church, there are also substantial variations within groups. Nevertheless, with few exceptions, teachers and principals in religious schools earn considerably less than their counterparts in most public and many non-sectarian schools. For principals, salary differences do not appear to be related to differences in years of administrative experience.

Committed religious educators often explain the motivation that draws teachers to accept modest salaries in religious terms, describing them as "called to the ministry of teaching." But others have questioned the extent to which mandatory certification requirements limit access to better paying jobs in public education, making a faculty appointment in a religious school the only option, rather than the preferred choice for some teachers. Some have suggested that private schools in general, and religious schools in particular, offer disciplined environments that support teaching and learning, and that climates conducive to teaching and learning play a large part in attracting and holding teachers in religious schools. The National Center for Educational Statistics spent some time and considerable statistical creativity in an examination of the interplay among these factors, and came to the conclusion that, while these issues explain some of the motivations of teachers in religious schools, they do not tell the entire story. Here, with its customary cautions and caveats, is the Center's summary of the untitled force that eluded its sophisticated statistical measures.

In summary, public school teachers earn substantially higher salaries than private school teachers. To some degree, these differences can be explained by differences in the characteristics of public and private school teachers that are rewarded by public and private school decision makers. Moreover, to some degree, these differences in earnings may be attrib-

Table 8.6. Principals' Experience in Teaching and Administering, and Salary in 1987–1988 and 1990–1991, by Affiliation

	Number of Principals		Yrs. Teaching		Yrs. Principal at School		Yrs. Principal Elsewhere		Salary	
	87–88	*90–91*	*87–88*	*90–91*	*87–88*	*90–91*	*87–88*	*90–91*	*87–88*	*90–91*
Total Private	25,401	23,881	9.7	9.4	5.1	5.5	2.9	3.2	$18,716	$25,562
Total Public	77,890	78,890	9.3	10.5	6.2	5.7	3.7	3.6	$40,809	$49,603
Catholic	9,211	8,098	14.0	13.7	4.7	4.7	4.0	4.3	$15,673	$21,840
Episcopal	315	367	11.1	11.1	4.7	5.8	3.0	3.4	$32,381	$38,327
Friends	74	54	8.7	9.9	6.6	5.5	0.8	2.1	$33,584	$44,275
Seventh Day Adventist	1,087	1,027	7.8	6.1	2.9	3.1	3.8	5.7	$20,576	$25,613
Hebrew Day	250	134	7.9	8.5	6.0	9.3	4.6	3.6	$29,688	$43,624
Solomon Schechter	—	46	—	9.6	—	4.0	—	4.6	$55,412	$52,774
Other Jewish	—	252	—	9.6	—	5.7	—	4.4	—	$42,612
Christian Schools Int'l.	306	388	7.7	7.6	5.4	4.6	6.4	4.5	$24,546	$30,939
Assoc. of Christian Schools Int'l.	1,756	1,741	6.1	7.1	4.2	5.3	2.2	2.2	$17,528	$22,131
Lutheran, MO Synod	1,162	981	7.9	8.0	7.7	8.0	6.1	6.0	$24,300	$29,551
Lutheran, WI Synod	—	405	—	3.0	—	6.8	—	3.9	—	$21,627
Evangelical Lutheran	—	105	—	10.5	—	4.9	—	1.5	$22,323	$27,139
Other Lutheran	406	—	3.5	—	6.1	6.5	2.5	—	$18,033	$18,617
Catholic	9,142	8,098	14.0	13.7	4.7	4.7	4.0	4.3	$15,724	$21,840
Parochial	6,337	5,039	14.7	13.6	4.6	4.8	4.5	4.5	$14,135	$21,076
Diocesan	1,841	2,238	12.3	13.9	5.0	4.4	2.7	3.7	$17,780	$22,320
Private Order	964	820	12.8	13.8	5.1	4.9	2.9	4.2	$22,245	$25,222
Other religious	10,287	9,862	6.4	6.2	4.7	5.4	2.6	2.9	$17,986	$22,738
Conservative Christian	3,939	3,534	5.2	5.8	4.0	5.1	2.0	1.7	$13,733	$18,809
Affiliated	4,019	3,868	7.5	7.5	5.5	6.3	3.9	4.2	$23,236	$28,523
Unaffiliated	2,329	2,460	6.5	4.9	4.2	4.6	1.2	2.3	$16,120	$19,289
Nonsectarian	4,611	3,802	8.4	8.4	6.6	6.9	1.5	1.8	$26,226	$40,392
All members NAIS	1,164	1,349	10.9	11.1	6.5	6.0	2.7	2.9	$39,121	$52,479

Source: United States Department of Education, Office of Educational Research and Improvement. *Private Schools in the United States: A Statistical Profile, 1990–91.* (National Center for Educational Statistics, Statistical Analysis Report, January 1995), p. 61.

uted to differences in the factors that characterize the work environments of public and private schools themselves. However, there is a residual difference in earnings that cannot be explained in terms of the models utilized in the present study. One hypothesis is that this residual difference in earnings may be explained by certification requirements that prevent the free flow of teachers between the two sectors. However, this does not explain the persistent differences between types of schools within the private sector. Further research is needed to understand why private school teachers do not move to the public sector given the differences in remuneration that are observed between these two sectors. Case studies or attitudinal surveys could perhaps yield some valuable insights into this teacher market phenomenon. Precisely, what is it about private schools or private school teachers that permits this salary difference to persist?[20]

Emerging Issues

The future of religious schools in the United States will be shaped by the interaction of a number of forces, some of which will undoubtedly prove as analytically elusive as the U.S. Department of Education's study of why people choose to work in these schools. The motivation of church leaders, parents and teachers to build new schools and to sustain and enlarge existing schools will be driven by the degree to which they continue to share the conviction that the good work done in these schools is an essential element of the Church's mission. Their faith will continue to be tested by a number of challenges, many of which have financial implications for the future of religious schools.

The Churched and the Unchurched

While most religiously sponsored schools were founded to serve the children of the sponsoring church community, a growing number of these schools find themselves serving the children of other faiths or children whose families are not committed to any religious community. Generally, religious schools insist that they are maintaining an institutional commitment to the sponsoring church by incorporating its religious vision into the climate and structure of the school. Families who choose the religious school do so with the full knowledge that the school makes no apology for its religious identity and intends to go about its educational business in ways that do not compromise its religious integrity. But the question persists: if significant numbers of children are drawn from outside the sponsoring religious community, will that community continue to see the school as an integral part of the church's ministry, worthy of the community's financial and moral support?

Catholic schools educate significant numbers of non-Catholic students, Lutheran schools educate significant numbers of non-Lutherans, and Friends schools educate students from a wide range of faith traditions. For many religious schools in inner-city areas, the arrival of large numbers of families of other faiths coincides with the movement of parishioners to the suburbs. An inner-city parish rarely generates sufficient revenues from its own tuitions and parish contributions to support its school without substantial help from the larger community. The Seventh Day Adventists are exceptional in providing a centralized funding mechanism through their regional conferences. Many Catholic dioceses serve a somewhat similar function, although the income distributed by dioceses to schools is increasingly generated by development and fund-raising activities, instead of redistribution programs based on universal tithing or interparish transfers.

In answering those who challenge the appropriateness of supporting schools that do not limit their enrollments to their own church members, some religious school leaders point to the church's mission to evangelize, to invite the world to consider the message of the gospel; others point to the church's mission to serve those in need, and see the church's educational effort as a powerful instrument for raising the poor and for building a humane and compassionate society.

Development and Fund-Raising

To generate the resources needed to support the church's educational mission, religious schools are becoming increasingly involved in fund-raising and development activities. Many schools continue to lean heavily on candy and bake sales. Bingo remains a fund-raising fixture for some Catholic schools, although a few voices have been heard to challenge the wisdom and appropriateness of dependence on what they see as a variant of *lottolust.* But, slowly and surely, religious schools are moving into more sophisticated and professional approaches to development. Often learning lessons from their bigger sisters and brothers in church-related colleges and universities, high schools have established development offices, staffed them with development directors, and nudged their principals to take a leadership role in shaping the institutional advancement effort. Elementary schools are more numerous, and usually smaller and more modestly staffed than the high schools. Nevertheless, annual funds are increasingly common at the elementary level, and a small but growing number of schools are building endowments.

National organizations are providing encouragement and training through publications and workshops. An increasing number of Catholic dioceses have mounted ambitious annual appeals, often focusing on the financial needs of elementary schools serving low income communities. Collaborative marketing efforts using print, radio, and television to promote the successes of religious schools are increasingly common in large urban areas. In 1994, privately funded voucher initiatives supported by individuals, corporations, and foundations were in place in a dozen cities, and planning groups had formed in thirteen other cities. These programs provided financial assistance for more than 5,000 students, most of whom attended church-sponsored schools.[20]

Public Support

Proposals to provide public support for parental school choice at the state or federal level have generated considerable discussion within the religious school community. Some of the opponents of comprehensive school choice initiatives which would include religious as well as nonsectarian private schools have raised objections that imply that religious schools do not serve the common good; that a parent's right to choose religious schools, while judged tolerable by the Supreme Court in 1925, should not be encouraged by society at large; and that public schools provide unique and unchallenged preparation for responsible citizenship in a democratic society. It is not surprising to find that most religious school leaders have a somewhat different view. They find it particularly difficult to hear their work challenged by some single-minded advocates of public education. Religious schools do not see themselves in a battle for market share with public education. Religious schools are not-for-profit organizations, rarely operated on a simple fee-for-service basis. In fact, most religious schools are viable only because they draw significant financial support beyond tuition income, and most of this additional support comes from the church community. In addition to educating students to live competent and decent lives, presumably prerequisites for responsible citizenship, these institutions are sustained by billions of dollars contributed by members of their church communities. If public support were to enable some parents to choose religious schooling for their children, and if the mechanism for providing that support did not require religious schools to compromise their religious identity, most religious school leaders would endorse the effort. The fiscal impact of such an initiative would vary from sector to sector and within religious groups. In some communities, religious schools are thriving, existing schools are expanding, and new schools opening. The Association of Christian Schools International, representing many newly organized evangelical Christian schools, reports continued growth in enrollments, waiting lists for some schools, and the establishment of new schools.

But for many older schools serving poor communities in inner-city and rural areas, the need to supplement their own church support and development efforts with increases in tuition revenues will make access, affordability, and viability problematic. In some communities, public support for school choice may make the difference between the continued presence of an oasis, a school providing both spiritual witness and academic success, and another abandoned building—soulless space and silence.

Numbers that represent average tuitions and salaries in religious schools hardly describe a network of unrelieved affluence. The call to service that characterizes the mission of many religious schools comes from a vision larger and older than *noblesse oblige*. It would be an especially perverse irony if the misrepresentation of the typical private school as a haven for the children of privilege became a self-fulfilling prophecy. Should the larger society reject the invitation to help parents choose religious schools for their children, it seems likely that many religious communities will find ways to continue to support their schools. It also seems likely that some of the most vulnerable and most valuable institutions will be lost, and the capacity of religious schools to serve children of modest means will shrink.

Notes

1. Timothy Walch, *Parish School: American Catholic Parochial Education from Colonial Times to the Present* (New York: Crossroads Publishing, 1996), 60–61.
2. *National Congress on Catholic Schools for the 21st Century*, National Catholic Educational Association (Washington, D.C.: 1991).
3. Ibid.
4. National Center for Educational Statistics, *Condition of Education 1995*. (Washington, D.C.: U.S. Department of Education, 1995), 52.
5. Richard Osborne, telephone interview with author, 27 March 1996.
6. The Lutheran Church-Missouri Synod, *Statistical Report Summary, Schools of the Lutheran Church-Missouri Synod 1994–95* (St. Louis: Lutheran Church-Missouri Synod, 1995).
7. John Scibilia, telephone interview with author, 15 February 1996.
8. Glen Schultz, telephone interview with author, 8 March 1996.
9. Daniel Vander Ark, letter to the author, 21 November 1995.
10. Michael Guerra. *Dollars and Sense: Catholic High Schools and Their Finances, 1994* (Washington, D.C.: National Catholic Educational Association, 1995), 30.
11. Robert Kealey. *Balance Sheet for Catholic Elementary Schools: 1993 Income and Expenses* (Washington, D.C.: National Catholic Educational Association, 1994), 17.
12. National Center for Educational Statistics, *Private Schools in the United States: A Statistical Profile, 1990–91* (Washington, D.C.: U.S. Department of Education, 1995), 52.
13. National Center for Educational Statistics, *Private Schools in the United States*, 52.
14. Kealey, *Balance Sheet*, vi.
15. Guerra, *Dollars and Sense*, vi.
16. Schools of the Lutheran Church-Missouri Synod, Unpublished statistics 1995.
17. The Seventh Day Adventist Church, Columbia Union Conference, *North American Division Financial Survey of Senior Academies, 1992–1993* (Columbia, Md.: The Seventh Day Adventist Church, Columbia Union Conference, 1993).
18. Christian Schools International, Unpublished statistics, 1995.
19. Schultz, interview.
20. National Center for Educational Statistics, *The Patterns of Teacher Compensation*, (Washington, D.C.: U.S. Department of Education, 1996), 22.
21. The National Scholarship Center, *JUST DOING IT: First Annual Survey of the Private Voucher Movement in America* (Washington, D.C.: The National Scholarship Center, 1995), 4.

Contributors

James C. Carper is associate professor of foundations of education at the University of South Carolina, Columbia; Education Advisor to Governor David M. Beasley of South Carolina; recently served as director of the Education and Society Division, Office of Research (OERI), U.S. Department of Education; and is a past president of Associates for Research on Private Education. Professor Carper is co-editor with Thomas C. Hunt of *Religious Schooling in America* (1984) and of a three-volume series of selected bibliographies on religious educational institutions in America and the author of many journal articles. Dr. Carper's research interests include the history of American education and church/state conflicts in the educational arena.

Bruce S. Cooper is professor of administration, policy, and urban education at Fordham University Graduate School of Education and has taught previously at Dartmouth College and the University of Pennsylvania. His recent publications include articles in the *Journal of Education Finance* and the forthcoming *Yearbook of the American Education Finance Association.* He has written several books including two studies of Chapter 1, an international study of teacher unions, a book on magnet schools, and a forthcoming book on the New School Finance. He has served as president of Associates for Research on Private Education (ARPE), a special interest group of the American Education Research Association, and editor of the *Private School Monitor.* His scholarly interests include private and religious education, school politics, reform, and finance.

William F. Davis, O.S.F.S., is a member of the Oblates of St. Francis de Sales and since 1990 has served as the representative for Catholic Schools and Federal Assistance in the Department of Education of the United States Catholic Conference. Prior to assuming his current position, he served as director of personnel and education for the Eastern Province of the Oblates of St. Francis de Sales (1986–1990) and superintendent of schools for the Catholic Diocese of Arlington, Virginia (1978–1986). He was also a high school administrator and teacher for eighteen years. Father Davis has an Ed.D. degree in educational administration.

Rita E. Guare is an assistant professor in the division of administration, policy, and urban education in the Graduate School of Education at Fordham University. Before assuming her teaching position, she directed the Center for Non-Public Education at Fordham. She works with doctoral students in both the Church Leadership Program and the Executive Leadership Program. Her research interests include spirituality and leadership, religious education, the arts, and teacher leadership.

Michael J. Guerra has served as the National Catholic Educational Association's executive director for secondary schools since 1982. During that time he has written and spoken about a wide variety of issues, including Catholic educational research, leadership, and public policy. He played a major role in organizing the National Congress on Catholic Schools for the 21st Century. He has published a number of original research studies, most notably "The Heart of the Matter," a study of the impact of schooling on student beliefs and values, and "Lighting New Fires," a summary and analysis of the prospects for Catholic schools in the post-conciliar era. In 1993 he was appointed to the National Assessment Governing Board by the U.S. Secretary for Education to fill the seat provided for a representative of nonpublic education. He serves as private education's representative among the resource experts appointed to advise the National Education Goals Panel. He has also served as headmaster of Loyola School in New York City and worked as a teacher and director of a church-sponsored youth center for the predominantly Hispanic community of New York's Lower East Side.

Thomas C. Hunt currently holds the position of professor and researcher in Catholic education at the Center for Catholic Education, School of Education, University of Dayton. Until recently he was professor of foundations of education at Virginia Tech. His major interest is the history of American education, with an emphasis on religion and schooling, particularly with Catholic schooling. He is the co-editor of *Religion and Morality in American Schooling* (1981); co-edited, with James C. Carper, *Religious Schooling in America* (1984), and numerous bibliographies and sourcebooks of religious educational institutions in America; and co-authored with Mary A. Grant *Catholic School Education in the United States: Development and Current Concerns* (1992). His articles have appeared in many educational and religious education journals. He received the Thayer S. Warshaw Award in 1986 for his essay "Religion, Moral Education and Public Schools: A Tale of Tempest." Currently he serves as president of the Associates for Research on Private Education, an affiliate of the American Educational Research Association.

Charles R. Kniker is professor of religion and education and former president at the Eden Theological Seminar, St. Louis, Missouri. Before assuming the presidency at the Eden Seminar, Dr. Kniker completed twenty-four years of service as a professor of curriculum and instruction at Iowa State University in Ames. While at Iowa State, Professor Kniker founded the journal *Religion & Public Education;* he served as its editor-in-chief from 1983 to 1993 and since then has been its senior editor. Author of numerous books and articles, his fields of interest include values education, assessments of teachers, and religion and public life.

E. Vance Randall is an assistant professor in the Department of Educational Leadership at Brigham Young University. He is the author of the book *Private Schools and Public Power: A Case for Pluralism* (1994) and has published articles in education and law journals. His research interests are in the fields of social philosophy, private education, policy analysis, and the influence of culture on education.

Mary Angela Shaughnessy, S.C.N., is professor of education and university legal counsel at Spalding University in Louisville, Kentucky. She has served as a teacher and principal in church-related schools and holds a Ph.D. in administration and supervision and a J.D. She is a member of the Sisters of Charity of Nazareth.

Index of Persons

Ackerman, James S., 15

Barnard, Henry, 5
Bischoff, Guntram, 11
Blaine, James, 167
Bodin, Wes, 19
Bohm, Winfried, 77
Boyd, William L., 128
Brennan, Supreme Court Justice William, 7–8
Buetow, Harold, 159
Burgess, Charles, 90

Carter, Stephen, 40, 116
Clark, Supreme Court Justice Tom, 33
Clinton, President William, 31, 35

Dewey, John, 91
Dilzer, Robert, 19
Doyle, Denis P., 127
Durkheim, Emile, 112

Erickson, Donald, 126, 134

Geertz, Clifford, 62–63, 113
Giroux, Henry, 116
Glenn, Charles, 123
Grant, Ulysses S., 167

Hatch, U.S. Senator Orrin, 100
Haynes, Charles, 10, 18
Hunter, James Davison, 60, 64, 69
Hyde, U.S. Representative Henry J., 32, 100

James, Estelle, 113, 115, 128, 132

Karlinger, Sr. Mary Jessica, 18
Kniker, Charles, 8, 10, 18
Kozol, Jonathan, 11

Lin, Maya, 20

Mann, Horace, 5
Mason, Peter, 119, 129
McDonald, Sr., Dale, 171

Nord, Warren, 5, 10, 17

Simmons, John, 20
Sloan, Douglas, 22
Smith, Lee, 19

Thomas, Oliver, 48
Tillich, Paul, 4, 113
Tylor, Edward Burnett, 62

Van Eyck, Jan, 20

Warhol, Andy, 20
Warshaw, Thayer S., 12, 14–15
Woodruff, Michael, 45

Yeats, William Butler, 60

Index of Subjects

Abington v. Schempp, 4, 7, 12-14, 19, 22, 33, 39, 95
adaptation theory (of religious schools), 108
Aguilar v. Felton, 170, 173
alternative schools, 95
American Academy of Religion, 8
American Association of School Administrators, 36
American Center for Law and Justice, 37
American Civil Liberties Union, 37, 46
American Federation of Teachers, 36
American Jewish Commitee, 37
Americans for Separation of Church and State, 37
Annunciation, The (Jan van Eyck), 20
Anti-Defamation League, 37
Apostolos-Cappadona, Diane, 20
Association for Supervision and Curriculum Development, 9, 17, 36

Baltimore, Councils of
  First Plenary, 88
  Third Plenary, 88
Bartels v. Iowa, 94
Beliefs and Believers (Public Broadcasting System), 20
Bender v. Williamsport Area School District, 43
Bennett Law, 90
Berger v. Rensselaer Cent. School Corp., 48
Bible as Literature, The (James S. Ackerman and Thayer S. Warshaw), 15
Bible in American Culture, The (Society of Biblical Literature), 15
Bible in Literature Courses: Successful Lesson Plans, The, (Linda Meixner), 15
Bischoff v. Brothers of the Sacred Heart, 147
Bischoff, Guntram, 11
Blaine Amendments, 167, 177
Bloch v. Hillel Torah North Suburban Day School, 148
block grant, 177
Board of Education v. Mergens, 44
Bob Jones University v. United States, 143
Bohning v. State of Ohio, 94
Bright v. Isenbarger, 141
Brown v. Board of Education, 95

Catholic bishops, 183
Catholic schools. *See* religious schools
charter schools, 130
child abuse, 153
Child Care Development and Block Grant Act, 173
choice, school, 130
Christian Coalition, 37
Christian Schools International, 186, 190
church and state, background, 33
churched and unchurched population, 193
Civil Rights movement, 16
Civil Rights Act, 1871, 141
colonial schools, 84-85
common school, 72, 84, 86-87
  sectarian nature of, 89
community service in churches, 183
compulsory school laws, 89, 93
contextualization of religious education, 113
corporal punishment, 149
creationism in teaching science, 21
  theory of evolution, 21
cultural conflict, 73-77
  monism in, 74-75
  pluralism in, 114
  relativism in, 74
cultural differences, responses to
  accommodation, 75

acculturation, 75
annihilation, 75–76
assimilation, 75–76
segregation, 75–76
culture
definition of, 61-62
and personal identity, 63
and society, 63
role of, 62-65
Culture Wars: The Struggle to Define America (James Davison Hunter), 60

Danish Evangelical Lutheranism, 127
Darwinism, 16
defamation of character, 151
development offices in religious schools
fund-raising, 195
marketing, 195
discipline of students, 154
Dixon v. Alabama, 141
due process, 141

education
definition of, 71
role of in society, 71-73
Edwards Law, 90
Elementary and Secondary Action Act, 169
Employment Division, Dept. of Human Resources v. Smith, 68, 99
employment practices in church-related schools, 153
Engel v. Vitale, 38-40, 95
equal access and use of school facilities, 32, 35, 42-44
Equal Access Act, 36, 43-44, 51
Establishment Clause, U.S. Constitution, First Amendment, 33, 42, 48, 51, 167
European Council of National Councils of Independent Schools, 119

Fifth Amendment, 141
First Amendment, 33, 85, 167
Florey v. Sioux Falls School District, 46
Focus on the Family, 37
Fourth Amendment, 141, 150
Free Exercise Clause, U.S. Constitution, First Amendment, 33, 51

Geraci v. St. Xavier High School, 148
Great Society (President Lyndon Johnson), 169

Holy Name School v. Dept. of Industry and Mary Retlick, 146
home schooling, 35

Illinois v. Burdette Wehmeyer, 149
Improving America's Schools Act, 177
Ingraham v. Wright, 149
injury. *See* negligence
in loco parentis, 90, 141
Islam, 113

J.M. Dawson Center for Church-State Studies, 37
Jones v. Clear Creek, 41-42
Journal of Church and State, 8
Journey of the Magi (T.S. Eliot), 14

Kniker, Charles, 8, 10, 18
Know-Nothing Party, 166
Kozol, Jonathan, 11

Laws, in education
case law, 34
common law, 140, 143, 154, 161
constitutional law, 140–141
contract law
breach of contract, 145
consideration, 144
legal subject matter, 145
mutual assent, 144
statutory law, 34
compelling interest, 143
statutes and regulations, 140, 143
torts, 149
Lee v. Weisman, 41
Lin, Maya, 20
Little v. St. Mary Magdalene Parish, 148
Living with Our Deepest Differences (Williamsburg Charter Foundation), 18

McCollum v. Board of Education, 6
McGuffey Reader, 6, 161
Meyer v. State of Nebraska, 94, 168
moments of silence. *See* prayers, school-sponsored
Moral and Spiritual Values in the Public Schools (NEA report), 7
moral education, 9
moral laws, 69
moral vision, 69
Morman schools, 114
Mueller v. Allen, 172

multiculturalism, 5
Murray v. Curlett, 7-8, 13-14, 19, 22, 39

Nation at Risk, A, 130
National Association of Evangelicals, 40
National Center for Educational Statistics, 182, 191-192
National Council of Churches, 37
National Council for History Standards, 17
National Council on Religion and Public Education, 8, 20
National Council for the Social Studies, 8, 16, 36
National Council for Teachers of English, 36
National Defense Act, 169
National Education Association, 36
National School Board Association, 36
National School Lunch Act, 168
Nebraska Lutheran Synod of Missouri v. McKelvie, 94
negligence, in litigated torts, 151
  field trips, 153
  injury, 152
New Age, 39
Nord, Warren, 5, 10, 17

Old Man and the Sea, The (Ernest Hemingway), 14
Orthodox moral vision, definition of, 69

Paradise Lost (John Milton), 14
parens patriae, 14
Pathways to Pluralism (teacher guide), 18
People for the American Way, 37
personalism, 77
Pierce v. Society of Sisters, 6, 93, 120, 140, 168
Pierce v. Hill Military Academy, 93
pluralism, 4, 5, 77
Pohl v. State of Ohio, 94
Political Responsibility: Proclaiming the Gospel of Life (U.S. Catholic Conference), 165
prayers, school-sponsored, 32, 36, 37–42
Preparing Social Studies Teachers to Teach About Religion (Thayer S. Warshaw), 18
Principles for Educational Reform in the United States (U.S. Catholic Conference), 165
private schools
  compensation for teachers, 187-190
  development and fund-raising, 194-195
  existence in the U.S., 182
  expenses, 187-191
  per pupil costs, 187
  principal's background, 192
  sources of revenue, 185
  tuition, 184
  See also religious schools
privatization of schools, 130
Prodigal Son (Gospel of St. Luke), 14
Progressive Era, 72, 91-92
progressive schools, 86
progressivism, 69
Protecting the Least Among Us, and Pursuing the Common Good (U.S. Catholic Conference), 165
Protestant beliefs and virtues, 67, 161-162
proximate cause, 152
public policy and political responsibility, 164, 168
public schools, religion curriculum in, 18–19

Reardon v. LeMoyne, 147
Religion and Public Education (journal), 8, 15, 17-18, 20, 37
religion
  activities ban, 119
  art and symbols, 32, 50
  in the curriculum, 17
  definition of, 4, 8-9, 65, 70
  diet and dress, 32, 49
  holidays, 32, 35, 44-47
  impact on culture, 13, 15
  materials, 32, 35, 47-48
  pluralism, 5, 67-68
  reasons and excusals, 47
  studies of, 12
  teaching of, 10
Religion in American History (teacher guide), 18
Religion in Human Culture (Lee Smith and Wes Bodin), 19
religion studies
  in art, 20
  in economics, 21
  in health, 21
  in history and social studies, 15-16
  in literature, 13, 14
  in music, 20
  in science, 21

Religious Contours of California (professors at University of California at Santa Barbara), 20
religious education
challenges, 110-111, 133, 135
constitutional legal context, 112, 119-125
cultural and linguistic context, 111-119
definition, 109-110
financial support and public funding, 112, 126-129, 160
identity, equity, quantity, and reform, 112, 129, 131
indoctrination of prejudice, 118
role of in spiritual development, 132
South Africa, religious education in, 114
teacher preparation in, 10
Religious Freedom Restoration Act, 36, 68, 99
religious practices, source materials, 36
Religious Quality Amendment, 32
Religious Right, 37
religious schools, denominations
Amish, 96
Calvinist, 87, 95, 163
Catholic, 88, 93, 117, 122-123, 163, 182-189
Dutch Reformed, 87, 163
Episcopalian, 87
fundamentalist, 98
Lutheran, 87, 163, 182, 186
Missouri Synod, 182, 190
Muslim, 163
Quaker (Friends), 87, 163, 182
Seventh Day Adventist, 95, 163, 186, 190
religious schools, financial aid for, 170–177
religious schools, location of, 181
Australia, 124, 126
Canada, 122, 125
Czechoslovakia, 121
Denmark, 123
France, 123
Germany, 121
Holland, 125
Romania, 120
United States, 124, 126
Rendall-Baker v. Kohn, 139, 142
respondeat superior, 149
Rutherford Institute, 37

"Second Coming, The" (William Butler Yeats), 60
separation of church and state, 35, 85, 148
Sheridan Road Baptist Church v. Dept. of Education, 98
slander, in schools, 151
Sloan, Douglas, 22
Smith v. Archbishop of St. Louis, 152
Social Gospel movement, 16
state action in private school cases, 141-142
state schools, 86
regulation of, 89-96
Supreme Court, position on religion, 10

teacher certification, 98
Teaching Values in the Literature Classroom (Charles and Bernard Suhor), 15
Ten Commandments, 143
Tenth Amendment, 34, 166
Thrasher v. General Casualty Company of Wisconsin,
Tinker v. Des Moines Independent School District, 42, 139, 141
torts. *See* laws, in education
tuition tax credits, 170-173

United States Catholic Conference, 165
U.S. Department of Education, guidelines for religious studies, 35
U.S. Department of Education Report of 1995, 188

Vietnam Veterans Memorial, 20
vouchers, school, 130, 173–177

Wallace v. Jaffee, 39
Warhol, Andy, 20
Warshaw, Thayer, 12, 14-15
Weithoff v. St. Veronica's School, 146
Weithoff, Steeber v. Benilde-St. Margaret's High School, 146
Widmar v. Vincent, 43
Williamsburg Charter, 17
Wisch v. Sanford School, 142
Wisconsin v. Yoder, 96-97
Wood v. Strickland, 139
Woodruff, Michael, 45
World Religions in America, textbook by NCRPE, 20
Wright State University, 8, 11

Zorach v. Clauson, 7

Source Books on Education

School Play
A Source Book
by James H. Block and Nancy R. King

Adult Literacy
A Source Book and Guide
by Joyce French

Black Children and American Institutions
An Ecological Review and Resource Guide
by Valora Washington and Velma LaPoint

Sexuality Education
A Resource Book
by Carol Cassell and Pamela M. Wilson

Reforming Teacher Education
Issues and New Directions
edited by Joseph A. Braun, Jr.

Critical Issues in Foreign Language Instruction
edited by Ellen S. Silber

The Education of Women in the United States
A Guide to Theory, Teaching, and Research
by Averil Evans McClelland

Materials and Strategies for the Education of Trainable Mentally Retarded Learners
by James P. White

Educational Testing
Issues and Applications
by Kathy E. Green

Teaching Thinking Skills
Theory and Practice
by Joyce N. French and Carol Rhoder

Teaching Social Studies to the Young Child
A Research and Resource Guide
by Blythe S. Farb Hinitz

Telecommunications
A Handbook for Educators
by Reza Azarmsa

Catholic School Education in the United States
Development and Current Concerns
by Mary A. Grant and Thomas C. Hunt

Secondary Schools and Cooperative Learning
Theories, Models, and Strategies
edited by Jon E. Pederson and Annette D. Digby

School Principals and Change
by Michael D. Richardson, Paula M. Short,
and Robert L. Prickett

Play in Practice
A Systems Approach to Making Good Play Happen
edited by Karen VanderVen, Paul Niemiec,
and Roberta Schomburg

Teaching Science to Children
Second Edition
by Mary D. Iatridis with a contribution by Miriam Maracek

Kits, Games and Manipulatives for the Elementary School Classroom
A Source Book
by Andrea Hoffman and Ann Glannon

Parents and Schools
A Source Book
by Angela Carrasquillo and Clement B.G. London

Project Head Start
Models and Strategies for the Twenty-First Century
by Valora Washington and Ura Jean Oyemade Bailey

Early Intervention
Cross-Cultural Experiences with a Mediational Approach
by Pnina S. Klein

Educating Young Adolescents
Life in the Middle
edited by Michael J. Wavering

Instrumentation in Education
An Anthology
by Lloyd Bishop and Paula E. Lester

Teaching English as a Second Language
A Resource Guide
by Angela L. Carrasquillo

The Foreign Language Classroom
Bridging Theory and Practice
edited by Margaret A. Haggstrom, Leslie Z. Morgan, and Joseph A. Wieczorek

Reading and Learning Disabilities
Research and Practice
by Joyce N. French, Nancy J. Ellsworth, and Marie Z. Amoruso

Multicultural Education
A Source Book
by Patricia G. Ramsey, Edwina B. Vold, and Leslie R. Williams

Religious Higher Education in the United States
A Source Book
edited by Thomas C. Hunt and James C. Carper

Teachers and Mentors
Profiles of Distinguished Twentieth-Century Professors of Education
edited by Craig Kridel, Robert V. Bullough, Jr., and Paul Shaker

Multiculturalism in Academe
A Source Book
by Libby V. Morris and Sammy Parker

At-Risk Youth
Theory, Practice, Reform
edited by Robert F. Kronick

Religion and Schooling in Contemporary America
Confronting Our Cultural Pluralism
edited by Thomas C. Hunt and James C. Carper